ESTABLISHED CHURCH, SECTARIAN PEOPLE
ITINERANCY AND THE TRANSFORMATION OF
ENGLISH DISSENT, 1780–1830

This book examines a neglected aspect of English social history – the operation of itinerant preachers during the period of political and social ferment at the turn of the century. It investigates the nature of their popular brand of Christianity and considers their impact upon existing churches: both the threat apparently posed to the Established Church of England and the consequences of their activity for the smaller Protestant bodies from which they arose.

The particular strength of the book lies in the extensive use it makes of untapped local archives drawn from many English counties – records which include numerous parochial, legal, associational and congregational sources. This is a study of religion in transition which is set against the wider canvas of social change attendant upon the early Industrial Revolution and the political shock waves emanating from France.

Established Church, Sectarian People

Itinerancy and the transformation of English Dissent, 1780–1830

DERYCK W. LOVEGROVE

Lecturer in Ecclesiastical History,
University of St Andrews

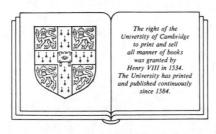

The right of the
University of Cambridge
to print and sell
all manner of books
was granted by
Henry VIII in 1534.
The University has printed
and published continuously
since 1584.

CAMBRIDGE UNIVERSITY PRESS

CAMBRIDGE

NEW YORK   NEW ROCHELLE

MELBOURNE   SYDNEY

Published by the Press Syndicate of the University of Cambridge
The Pitt Building, Trumpington Street, Cambridge CB2 1RP
32 East 57th Street, New York, NY 10022, USA
10 Stamford Road, Oakleigh, Melbourne 3166, Australia

First published 1988

Printed in Great Britain at
the University Press, Cambridge

British Library cataloguing in publication data
Lovegrove, Deryck W.
Established Church, Sectarian People: Itinerancy and the transformation
of English Dissent, 1780–1830.
1. Dissenters, Religious – England – History – 18th century
2. Dissenters, Religious – England – History – 19th century
3. Preaching – England – History
I. Title
322'.1'0942   BX5203.2

Library of Congress cataloguing in publication data
Lovegrove, Deryck W.
Established Church, Sectarian People: Itinerancy and the transformation
of English Dissent, 1780–1830.
Bibliography.
Includes index.
1. Circuit riders – England – History.
2. Dissenters, Religious – England – History.
3. Church of England – History.
4. Anglican Communion – England – History.
5. Christian sects – England – History.
6. England – Church history – 18th century.
7. England – Church history – 19th century.
I. Title.
BR758.L68   1988   274.2'081   87-21872

ISBN 0 521 34457 3

For Barbara

The Church of England must ever be considered, both by Protestant and Dissenter, as that steady guide which direct[s] the opinions and judgment of the whole nation. But if this part of our national constitution [i]s not better attended to, we sh[all] be in danger of having a nominal Established Church, and a sectarian people.

Viscount Sidmouth proposing the Protestant Dissenting Ministers Bill before the House of Lords, 9 May 1811. *Cobbett's Parliamentary Debates*, 19 (1811), 1131.

Contents

Figures

Preface

There exists within historical scholarship a natural bias towards the great and the powerful. Historians have always concerned themselves with the affairs of leading politicians, society figures and churchmen, persons who by their very nature have tended to leave the most visible testimony to their own importance. Yet, in order to speak with authority, the student of history must also investigate the lower levels of society, asking questions concerning the economic, social and religious practices of ordinary people. The study of English Dissent during its most expansionist and popular phase accords well with this aim, promising to shed light upon the religious habits and circumstances of a large section of English society at a critical point in its evolution. It has the additional attraction of offering authoritative detail chosen from the rich and largely untapped resources of local history.

Yet mere localism, however carefully employed, is inadequate for the wider task. It cannot support useful generalizations. It can only point with certainty to the situation prevailing in a given area. In seeking to avoid this limitation this study attempts to investigate a wide variety of contrasting localities, making equal use of local and national records, as well as the written material left by individuals. The use of these records, drawn as they have been from all parts of the country, has rendered my obligations to individuals and institutions very extensive, and I would like, therefore, in the following paragraphs to record my thanks to those who have helped me.

In the first place, I owe an immense debt to my two former teachers: Professor Alec Cheyne of Edinburgh University who fostered in me a deep and abiding love of ecclesiastical history, and Dr David Thompson of Fitzwilliam College, Cambridge who patiently helped and guided me through my postgraduate work. Both sought to instil into me a concern for sound conceptual analysis based upon meticulous scholarship, both gave unstintingly of their time and wisdom, and to both for their continuing friendship and counsel I am most deeply grateful.

At an early stage in this study I was privileged to make the acquaintance of Dr Geoffrey Nuttall. Apart from facilitating my investigations within the archives then located at New College, London, he allowed me to benefit from his own renowned expertise in the field of English Dissent.

Among the many institutions to which I am indebted two groups in particular deserve special mention. From Preston to Maidstone and from Durham to Dorchester the archivists in almost a score of county record offices have made available by means of diligent collection and preservation many important manuscripts whose existence and whereabouts might otherwise have remained uncertain. In addition a further invaluable institutional source has been the various collections held in denominational archives. In this regard I would like to pay tribute to the unfailing assistance and kindness shown by the staffs of the Baptist Missionary Society, the Baptist Union of Great Britain and Ireland, Bristol Baptist College, Manchester Congregational College, the former New College, London, Regent's Park College, Oxford, and Westminster College, Cambridge, including the Governors of the Cheshunt Foundation for permission to use the papers of the Countess of Huntingdon's Connexion. Other research centres which have played an important part in the evolution of this book include: in London, the British Library, the Congregational Library, Dr Williams's Library, the Guildhall Library and the Public Record Office; in Oxford, the Bodleian Library; the University Libraries of Cambridge and Southampton; the John Rylands University Library, Manchester; New College Library, Edinburgh; and the University Library, St Andrews. For the help afforded by these bodies and by private custodians who have granted me access to important material I would like to record my sincere gratitude.

Apart from the help received from these sources I have also benefited from the expert advice of a number of scholars whose interests bear upon my own. Among these I would mention Dr John Walsh of Jesus College, Oxford, and Mr Robert Elliot of the University of Dundee. My own university at St Andrews furthered the work by granting a period of study leave which enabled me to examine the episcopal visitation returns for several dioceses. More recently my colleague, Professor James Cameron, very kindly read the completed manuscript. The final stage, the production of the typescript, was relieved of most of its difficulty by the effort of Mrs Helen Smith. For her helpfulness and the quality of her work I wish to express my appreciation.

Finally, it is my greatest pleasure to thank my wife for her love, support and help during the years in which this work has been in preparation, and my sons, Philip and David, for their willingness to tolerate its encroachment upon family life.

DERYCK LOVEGROVE

St Mary's College
University of St Andrews

Acknowledgements

The author would like to thank the following bodies for permission to use quotations from records in their possession or keeping:

Norfolk Record Office, for extract on p. 11 from the Norwich Diocesan Papers, ref. VIS/35d.

The Cheshunt Foundation, Westminster College, Cambridge, for extract on p. 28 from the Plan of Association of the Countess of Huntingdon's Connexion, also published in C. E. Welch (ed.) *Two Calvinistic Methodist Chapels, 1743–1811: the London Tabernacle and Spa Fields Chapel*, (London, 1975), p. 94.

The Lancashire Congregational Union (Inc.), for extract on pp. 44, 46, from the Lancashire Congregational Union minutes, 9–10 April 1816 (CUL 2.2).

United Reformed church, Andover, for extract on p. 60 from Andover Congregational church minutes, 5 December 1817.

Northern College (United Reformed and Congregational), Manchester, for extract on p. 69 from Sketch for projected autobiography, p. 6, William Roby Papers.

Dr Williams's Library, London, for extracts on pp. 72, 77, 160 and Figure 5 from: (a) English Evangelic Academy, minutes pp. 2, 9, New College MS 126/1; (b) Village Itinerancy, minutes 20 September 1813, New College MS 56/1; (c) Village Itinerancy, report 1811, New College MS 47; (d) Hoxton Academy, report 1824, p. xvii, New College MS 546/3/5; (e) Itinerancy plan enclosed with letter from William Church to John Eyre, 21 February 1797, New College MS 41/7.

Baptist Union of Great Britain and Ireland, for extract on p. 121 from the Essex Baptist Association minute book, 1805–64.

Baptist Missionary Society, for permission to print the 'Journal of T. Wastfield, June 1797–April 1798' in its entirety. (See Appendix A.)

Abbreviations

BBC	Bristol Baptist College
BL	British Library
BMS	Baptist Missionary Society
BU	Baptist Union
CL	Congregational Library, London
CRO	County Record Office
DWL	Dr Williams's Library, London
GL	Guildhall Library, London
MCC	Manchester Congregational College
PRO	Public Record Office
RPC	Regent's Park College, Oxford
WC	Westminster College, Cambridge

1 · The Established Church and English Separatism

In May 1660 an important declaration of religious intent by Charles II, king in exile, then at Breda in the Netherlands, was read to the assembled members of the English Parliament. In the most famous passage of the declaration the king acknowledged the divided state of religious opinion within the country and expressed the conviction that free discussion would resolve many of the differences: '... we do declare', he wrote, 'a liberty to tender consciences, and that no man shall be disquieted or called in question for differences of opinion in matter of religion, which do not disturb the peace of the kingdom'.[1] Already more than a century had elapsed since the acceptance of Protestantism, and in the intervening years, as the declaration noted, a bewildering range of belief had surfaced in English society offering religious alternatives which seemed increasingly to challenge the basic pretensions of the national church.

The English version of the Reformation, which reappeared after the unsettled years of Mary Tudor, was conservative in its approach to theology and worship, territorial in organization and, above all, monopolistic in its claims upon the religious allegiance of the nation. The reformed Church of England remained the only recognized ecclesiastical body within the realm. Like the majority of European leaders in the sixteenth century, English monarchs, ministers and ecclesiastical dignitaries accepted without question the idea of a single, undivided Church coterminous with civil society. Unlike the Continent, however, England did not experience the bitter factional struggles which marred the religious development of later sixteenth-century society. But the absence of confessional warfare did not imply any greater regard for the principle of religious toleration.[2]

Between 1549 and 1559, interrupted only by the short-lived return to Catholicism under Mary, three Acts of Uniformity were entered upon the statute-book, each designed to prescribe a form of worship and to ensure by means of penalties the minimum of deviation from the new devotional practices. Yet the success of the new order was by no means instantaneous. For many of Elizabeth's subjects the 1560s and 1570s represented a period of uneasy readjustment to the new patterns of worship. Professor Bossy, who assumes for the sake of statistical analysis the existence of a radical break between the earlier Roman order and the religious settlement of Elizabeth I, is careful to qualify the abruptness of the transition. He points to the ambiguity of those who in the period immediately following 1559 can be identified as continuing Catholics. Most conducted their religious affairs with a mixture of outward conformity to the new religious Establishment and private devotions according to traditional observance, earning in the process the abusive epithet 'Church-Papists'.[3]

Though the Elizabethan Prayer Book of 1559 with its restoration of traditional ceremonial and eucharistic language may have gone some way towards lessening the alienation felt by convinced Catholics, ardent Protestants detested the apparent return to popish practices implied by the latest set of liturgical changes. Under the Act of Uniformity passed in the same year members of the clergy who refused to use the new Prayer Book and its prescribed forms faced a range of penalties extending from limited fines and prison sentences for first offences to complete forfeiture of spiritual preferment and even to life imprisonment. Nor did dissentient parishioners escape unpunished, for the terms of the act dictated that every subject of the realm was to attend church on Sundays and holy days on pain of ecclesiastical censure and the exaction of twelve pence for every offence.[4]

At the start of Elizabeth's reign those who raised their voices in religious protest were not to any significant extent questioning the principle of establishment. Religious controversy within the Church of England concerned the degree to which old forms of worship and organization ought to be retained. The influence of international Calvinism especially over those who had fled into exile during the Marian persecution produced a generation of leaders whose preoccupation was with the achievement of a thoroughly reformed national Church free of superstitious practices; an ecclesiastical body that would exercise effective godly discipline throughout society, especially with regard to the administration of the sacraments and observance of the Lord's day. The views of this group contained inherent contradictions. On the one hand its members were prepared to recognize just authority and to treat the Church in non-sectarian fashion as a mixed community of saints and sinners. On the other hand they quickly showed themselves willing to criticize and resist the unjust use of power and to apply strict religious standards to the whole of life. They functioned as an inner circle separated to some extent from the mass of English society.[5] As the Puritan convictions held by individuals hardened into a formal position, a struggle for supremacy began to take place between those who followed the queen and episcopate in espousing traditional Catholic forms, and those who preferred the more austere Presbyterian ideal subsequently expounded by Thomas Cartwright. The chief problem for Elizabeth was that of securing from the latter group a proper acceptance of the 1559 formulary.

In order to be effective legislation on uniformity needed the support of internal discipline. The first significant move in that direction came in March 1566 with the promulgation among the clergy of Archbishop Parker's *Advertisements*. This document, which was produced in response to royal concern at the current diversity in religious ceremonial, consisted of a series of articles issued without specific royal approval. It insisted upon unity of doctrine and ceremonial and prescribed clear practical rules for the proper administration of public worship including the sacraments, and for the general conduct of the clergy. Preaching was to be restricted to those properly licensed by their bishop. The appropriate dress for ministers saying public prayers, administering the sacraments or conducting other rites was deemed to be the surplice. All communicants were to receive the sacrament in a kneeling posture.[6] Many may have disliked Parker's injunctions but comparatively few pressed their objections to the point of open defiance. Those that did were deprived of their livings.

Parker's *Advertisements* sought to protect internal uniformity, but a more serious development, the gradual appearance of alternative gatherings of Protestants outside the liturgical forms and buildings of the Church of England, the emergence of the religious conventicle, was not explicitly proscribed until 1593. In that year under the guidance of Archbishop Whitgift a harsh law was enacted against those who attended or encouraged others to attend 'any unlawful assemblies, conventicles, or meetings, under colour or pretence of any exercise of religion' to the neglect of the worship of the Established Church. Conviction under the act carried with it a mandatory prison sentence, release being dependent upon a declaration of conformity and attendance at divine service. After three months those who still refused to conform faced a choice between exile or punishment as a felon by means of forfeiture with no 'benefit of clergy'.[7]

Despite the comparatively late appearance of this statute the authorities had already begun to take action against those who were exploring alternative forms of worship. By the end of 1587 a number of London dissidents were languishing in gaol, their leaders John Greenwood and Henry Barrow being executed early in 1593 for the allegedly seditious character of their writings.[8] Their approach to religion seemed incompatible with the concept of a national Church. But in spite of repression religious Separatism with its independent conception of the Church became from this point onwards a serious and permanent feature of English religious life.

Although the Separatist views of Greenwood and Barrow arose directly from their own dissatisfaction with the Church of England, there are signs of a shadowy connection with earlier expressions of religious protest. The roots of English Separatism stretch back into the mediaeval period, to the poor preachers of the Lollard tradition, gaining a measure of encouragement from Radical ideas from the Continental Reformation which had made their way by means of trade contacts and exile to London and the south-east corner of England. Not only did Separatist conventicles spring up in the clothing communities of northern Essex, in the Kentish Weald and among the towns and villages of the Chilterns in the very places which had earlier been centres of Lollard activity, but the Kentish and Essex groups showed clear signs of theological influence by Continental Anabaptism, especially the teachings of the Christological heresiarch, Melchior Hoffmann.[9]

In spite of this very early appearance by Separatism one of the most obvious features of the English Reformation was its comparative unity. Unlike the situation in the German cities and principalities or in some of the Swiss cantons where the Reformation gave rise to a threefold division between traditional Catholicism, Magisterial Protestantism and Radical groupings, the English Church managed to negotiate the ecclesiastical watershed with few outward signs of schism. Unity was encouraged by the existence of a strong national government which decided as early as 1533–4 to reject Roman pretensions to authority.[10] It was also fostered by the relative isolation and insularity of English society and the consequent lack of influence by Continental Radicalism outside the south-eastern counties.[11]

Serious religious dissent was in consequence slow to develop. Where it did appear its chief preoccupation was not with matters of theology but with the nature of the Church, its relationship with the State and with society at large, and with the concomitant matter of internal organization and government. Most Protestants at odds with the leadership of the Church of England were Calvinists and desired only the removal of those aspects of religious life and organization that were redolent of the old order. They hoped for the replacement of episcopacy and the prelatical accoutrements of religion by a Presbyterian system of government based upon the centrality of the Bible rather than sacraments, the essential equality of ordained ministers, and a graded system of ecclesiastical assemblies. The territorial character of the Church, its monopolistic position in society and its co-operation with the secular authorities would have remained to all intents and purposes unchanged. Only when the reforming impetus showed signs of failing in the face of episcopal intransigence did some of the more determined Puritan elements turn towards the Separatist ideal.[12]

From the time of Greenwood and Barrow a number of English Protestants held the view that membership of Christ's Church was a voluntary matter. They believed that the Church consisted of those who gave their willing assent to its discipline, and that the exercise of biblical rules alone should govern their continuing membership. At the close of the sixteenth century those who adopted this radical viewpoint represented only a small proportion of the group which disliked the Elizabethan Settlement, yet their ideas contained ominous and far reaching implications. Their concept of membership clashed with the traditional view of the Church as a territorial body, a notion which had survived the Reformation almost unaffected and which seemed to most contemporary minds to be an essential ingredient in the cultivation of a Christian society. The emphasis upon voluntarism raised even more delicate issues including the proper allegiance to be expected by the State from its subjects, the extent of the power to be exercised by that body over the conscience of the individual believer, and the precise basis of authority, whether prescriptive or derivative. The latter question was to become especially important during the turbulent years of civil war in the 1640s when Protestant Dissenters of various kinds gave their allegiance to the parliamentary cause.

The fragmentation of English Protestantism had also economic causes. In his recent study of English Dissent Dr Watts suggests that there were important social differences between those who gave their wholehearted support to established religion and those who seceded from it. He points out that unlike the Puritan movement very few landowners embraced Separatism. Gervase Neville of Ragnall in Nottinghamshire was one of the rare exceptions. Religious dissent was associated characteristically with economic mobility. The Separatist congregation to which Greenwood and Barrow belonged was composed of two distinct groups: one whose members, in some cases as former clergymen, had received a university education and another much larger body of artisans which represented a wide variety of trades. Despite the discrepancy in education and status they shared a common familiarity with urban life, they possessed an important degree of economic flexibility, their skills were to some extent geographically transferable and at first many had active contacts with the Continent.[13] English Separatism was to retain its urban complexion throughout the seventeenth and eighteenth centuries, thriving most successfully in the comparatively unsupervised society of the pre-industrial town.[14]

If Protestant divisions had been slow to develop in the sixteenth century the same could not be said of the Stuart era. The mid-seventeenth century saw the first peak of non-established religion as Separatist congregations began to multiply in the wake of the parliamentary army. A variety of theological views appeared during the Civil War and Interregnum. Contact with the Continent produced the first English expressions of Fausto Sozzini's anti-Trinitarian rationalism. A number of radical army chaplains in the parliamentary cause contrived to push traditional Calvinism to equally heterodox conclusions of an antinomian character. The heady uncertainty of the Commonwealth inspired others to emphasize the millenarian aspect of Christian teaching. Ideas poured out of the ecclesiastical melting-pot as Quakers relying on the inward illumination of the Holy Spirit offered an

5

alternative source of authority to that provided by Church or Bible, and a variety of sects sought to apply egalitarian criteria to the structure of Christian society.[15]

The corollary of these outpourings was a growing belief in religious pluralism; a desire for the acceptance of diversity in the realms of faith and practice. In spite of the austere reputation acquired by the Cromwellian interlude, the Commonwealth and Protectorate gave England its first taste of genuine religious choice exercised within an overall climate of toleration.[16] Notwithstanding the brevity of the experiment and the Draconian legal measures enacted in the wake of the Restoration to end the sectarian divisions, which in the mind of High Churchmen provided a visible reminder of the connection between the sins of schism and regicide, the accession of Charles II merely confirmed the permanence of non-established religion. The Presbyterian element, hitherto contained within the Established Church, was compelled by the Ejectment of 1662 to come to terms with its position as an unintentional component of English Dissent. Ten years later many Presbyterian congregations had abandoned the dream of belonging to a thoroughly reformed version of the Church of England. The demise of that aspiration came finally in 1689 with the failure of the Comprehension Bill.[17] From that point onwards English Protestant Dissent included within its ranks both traditional Separatists and the lineal descendants of the Puritans.

For those outside the Anglican fold 1689 marked the attainment of a significant measure of religious toleration. Yet it also heralded the beginning of a slow decline into obscurity and theological introspection. It was the latter rather than continuing legal restrictions, heterodoxy or even the strength of the Established Church which led to the withering of the Dissenting community in the course of the eighteenth century.

Even after the passage of the Toleration Act substantial restrictions upon religious freedom remained. Those affected were required by law to register their places of worship and to ensure that only officially recognized preachers conducted public services.[18] In the civil sphere the sacramental test acted as a barrier to the more lucrative and prestigious public offices, although after 1745 the passage of annual indemnity acts mitigated the worst effects.[19] Those who openly espoused Unitarian ideas were denied the protection of the Toleration Act.[20] Behind the smiling facade of the 1689 act lurked the spectre of penal legislation enacted in the Stuart era; statutes which were still capable of inspiring individuals to interpret the law in a manner calculated to harm Dissenting interests. The records of the London committee of Deputies demonstrate unequivocally that in spite of the complacent atmosphere of the early Hanoverian period many infringements of Dissenting rights took place. The offences ranged from the refusal to marry or bury church members and attempts to prosecute ministers and schoolmasters for running independent schools and academies, to cases of riot, disturbance and even arson directed against the property of individual congregations.[21]

Deviant theological opinions, whether openly heterodox[22] or extreme in their logical conservatism,[23] offer a persuasive explanation for the dwindling of many eighteenth-century congregations and the dearth of ministerial candidates. But the frequent secessions of orthodox worshippers from heterodox congregations and the vigorous debate aroused in Northamptonshire by 'the Modern Question'[24] suggest that the more overt manifestations of rational thought may have exercised a healthy influence upon belief by way of stimulating reaction. The real problem lay elsewhere, in the matter of isolation. The very strength of independency, the internal cohesion of the gathered church, became its weakness as geographical remoteness conspired with autonomy and lack of common purpose to foster numerical decline.

If the history of eighteenth-century Dissent was that of toleration followed by decay, the course of the national Church was marked by a similar discrepancy. Outwardly strong and confident the religious Establishment contained within it the seeds of popular alienation and ineffectiveness. In 1736 when William Warburton wrote his classic account of the alliance between Church and State, the Church of England was approaching the height of its formal power and influence. The bench of twenty-six bishops operated within the House of Lords as an important constituent of the process of government. Intellectually the Hanoverian Church retained the respect earned in the previous century by the theological contribution of the Caroline divines and the powerful sermons of Tillotson and Stillingfleet.[25] That earlier momentum was maintained throughout the difficult years which followed the reign of Queen Anne by the effective philosophical rebuttal of Deism. The English Church met the challenge of rationalism with little if any sign of the antagonism seen in France between religious and secular viewpoints.[26] The situation in England, despite the presence of an ecclesiastical establishment, drew favourable comment from no less a critic of state religion than Voltaire on account of its tolerance and lack of persecuting zeal, characteristics he was inclined to attribute to the breadth of religious practice allowed under the Hanoverian monarchy.[27]

Yet even such distinguished Gallic approval cannot conceal the more negative elements. The absence of persecuting zeal owed much to the general spirit of complacency. Toleration of religious diversity merely masked the decline of the territorial ideal. The intellectual prowess of eighteenth-century apologists has to be set against the unemotional coldness of public worship. Episcopal prominence in the political arena diverted attention from the loss of effective leadership within the Church. To the modern observer instances of mob support contrast sharply with the much wider failure to understand and respond to the popular appeal of

7

Methodism. Most important of all in the longer term, close identification with the State appeared with hindsight to entail a dangerous degree of erastianism.[28]

Most Hanoverian Churchmen followed Warburton in regarding the religious Establishment as resting upon a compact between two free and equal sovereign bodies for their common benefit. 'Such', he argued, 'is the nature of that famous union which produces a Church Established, and which is indeed no other than a political league and alliance for mutual support and defence.'[29] The erastianism which to nineteenth-century critics seemed implicit in this relationship appeared to Warburton in a different guise; as the guarantee of security, disciplinary power and influence in the life of the nation.[30]

At first sight the Glorious Revolution may appear to have brought about a reduction in the independence of the English Church. As if to confirm this impression the future primate, William Wake, in his reply to Francis Atterbury's High Church plea for the summoning of Convocation (a request granted during the reign of William and Mary) showed himself prepared to subordinate the authority of the ecclesiastical courts to that of Parliament.[31] Yet the level of erastianism expressed in the Revolution Settlement and even by theorists such as Wake was nothing new. Charles II and James II between them had ruled for twenty-four years without recourse to Convocation. The fatal act of submission by the Church had occurred much earlier, in 1664, when Archbishop Sheldon had surrendered to Parliament the traditional right of the clergy to tax themselves. With the disappearance of this vestige of autonomy any remaining necessity for the later Stuart monarchy to summon Convocation had vanished.

The essential difference between the post-Revolutionary position of the Church of England and that which obtained earlier was not one of increased erastianism, so much as change in the nature of the political power to which the Church was subject.[32] Prior to the accession of William and Mary authority was prescriptive, being seen to repose in a divinely appointed ruler. With the rejection of the Stuart dynasty in the bloodless coup of 1688 control of ecclesiastical as well as secular affairs passed in some measure to the will of Parliament. Royal fiat was replaced, especially after the reign of Queen Anne, by the corporate decision-making of Lords and Commons. The preference for the Stuart monarchy expressed by the more conservative section of the clergy merely obscures the fact that the new political circumstances did not immediately signify any practical increase in secular interference.

There were, nevertheless, ominous portents of things to come. In 1717 the king in order to deal with internal dissensions among the clergy and to prevent a formal confrontation with the government silenced the independent voice of the Church by the simple expedient of proroguing Convocation.[33] From then on the only official medium for the expression of ecclesiastical opinion was the House of Lords where matters affecting religion vied with other issues for the attention of government. During the early years of the Hanoverian monarchy the practical implications of erastianism became obvious as the bench of bishops was increasingly transformed into a special group of political functionaries.

The effect of the secular role of the bishops upon the Church was highly ambiguous. On the one hand their corporate presence in the Upper House ensured that they were able to exercise greater political power than at any time in post-Reformation history. Eighteenth-century parliaments met regularly, and as a result of the Revolution Settlement their authority was far greater than that of their predecessors. The bishops with their tendency to act unanimously constituted an important block vote in a chamber which rarely had more than 145 members in attendance.[34] Their influence was particularly important at a time when politics tended to be characterized by factions rather than formal parties.[35] Benjamin Franklin, noting the unequivocal support given by the bishops to Lord North in his preparations for war against the American colonists, observed bitterly: 'Twenty-four bishops with all the lords in possession or expectation of places, make a dead majority which renders all debating ridiculous.'[36] The bishops, remaining as they did in London throughout the parliamentary session, ensured at least from one point of view that on matters of national concern the Church's voice was heard, if not in its own right then at least in the decisions taken by Parliament.

Against this positive interpretation the expectation of political loyalty and service severely circumscribed the exercise of spiritual leadership within the Church of England. The operation of patronage promoted an unseemly scramble for translation to wealthy sees. The demands of patrons both in London and at the local level served to divert the attention of bishops from their administrative and spiritual responsibilities, encouraging perfunctory attention to such important duties as diocesan visitation, confirmation and the examination of ordinands. One of the most notorious cases was that of the Latitudinarian bishop, Benjamin Hoadly. During his six-year incumbency of the see of Bangor, Hoadly, who was a cripple, only once visited his remote, mountainous and entirely unsuitable Welsh diocese, and then only by sea.[37]

Close integration with politics and the ruling class may have compromised the Church's leadership but the vitality of the religious Establishment was also sapped by economic malaise. Lay impropriation of ecclesiastical revenues was directly responsible for the abject poverty of many parochial livings. The efficient functioning of the priesthood depended upon a secure base of tithes and endowments, but the reforms carried out by Henry VIII, whilst stripping impropriated revenues from monastic foundations, had merely delivered these assets into lay hands, thus consolidating the problem of alienation. Professor Best has estimated that more than 50 per cent of eighteenth-century benefices belonged to lay patrons, a fact which had a direct bearing upon the economic condition of the parish clergy.[38] The financial status of vicars varied widely depending upon their right to the greater and lesser tithes, but the class of stipendiary curates, by far the most numerous clerical category, suffered almost universal impoverishment. As well as inadequate remuneration many lacked security of tenure either by the design of the patron or by their own neglect to obtain an episcopal licence.[39] The condition of the ordinary curate spoke eloquently of the need for further reform.

The end product of the remorseless drain upon resources was a parochial system whose abuses mirrored the failings of the higher clergy. By the establishment of Queen Anne's Bounty in 1704 for the redirection of the Crown's exactions of first fruits and tenths towards poor livings some attempt was made to rectify the ill effects of secular control, but the ad hoc nature of the distribution system, with its reliance upon the lot, and the inadequacy of the sums available meant that little impression was made upon the overall problem.[40] Indeed, in at least one diocese there are signs that towards the end of the century the situation was growing worse.[41] While there was no automatic guarantee that higher salaries alone would ensure a more effective parochial ministry, the root of the problem lay in the impropriation of tithes. They were regarded in common with advowsons as a species of private property and, therefore, in Hanoverian eyes as being inviolable.

By the 1790s the practical weaknesses associated with financial stringency were obvious to critics and supporters of the Church alike, even though the tension provoked by events in Europe prevented the application of any significant remedies. Pluralism was endemic in the English countryside. Curates, both fully priested and at the preliminary stage of deacon's orders, were in a permanent and impecunious state of over-supply. As a consequence aspiring candidates competed for the doubtful privilege of serving country parishes at a level of remuneration which made it necessary to unite the work with the cure of one or more neighbouring livings.

The financial hardship of the lowest sector of the clergy can be illustrated from the visitation returns of many dioceses. The enquiry form sent to incumbents in the Norwich diocese at the triennial visitation held in 1794 included a typical section dealing with the employment of stipendiary curates. Section VII of the form enquired of incumbents: 'Have you a licensed Curate residing in your Parish? or what Distance from it? What is his Name? What Salary do you allow him? Doth he serve any other and what

Cure?'[42] Of the 41 returns examined by the author 14 (34 per cent) indicate that the incumbent served the cure himself with no clerical assistance. In 2 cases (5 per cent) curates were employed at a salary of £50 p.a. or more, while 12 other returns make no specific mention of the level of remuneration. The remaining 13 parishes (32 per cent) received the attention of more poorly paid curates, the normal stipend being £25 p.a. but in one case dropping to as little as 12 guineas p.a.[43] In this situation the return made by the Rev. George Deane of Kenninghall parish typified the practical choice that had to be faced by the underpaid stipendiary curate:

VI [Vicar not resident]   He resides at Littleport near Ely – He has another Benefice – I do not know what Church he serves.
VII   I am a licensed Curate, I do not reside in the Parish, I live two Miles Distance from it. Geo. Deane is my Name, my salary is 21 Pounds a year – I serve two other Cures, Shropham and Snetherton – I have served the Cure of Kenninghall above Twenty one Years.[44]

In response to further questions concerning the frequency of administration of the Lord's Supper and the number of communicants, Deane indicated a quarterly celebration involving twenty to thirty parishioners. Given the population of this lowland parish of 128 houses and the total absence of Dissenters, Quakers or Roman Catholics, it is hard to avoid the conclusion that the small communicant figure points to a certain religious lethargy; a lack of involvement which may or may not have been associated with the need to share the services of a clergyman with two neighbouring cures.[45] Attendance at communion varied widely within the diocese. Hintlesham, which enjoyed the advantages of a resident rector, was able to produce fifty communicants from a total of fifty-four dwellings.[46] At the other extreme the situation at Aldeburgh, a parish of 300 houses and tenements on the Suffolk coast with no Quakers or Catholics and only one Dissenter, prompted the non-resident vicar, Robert Blayney, to write from his London home lamenting the scale of rural irreligion. Replying to the bishop's question concerning habitual non-attendance at public worship Blayney remarked, 'There are too many in this Parish as in many others, who absent themselves from public worship.'[47]

The relative poverty of many incumbents over and above the plight of stipendiary curates combined with changing social values to affect on a wide scale the provision of parsonage houses. Notwithstanding their importance to an effective religious establishment organized on territorial lines, many diocesan returns mention their non-existence, dilapidation or total unsuitability. In some cases the poor state of repair or the lack of a house was used as a reason for non-residence; in other instances the material neglect seems to have been caused by prior disuse or by the absence of a resident clergyman. In either case insufficient attention to maintenance was compounded by financial restriction. Repair or rebuilding on a scale deemed to be appropriate to the office of a parish clergyman could by the end of the century involve an incumbent in considerable outlay. In 1778 the Vicar of Leigh in Lancashire reported to his bishop that he had rebuilt and repaired the vicarage house and outbuildings at 'great' though unspecified expense.[48] Nine years later the estimate for rebuilding the ruinous parsonage at Godington in Oxfordshire in 'proper and fitting' fashion amounted to £200 not including reusable materials valued at £20.[49]

The result of these developments was a decline in the effective supervision of many parishes at a time when the population of the country was increasing rapidly. The absence of clerical supervision was not a new phenomenon, but the growth of pluralism and non-residence in the course of the eighteenth century exacerbated the problem. As many poor livings developed patterns of worship based on protracted periods of administration from neighbouring parishes, a sizeable segment of the population grew up with no experience of a resident clergyman.

Paradoxically, the improving economic condition of other more fortunate members of the rural clergy tended to diminish still further the effectiveness of the Church at the parochial level. From the 1760s onwards agricultural improvements combined with land enclosure to benefit greatly those incumbents who were fortunate enough to remain in possession of their tithes. Enclosure, which in the years after 1759 became a widespread practice in the arable lowland counties, was normally accompanied by the commutation of tithe. Landowners were only too willing to exchange what would have become a sliding clerical tax on their improvement for a fixed payment, accompanied in many instances by a settlement of land. The latter increased considerably the size of the traditional glebe. Professor Ward has estimated that in spite of the depressive effect upon the overall statistics exercised by unenclosed land, the figures for commutation suggest that the average glebe multiplied during the enclosure period by a factor of 2 or 3.[50]

Those affected by this transfer of property could experience a dramatic change of fortunes. In his report on Oxfordshire agriculture published in 1794 Richard Davis gave particulars of a vicarage near Banbury which was subject to an immediate increase in value from £105 to £220 p.a.[51] Others were less spectacular but the gains made were still substantial. The new-found wealth imparted an enhanced social status represented in bricks and mortar by a generation of ostentatious parsonages and rectories far removed in character from their predecessors. Apart from gaining an entrance to the ranks of the landed proprietors the newly improved clergy as men of learning and possessions found their way in increasing numbers onto the local bench of magistrates. If non-resident, demoralized and overworked stipendiary curates in the poorer impropriated livings were unable to maintain effective contact with the majority of the rural population, their wealthier brethren were no more favourably situated. For them the difficulty of communication stemmed from economic success and from their consequent willingness to participate in the structure of social control.

There was, however, another side to the parochial ministry. Visitation returns show clearly that many clergymen, even if technically non-resident, approached their parish duties with diligence and a sense of responsibility. Divine service was normally performed at least once every Sunday, while some of the more populous parishes enjoyed morning and afternoon worship. John Barlow, the Vicar of Leigh in Lancashire, reported in 1778 that in addition to two Sunday services in the parish church, prayers were said during the week.[52] Most incumbents or curates made some attempt to catechize the young even if their efforts were confined to the period of Lent or to a few weeks in the summer months. The sacrament of communion varied in its observance from the minimum established by the great festivals of the Christian year to a regular monthly celebration.[53] In the strongly nucleated villages of the midland and southern counties with their focus upon the parish church the clergyman was still able to exercise a dominating influence in rural society. If he did not command the active allegiance of every parishioner he could at least ensure that his parish did not experience the religious pluralism found in areas of greater economic diversity such as southern and central Lancashire. There by the end of the century a number of parishes and chapelries contained 5,000 or more inhabitants distributed among as many as a dozen townships, a situation which made close supervision of religious life impossible.[54] But in the vast majority of country parishes clerical influence, if only in a restraining form, remained an important feature of social life.

The twofold weakness of the Hanoverian Church, the social alienation arising from clerical poverty and that which stemmed from the opposite condition, combined by the end of the century to enhance the attractiveness of newer, more vigorous and more socially relevant forms of Christianity. Lord Sidmouth's awareness of the loss of popular support prompted him in May 1811 to warn his fellow peers that if steps were not taken to redress the situation they would soon discover to their consternation that while the outward form of a religious Establishment remained, the affections of the people had been given to other bodies; to ecclesiastical groups that were by definition sectarian. It is in this context that the phenomenon of Dissenting evangelism has to be considered.

2 · Itinerancy and Dissent

THE PERIOD AFTER 1780 was as important for ecclesiastical life as it was for the evolution of English society as a whole. For Protestant Dissent the historical significance of the ensuing decades was if anything even greater than for those groups which sought to defend the privileges of the Established Church. For the former the late eighteenth century represented the crucial stage in its development; the process of change from contemptible insignificance to the full flower of Victorian Nonconformity. The point of transition was marked by a new and highly visible phenomenon; the widespread employment of itinerant evangelism. Itinerancy had operated in desultory fashion since the mid-seventeenth century, but for the majority of congregations the age of the field preacher did not commence until the period of conflict with Revolutionary France. As the practice began to spread during the 1790s the gains resulting from its application were immediate and obvious. Long before the defeat of Napoleon in 1815 it had enabled Dissent to penetrate deeply into the fabric of rural society, especially in areas where Methodism was weak. In the light of this achievement and the degree of anxiety aroused in contemporary minds by the undeniable success of popular preaching, it is all the more surprising that its social prominence during a period of unprecedented tension has been almost entirely overlooked.

One important break in this silence was made in the early twentieth century by the French historian, Elie Halévy. Though his study of the English people gave only passing attention to the religious aspect of Napoleonic society, the author remarked upon the adoption of the Methodist practice of itinerancy by Calvinistic Dissent. In his observations concerning the extent of the religious transformation involved, itinerancy was linked with the abandonment of the inveterate autonomy of local congregations and the evolution of a new form of academy shaped explicitly on evangelical lines.[1] But Halévy's remarks remained little more than allusions. He offered no assessment of the extent of change, nor did he investigate the adaptation of the traditional pastorate which lay at the heart of the process. His appreciation of the role and significance of the new academies was at best only partial, and he provided no indication of the importance of Dissenting itinerancy for the development of mature Nonconformity.

Despite these limitations the degree of insight shown by Halévy was quite exceptional. Prior to the 1960s scholarly interest in Dissent was largely confined to the parochial sphere of denominational journals and histories and to the equally limited area of religious biography. More recently the balance of historical scholarship has changed and these restrictions have been pushed aside. An increasing volume of published material attests to the significant growth of interest in non-established forms of Protestantism.

Among these publications the most prominent treatment of Dissenting itinerancy is that by Professor Ward in *Religion and Society in England 1790–1850*. Some impression of the scale of the movement is conveyed by this work, but as the author's references are designed to serve a wider theme, the reader is offered only a glimpse of the practice. Although itinerancy is not presented as a regional phenomenon, the examples given are largely drawn from the southern and midland counties. Less well known and still more restricted in geographical scope is a study of the Salisbury village preaching controversy by David Jeremy.[2] This article, which takes as its source a series of polemical tracts published in 1798, is concerned with only one provincial centre, but it contains analysis of a more general character. A third important contribution comes from a short study by Dr Nuttall dealing with the significance of Trevecca College.[3] In contrast to the normal preoccupation with the earlier generation of Dissenting academies, this work directs the attention of the reader to the neglected subject of the late eighteenth-century evangelical seminary, an institution displaying a strong partiality for the distinctive practice of itinerant preaching. More recently an interesting comparison has been drawn between evangelical revival in the English context and North American revivalist preaching.[4]

Elsewhere significant scholarly attention is confined to the realm of academic dissertations.[5] The Calvinistic Methodist roots of the movement are exposed, for example, in P. E. Sangster's study of Rowland Hill, the notoriously irregular minister of Surrey Chapel, while the development of itinerancy within Particular Baptist circles is given a brief examination by O. C. Robison.[6] In addition a number of studies deal with the political context of Dissenting expansion.[7]

This brief historiographical survey demonstrates the scant attention so far paid to the subject. Even the most direct consideration to date in a recent article by Roger Martin ignores the change which overtook the traditional pastorate, arguably one of the most important results of the adoption of itinerancy.[8] The silence of the historians prompts a number of questions. What interpretations of the period have been offered? How did the staid and introspective Dissenting community of the eighteenth century react to the appearance in its midst of itinerant preaching? Perhaps most important of all: what effect did the practice have upon the traditional features of Dissenting life?

The social turmoil of the Revolutionary era presented unique opportunities for experimentation. If innovation was to characterize Dissent during the 1790s what more natural source of inspiration was there than that provided by the earlier Methodist Revival? Amid growing signs of weakness on the part of social and religious authority Methodism bequeathed to evangelical Dissent a pattern of activity which presented an abrupt challenge to existing ideas. The probability of influence is obvious for the points of contact between Independents, Baptists and Methodists, especially those of the Calvinist variety, were numerous. A number of the rising generation of Dissenting ministers attributed their Christian conversion to the evangelical preaching of 'Methodist' clergymen like William Grimshaw of Haworth and John Berridge of Everton. Indeed the origin of many independent congregations can be traced to a similar source, while to that influence must be added the more general contribution made by Wesley and Whitefield.

Several factors account for the particular influence of George Whitefield on English Dissenters. Apart from the natural doctrinal affinity that existed between fellow Calvinists, his extensive ministry overcame their spatial isolation. His peculiar tolerance, which posed no threat to their prosperity but rather encouraged membership of local congregations, helped to break down the reserve they felt towards enthusiasm. Moreover, the geographical coincidence of Calvinistic Methodism with the traditional centres of Baptist and Independent strength at Bristol, Birmingham and London, encouraged the development of close relationships. In the longer term the comparatively loose structure of the former enabled many Whitefieldite congregations to become Independent churches, and even the Countess of Huntingdon's Connexion with its greater degree of central control was not always successful in preventing the drift into independency, whether at the personal or the congregational level.[9] More subtle than the direct accession of Methodist converts was the influence which emanated from seminaries whose early development had links with Calvinistic Methodism. The list includes such names as Trevecca, Marlborough–Painswick, Oswestry–Newcastle-under-Lyme, Mile End–Hoxton, and Hackney.

Yet to attribute every evangelistic development to the example of Methodism would be almost as unsatisfactory as to ignore the influence of Whitefield and his fellow-travellers altogether. The provenance of certain patterns of activity has to be sought within the life of Dissent itself. In the West of England a tradition of evangelical Calvinism associated with the Bristol Academy and the Baptist Western Association reached back to the earlier part of the eighteenth century.[10] Similarly in Essex the formation in 1798 of a Congregational union for the evangelization of the county was the work of a group of ministers who were almost without exception products of Homerton Academy and who therefore represented the old Independent tradition.[11] Some external influence has to be acknowledged in the latter case in so far as the formation of the London Missionary Society provided the immediate inspiration for the union, but the importance of the local Dissenting attitude must not be overlooked.

In many ways itinerancy seems to have constituted the most effective vehicle for the communication of ideas. Its importance is demonstrated by its widespread use. Not only Methodists and Dissenters but also that other branch of religious nonconformity, the English Roman Catholic community made use of its flexibility. Roman Catholicism possessed a tradition of peripatetic ministry dating back to the earliest days of the Jesuit mission in England.[12] Moreover, with the rise of 'the Platform' itinerant proselytizers for political causes began to appear; the advance guard of those later educators of public opinion, the lecturers of the Anti-Corn Law League.[13]

In the historiography of Dissent lineal development and the maintenance of traditional principles form two important themes. Interruptions to the ecclesiastical inheritance caused by external influences tend to be minimized. The numerous histories of local congregations provide the most obvious and understandable examples of this concern for continuity, but they are not unique. Similar attitudes can be found in works of much wider interest. Their presence has resulted in an unhealthy deference to received opinion, and a tendency either to ignore inconvenient historical developments, or to offer unsatisfactory explanations of their significance.

At the heart of late-eighteenth-century Dissent there is a suggestion of theological change: an apparent mutation in the earlier unswerving allegiance to classical Calvinism. Yet denominational historians in their concern to demonstrate the strand of internal development have invariably misrepresented its real significance. Even the great Congregational scholar, R. W. Dale, is guilty of this, for he describes the 'Moderate Calvinism' of those responsible for early nineteenth-century itinerancy as 'Calvinism in decay'.[14] By resorting to the notion of decline he ignores the positive nature of their theology and the infusion of practical evangelicalism by which it was accompanied. Though comparison with the developed concepts of the previous century may be valuable, Dale's comments do little justice to the seriousness with which the new theological consensus was held. Its viability, by contrast, was in no doubt among its adherents. In 1791 John Stanger, a noted village preacher in Kent and pastor of the Baptist church at Bessels Green, led his congregation away from Arminianism, submitting a declaration of Calvinist belief which was sufficient to satisfy the rather conservative Kent and Sussex Association of Baptist Churches.[15] Moreover, in spite of Dale's opinion that moderate Calvinism represented a step towards the complete eclipse of Calvinist belief, William Roby of Manchester, an ardent exponent of the new position, was still able in 1819 to produce a strong defence of the doctrine of predestination; a theological argument in which he insisted, 'That God, after reasonings and remonstrances, does actually "leave some to a final continuance in sin, and to the dreadful consequences of their guilt", is a manifest fact.'[16] Elsewhere he described evangelical Calvinism as the difficult 'middle path of truth' between the unpalatable Huntingtonian views and Arminianism.[17] For a theological position which represented decay moderate Calvinism received surprisingly frequent and enthusiastic exposition both on account of its doctrines and its practical tendencies.[18]

Although Dale's assessment of the theological basis of evangelical Dissent may raise considerable doubts, his analysis of the changes in polity which accompanied the growth of evangelism is both perceptive and convincing. He argues that even before Congregational churches experienced the full impact of revival their traditional regard for independency had been diluted by the accession of Presbyterians disenchanted with heterodoxy. The remnants of congregational polity finally succumbed to the undenominational spirit of evangelism sweeping the churches at the end of the century. In the new climate congregational polity continued to receive lip service but the vitality of the principle had largely disappeared.[19] A more recent survey of English Congregationalism suggests that a continuing sense of denominational character is discernible in the contemporary interest in Puritanism and in the shape of the infant county unions.[20] It would be pointless to deny the existence of a strong and growing sense of denominational identity by the third decade of the nineteenth century, but the survival of earlier Dissenting characteristics is another matter. Dale's thesis concerning the demise of congregational polity is not, therefore, necessarily impaired. It is arguable whether the traditional pattern was even compatible with a period of aggressive evangelism whatever stage denominational consciousness had reached. The later work ultimately appears to concede the very point that Dale is making by using the chapter title 'Gardens Walled Around' as a description of Congregationalism in the period prior to 1760.

In Baptist historiography Underwood identified a shift in theology which he associated with the work of Andrew Fuller of Kettering. The change apparently came about as Fuller's views became accepted in the east midland counties and further afield, especially following the publication of his book *The Gospel of Christ worthy of all acceptation* in 1785.[21] More recently the uniqueness of 'Fullerism' has been called into question by the discovery of the similar tendencies affecting Calvinistic Baptist circles in the West of England.

While these examples demonstrate a certain capacity to accept ideas of innovation and change, denominational historians have tended to favour the concept of gradual development and continuity. A more questioning approach is found among contemporary observers and in the writings of modern scholars whose wider interests have prompted a fresh appraisal of ecclesiastical events. In a tract defending village preaching, Samuel Clift, an Independent minister at Chippenham, commented upon the striking contrast between the introspective spirituality of his Dissenting forebears and the mood of evangelical zeal derived from Methodism.[22] Awareness of this transformation was not confined to sympathetic observers: few were more conscious of the changes taking place than those High Churchmen who fulminated against the growing activity of itinerant preachers. Richard Mant, Rector of All Saints parish Southampton, regarded much of contemporary Dissent as being indistinguishable from Calvinistic Methodism. He insisted that it had more in common with radical Puritanism than earlier eighteenth-century independency.[23] A similar vein of criticism can be traced among orthodox Dissenters of the more traditional kind. There the process of innovation was noted without approval, while the new patterns of churchmanship were greeted with hostility rather than enthusiasm.[24]

In recent years a fresh understanding of the period has emerged. The earlier emphasis upon doctrinal development is now treated as part of a much wider change of outlook affecting many congregations during the later part of the century. From the older viewpoint, epitomized by John Gill of Southwark, life appeared to be a closed system in which the continuous cycle of prosperity and adversity experienced by God's people was closely linked with the various stages of biblical eschatology. The later position adopted by evangelical Calvinism was entirely different. With its open-ended, progressive view of the divine purpose in human affairs, it turned the prevailing introspection into a mood of expansion and optimism.[25] It represented the marriage of traditional theology with the more positive concerns of the Enlightenment. The revolution in thought forms explains how the late eighteenth-century preoccupation with evangelism became possible within the context of a continuing Calvinist theology.

Another approach to the problem of historical continuity is suggested by Edward Thompson who tentatively attributes the unusually high working-class response to Methodism during the Napoleonic era to 'political' and temporal frustration.[26] Against a background of unachieved aspiration the increased involvement of working men in evangelism is treated as an essentially negative phenomenon. The question naturally arises as to the relevance of this interpretation to Calvinistic Dissent. While Thompson implies the existence of clear distinctions between those who responded to these differing forms of extra-Establishment religion he does not qualify his basic thesis.[27] By contrast contemporary evidence suggests that, whatever the circumstances of other religious groups, the frustration theory cannot account for the wave of Dissenting itinerancy which developed in the late

1790s. Apart from chronological difficulties the village preachers and their adherents displayed an air of confidence and optimism which sprang from a sense of social and material progress rather than failure. The growth in their activity certainly coincided with the rising tide of millennialism which reached its height at the turn of the century, but there was little of a chiliastic flavour about their preaching.

If the idea of a religious substitute for political fulfilment proves unsatisfactory, Professor Hobsbawm has an alternative ready to hand: he offers a cyclical pattern of closely connected political and religious activity based upon the behaviour of the early Primitive Methodists.[28] But what may apply to Methodism has no necessary relevance to Calvinistic Dissent. In the case of the latter there is nothing to suggest any significant political involvement either among the preachers or the hearers.[29] Nevertheless the chronological coincidence between the two spheres can hardly be overlooked, and as such continually invites close scrutiny.

While historiography can offer valuable insights, an understanding of the full implications of itinerancy requires a more detailed examination of Dissenting life. For this a convenient starting point is offered by the theoretical element mentioned earlier: the issue of theology and related attitudes. Much has been written about the theological changes evident in the period after 1750. From the now customary account of the rejection of high Calvinism it is possible to assume the adoption of a quite different set of beliefs; ideas more compatible with the needs of practical evangelism. Yet it is difficult to differentiate on doctrinal grounds between the so-called high Calvinists led by Gill and Brine and their more moderate successors.[30] There is a further suggestion that the need for theological moderation was a problem peculiar to Particular Baptists, since Independents were able to negotiate the middle years of the eighteenth century with a doctrinal flexibility derived from the influence of Richard Baxter and Philip Doddridge, but even this is too simple. The theological situation does not submit to easy analysis and it must be sufficient to notice some of the salient features.

Joseph Ivimey, who belonged to the second generation of moderates, depicted in vivid terms the stultifying effect of mid-century orthodoxy among Particular Baptists. While he criticized Gill and Brine for their failure to apply to their hearers the doctrines they expounded, he admitted that Gill did not openly espouse the high Calvinist view that invitations to repentance should not be given to unbelievers. But it was widely believed that those who insisted upon the obligation of Christians to urge upon the unconverted the duty of repentance detracted from the grace of God and demonstrated strong Arminian and Semi-Pelagian tendencies.[31] Independents were no less inclined to theological introspection than their Baptist counterparts and the change within their circle accomplished by the growing concern for evangelism was equally pronounced. Theological change was merely part of a general transformation of attitude affecting the whole of Dissent; the appearance of an outlook upon the world which contained the realization that not only was it the duty of Christians to communicate the gospel to the unconverted, but also their responsibility to take the initiative in overcoming those barriers which separated them from the majority of their fellow countrymen. From this new theological conviction stemmed the widespread use of itinerancy.

From this point onwards Dissenters displayed a diminishing sense of incongruity in associating the doctrine of election with an acknowledgement of the Christian duty of evangelism. The 'Declaration of the Faith and Practice' of the Particular Baptist church formed at Waterbeach in Cambridgeshire in 1826 added to a full statement of Calvinist doctrine the following rider: 'We believe ... That we are bound to support to the utmost of our ability the ordinances of God's House among ourselves, and to assist in spreading abroad the knowledge of the Gospel of Christ.'[32] But it was one thing to place election and evangelism in juxtaposition and quite another to present that doctrine as the basis for a sustained programme of village preaching. Yet even that approach to the once forbidding realm of divine prerogative was by no means uncommon in the association literature produced after 1800. Concerning the doctrine of election the Baptist Midland Association letter of 1817 commented:

How encouraging is the thought to ministers, to missionaries, to the teachers of youth, to village preachers, to the visitors of the sick, that God will gather together the number of his elect! And perhaps the words we are speaking in a barn, or a sunday school, or the cottage of affliction, at a dying bed, may be the word which the Holy Spirit will bless to the conversion of a soul, who will shine for ever among the angels of glory. God will fulfil his designs: let us be workers together with God.

The new Calvinists took a more optimistic view of the outcome of predestination than their predecessors had done; a point which was raised in several contemporary sermons. William Roby, the Independent minister at Grosvenor Street Chapel, Manchester, insisted that Calvinism was not necessarily pessimistic concerning the number of the elect: in his opinion many of its proponents entertained an entirely contrary conviction.[33]

The examples of William Huntington and William Gadsby prove that some high Calvinists were prepared to engage in itinerant preaching, and it is possible, therefore, that no simple equation can be drawn between moderate evangelical Calvinism and attention to the unconverted. Nevertheless, Gadsby rejected any idea of faith as a duty to be urged upon the unregenerate,[34] and it appears that the content and approach of his preaching differed considerably from that of his evangelical contemporaries. It would seem unwise in any case to generalize from two untypical exponents of the strict position. In most cases high Calvinism remained a local and introspective phenomenon, as at Sandy in Bedfordshire where in 1827 a short-lived splinter group separated from the local Dissenting churches connected with the Bedfordshire Union of Christians.[35] Where evangelistic agencies encountered these views the noisome doctrines were firmly resisted. In one case involving the London Itinerant Society this led to the rejection of a prospective preacher on the grounds that the man concerned, a Mr Alderson, 'denied the Doctrine of the General Call to Sinners'.[36]

By their very nature the theological issues emphasize the suddenness with which itinerancy entered Dissenting life. They offer an interpretation which accords with the allegations of past neglect made by leading participants in the movement.[37] Yet firm historical precedents did exist, and so far as it is possible to distinguish the contributory elements, three strands of practical influence stand out.

The first comprised a tradition of itinerancy wholly indigenous to Dissent, a practice noted by William Kingsbury in his *Apology for Village Preachers* as dating from the seventeenth century.[38] In the years immediately prior to the Commonwealth, itinerants holding Baptist views could be found in the southern counties of England, among them Thomas Collier a native of Surrey. Collier, whose theological sympathies lay in a Calvinist direction, worked as an evangelist over a wide geographical area. Between 1634 and 1646 he visited places as widely separated as York, London and Taunton before settling eventually as pastor of a congregation at Upottery in Devon.[39] In other cases the motive for seventeenth-century itinerancy was more explicitly pastoral. In 1689 the first general assembly of Particular Baptist ministers meeting in London commissioned itinerant preachers for the task of collecting and reorganizing those congregations which had been scattered during the years of persecution.[40] There was in this step no obvious commitment to expansion, merely a desire to restore the status quo ante.

In 1662 the ejection of Puritan clergy under the Act of Uniformity gave a further important stimulus to evangelism. The following years saw a number of deprived clergymen turning to itinerancy. In Cambridgeshire Joseph Oddy and Francis Holcroft[41] pursued a peripatetic ministry within the county, earning themselves long periods of imprisonment, but at the same time laying a foundation for the subsequent penetration of many remote fenland villages by Dissent.[42]

Even during the long eighteenth-century decline occasional examples of itinerancy continued to appear. In Dorset the villages of the Maiden Newton area received the attention of a local family named Reed, who, in an apparently isolated initiative, held meetings during the 1760s both in cottages and the open air.[43] It was, perhaps, not entirely coincidental that the

Dorset Missionary and Itinerant Society, which commenced its work in 1795, stationed its first full-time evangelist at Maiden Newton.[44] Nor were the eighteenth-century examples confined to laymen, for some ministers demonstrated a firm commitment to itinerant evangelism. Benjamin Francis, a product of the Bristol Academy and pastor of a Baptist congregation at Horsley in Gloucestershire, for many years undertook regular monthly preaching excursions to towns and villages with no existing evangelical ministry.[45] As the academy at Bristol encouraged Baptist evangelicalism, so among the Independents a similar influence was exerted by James Scott's seminary at Heckmondwike near Leeds, an institution which flourished for almost three decades until its tutor's death in 1783.

A second practical stimulus came from the many contacts with early Methodism. The theological proximity encouraged a synthesis in which traditional Dissenting features were linked to a more flexible concept of ministry. In Staffordshire and the neighbouring counties the activity of Jonathan Scott, a former captain of the 7th Dragoons, who was ordained at Lancaster in 1776 as a 'presbyter at large', provides a clear example of this concatenation.[46] For thirty years Scott itinerated widely, establishing congregations which in due course evolved into Independent churches, but he himself eschewed any pastoral commitment. With the opening of Surrey Chapel in 1783 Scott's influential and eccentric contemporary, Rowland Hill, appeared to adopt a more normal pastoral role. Yet he too had little time for pastoral responsibilities, spending months at a time engaged in lengthy preaching tours.[47] More important than the isolated influence of Hill and Scott was the wider contribution made by converts from Methodism who, as a matter of conviction, endeavoured to combine missionary zeal with genuine pastoral concern.[48]

By the end of the century the number of Dissenting academies which owed at least an inspirational debt to Methodism had increased considerably. Their work tended to obscure the more direct influences. The majority of new or revived foundations expected students to take part in a regular programme of itinerant preaching and to regard that work as an integral part of the Dissenting minister's responsibilities. Even the Baptist academy at Bradford, whose links with Methodism were rather tenuous, ensured that its men were well grounded in the practice.[49] William Steadman, the first president of the academy and a lifelong exponent of evangelism, had himself witnessed during the 1790s the striking achievements of Methodist itinerancy in Cornwall.[50]

The third and most decisive practical stimulus emerged in the 1790s with the initiation of overseas missions: the Particular Baptist Missionary Society in 1792 followed three years later by the predominantly Independent London Missionary Society. Organized home mission appeared almost

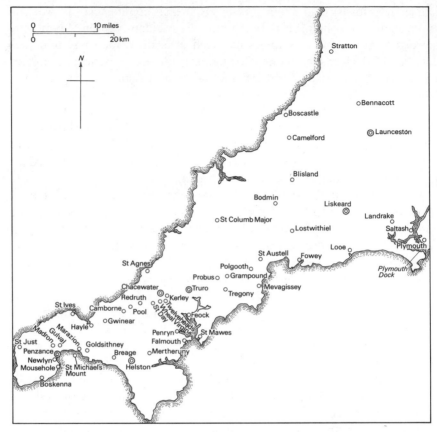

1   Occasional evangelistic tours. Cornish mission, Steadman and Franklin, July and August 1797.

During this eight-week tour sponsored by the Baptist Missionary Society, both men travelled the length of Cornwall twice, frequently preaching in separate places for several days at a time. Certain towns formed obvious centres for the evangelization of the rural hinterland; these are indicated on the map by means of a double circle. Mention of a preaching stop at St Michaels between Truro and St Columb Major may be a reference to the village of St Michael Penkevil, three miles south-east of Truro. The preaching activities of both men in the vicinity of Chacewater included visits to the miners of Wheal Virgin, a copper mine situated two miles to the south of the town.

Sources: Rippon, *Register*, vol. 3, pp. 56–9; R. Thomas, *Report on a Survey of the Mining District of Cornwall from Chasewater to Camborne* (London, 1819).

simultaneously, though a prototype already existed in the form of Societas Evangelica, a society formed to supply lay preachers to the suburban villages of the metropolis and which was in being as early as 1778.[51] Close relationships existed between home and overseas mission during the early phase of development. Independents such as Samuel Greatheed, David

Bogue and George Burder, and the Baptist leaders William Steadman, John Saffery and Samuel Pearce directed their energies towards both objectives from the mid-1790s. While they laid the foundations of the overseas work they were equally active at home creating local evangelistic unions and national societies for the support of itinerancy.

Apart from the obvious Christian concern for the religious well-being of fellow countrymen, one repeated theme of the early advocates of domestic evangelism concerned the need to counter the objection currently levelled at every attempt at overseas mission: 'What about the heathen at home?' When, in the wake of a proposal to the general meeting at Birmingham in September 1795, the infant Baptist Missionary Society agreed to the appropriation of part of its funds for the cause of home mission (thus anticipating the work of the Baptist Society in London, for the Encouragement and Support of Itinerant and Village Preaching[52] by almost two years), the reason given was the need to take account of the charge of domestic neglect.[53] The support given to home mission by the society was limited in scale and of comparatively short duration, but it represented the first attempt to organize the work on a national and denominational basis. Moreover, with this experiment home and overseas evangelism became for a short period the responsibility of a single body. In the society's accounts 1810 is the last year in which village preaching appears as an item of expenditure. Although the proportion allocated to home mission never approached the overseas figure, two Cornish preaching tours were financed in 1796 and 1797, help was afforded to various ministers for expenses incurred in local village preaching, and for several years Thomas Wastfield, a schoolmaster from Imber, was enabled to itinerate in the Vale of Pewsey and the upper Avon valley in Wiltshire.[54] Careful scrutiny of the early reports of the London Missionary Society provides no evidence of a similar involvement in home missionary enterprise, but that is hardly surprising since the financial commitments of the latter society were from the outset more extensive. In Independent circles the initiative in home mission belonged instead to the new and specifically evangelistic county unions.

The growth of itinerancy produced inevitable adjustments to the concept of ministry. Traditionally this had focussed upon the settled pastor ministering to the spiritual needs of the gathered company of God's elect, together with those regarded as serious enquirers. But the qualities of solidity and exemplary piety which characterized so many eighteenth-century ministers failed to compensate for their inflexibility. The limitations of the pastoral approach became increasingly obvious against a background of unprecedented social change. Within the Dissenting community the Independent congregations tended to make the most rigid distinction between lay membership and ministry and the concomitant spheres of

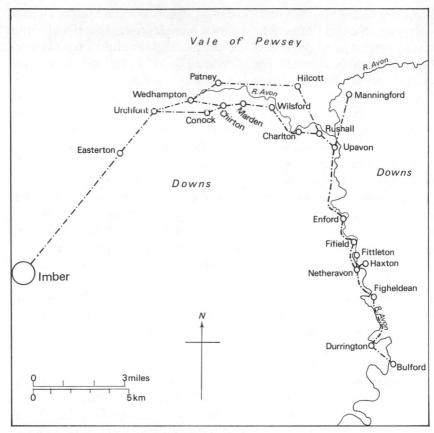

2   Circuit itinerancy. Wiltshire. Village preaching by Thomas Wastfield of Imber in the upper Avon valley, 1797–8.

The details of these fortnightly preaching journeys sponsored by the Baptist Missionary Society are taken from Wastfield's Journal which covers the period to April 1798 (see Appendix A). The precise route is sometimes difficult to ascertain, for, although in his early visits to the villages bordering the Vale of Pewsey Wastfield used the direct Lavington turnpike, the later pattern of visits encompassing only Netheravon, Fifield and Enford entailed a long journey by road, and on moonlit nights it would appear that the direct route was possible across the downs.

activity. In part this reflected the accession of erstwhile Presbyterians dissatisfied with the movement of many of their co-religionists towards Unitarian views; in part it was a consequence of the esteem felt by Independents for a learned and properly trained ministry. Whatever its origins may have been this dominant eighteenth-century view had undergone a dramatic change by the late 1790s. By then many settled pastors were, like John Adams at Salisbury and Thomas Hillyard at Olney, undertaking regular village preaching excursions in addition to their recognized commitments.[55] At the same time lay church members in increasing numbers were at work in ministerial and semi-ministerial capacities: preaching, exhorting, reading sermons and leading cottage prayer meetings. The conceptual transformation was completed by the appearance of the paid, full-time itinerant evangelist working in conjunction with certain of the newly formed evangelistic agencies.

These different categories express the true significance of contemporary change in ministry: a significance consisting not so much in geographical mobility and the capability of rapid extension, as in the melting down of professional attitudes and structures, and in the maintenance of the subsequent state of flux throughout the critical wartime period. This process, though uncomfortable to those of a conservative stamp, was vital for the growth that was already taking place by the turn of the century. The seeds of the closer approximation between the roles of pastor and church member are to be found, paradoxically, in earlier eighteenth-century practice. Within the tradition of English independency the use of the 'gifted brother' as occasional preacher, and the relatively simple procedure by which a man of proven gifts could be set apart for pastoral ministry, contributed to the ease with which mid-eighteenth-century conventions could be adapted. Particular Baptists, with no equivalent of the Presbyterian influx into Independent circles, and displaying a lesser concern for formal education than their fellow Dissenters, had tended to have the most radical tradition, embodying the greatest similarity of status between ordained pastor and ordinary church member.[56] Apart from the standard theological objections concerning the indiscriminate offer of the gospel, they had invariably accepted lay ministry more readily than Independents.[57]

But, as before, indigenous factors were supplemented by the example of Methodism. There is ample evidence to suggest that the Methodist use of lay resources to offer a wide range of preaching-related activities provided a pattern for the subsequent development of Dissenting ministry. In spite of the occasional appearance of itinerant preaching in earlier years, it was the influence of Methodism that led the new generation of Dissenters to link the traditional emphasis upon the settled ministry with a firm acceptance of the itinerancy principle.

Both Whitefield's Connexion and the churches supervised by the Countess of Huntingdon were committed to itinerancy as an integral part of the Christian ministry. The principle was enshrined in their very organization. The activity of the Rodborough Connexion in Gloucestershire and the personally directed itinerancy reflected in surviving correspondence between the Countess and her ministers and students demonstrate its centrality within Calvinistic Methodism. In the Plan of Association drawn up in March

1790 the Countess's Connexion gave permanent expression to its perceived importance:

XIX The Lord having in the present age much blessed itinerant preaching, it is proposed that circuits be formed in different parts of the kingdom, for the further spread of the Gospel of Christ; and that preachers be sent out and supported by the connection, as collectively considered, so far as the Lord enables and their finances will allow.[58]

Although there was a remarkable acceptance of the principle among Dissenting churches during the period 1780 to 1830, comments made by some Independent and Baptist leaders suggest that its value and importance were seen in different terms from those prevailing within Methodism. Leaders of the Methodist Revival on both sides of the theological divide regarded itinerancy as a matter of fundamental importance: its vigorous application was both a measure of the spiritual health of the Christian ministry and the means of maintaining its effectiveness. By contrast the Dissenting argument for the practice ignored the appeal to intrinsic merit, preferring the more obvious considerations of scriptural precedent and manifest utility.

William Roby, in many ways typical of the leadership after 1780, even to the extent of his early experience within the ranks of Calvinistic Methodism, demonstrates this approach. In a charge given at the ordination of Joseph Johnson at Warrington in 1803 he drew upon the example of Jesus to prove that a complete ministry must include itinerant preaching.[59] On another occasion he emphasized that no conflict should be involved in the fulfilment of this obligation. 'With respect to the propriety of an itinerant ministry', he wrote, 'let it be recollected that I recommend it, not in opposition to a stated ministry, but in connection with it.'[60] In commending the itinerancy principle on scriptural grounds Roby and his contemporaries pointed not only to the example of Jesus, but also to the apostolic commission and to the practice of the early Church.

Despite his lifelong commitment to evangelism, a certain declension from the Methodist ideal is apparent in Roby's career. His letters to Sarah Roper, his future wife, and the outline of a projected autobiography reveal an early dissatisfaction with a ministry in which itinerancy was not firmly related to a pastoral base.[61] Within the pastoral context he was prepared to admit that great benefits could accrue from the practice, not least to the minister involved, through the exercise of zeal, the development of an ability to speak freely and through familiarization with the first principles of the gospel.[62] But, as with many of his contemporaries, the primary consideration remained pragmatic: the conviction that local itinerant evangelism by settled ministers provided the only practical means by which large sectors of the population could be brought into effective contact with Christian teaching.[63]

The changes to which the conventional pattern of ministry was being subjected were also reflected in the wider issue of ecclesiastical polity. Yet developments in organization frequently passed unnoticed. Early nine-teenth-century association literature extolled the virtues of independency, ignoring the incongruity this created. Far from recognizing any need for qualification, articles dealing with the subject made exaggerated claims for its historical continuity. The 1826 circular letter of the Particular Baptist Berks and West London Association followed an unexceptionable remark about the general pervasiveness of religious decline in the eighteenth century, with the more controversial suggestion that of all the religious bodies 'the congregational felt [the decline] the least, and retained the largest measure both of vital godliness and effective usefulness'. This statement in favour of the congregational principle concluded with the confident assertion that 'as these societies were the first to arouse themselves from their slumbers, so their system afforded the only receptacle for those elements of revival which the hierarchy contemptuously expelled, but could not destroy'. In adopting this theme the letter openly disregarded the Anglican–Methodist base of the revival and the substantial adaptation of independency it had encouraged within Dissent. The comparison, though intended for internal consumption, was itself part of the historical process, for it has to be seen against a background of mounting public criticism of the Established Church.[64]

In spite of this contemporary emphasis upon the resilience and vitality of the congregational principle, it is impossible to ignore the real movement towards association, interdependence and the growth of external authority: a process not capable of reversal, arising as it did from the confluent pressures of permanent social change and the practicalities of concerted evangelism. The importance of these external factors to the changing concept of the church should not be underestimated. Their presence serves to correct any undue emphasis upon the theological element.

Though this change in ecclesiastical polity can be linked with growing evangelistic pressures, the earlier lack of interest in evangelism cannot simply be attributed to a mid-eighteenth-century predilection for true congregational autonomy. Mid-century Independents comprehended various elements, not all of them equally attached to the congregational principle.[65] All that can be said is that before the pioneering efforts of Jonathan Scott, George Burder and Joseph Cockin in Staffordshire and Yorkshire during the late 1770s, and, more generally, until the middle 1790s, little genuine evangelism or expansion took place. In consequence traditional independent polity experienced little pressure for change until late in the century.

From the 1770s a new focus of attention began to develop. Formerly the life of the individual church had centred upon the spiritual well-being of its members and adherents together with their families, but the new emphasis, especially evident after 1795, concerned itself with the conversion of outsiders, often the inhabitants of previously untouched communities. Dissent became expansionist, outward looking and welcoming, turning away from its earlier exclusivity. The traditional prayer meeting typified the transformation. From being '"a select company of Christians, [which] excluded others"' it became 'a congregational gathering open to all'.[66] The change is reflected in the source material. Eighteenth-century association literature had varied in its degree of introspectiveness but its primary concern had been with the spiritual calibre of member churches. This inward preoccupation did not entirely vanish with the coming of the new century, but the reader's attention was increasingly turned towards those still beyond the range of effective Christian teaching.[67] In 1819 the magnitude of the task confronting one of the first Home Missionary Society agents was presented to the readership of the *Congregational Magazine* in typically challenging terms: 'The other Missionary has been stationed in the vicinity of Farringdon, Berks, where, within a few miles are sixty towns and villages, containing a population of 25,000, of whom only 5,000 have been hitherto favoured with an Evangelical ministry.'[68]

Evangelistic involvement on any significant scale created a need for strategy, finance and manpower, and for suitable literature. An obvious prerequisite was the exchange of the old semi-isolationist polity for a more appropriate mode of organization; one which embodied active co-operation, mutual support, the pooling of resources, and increased scope for the ordinary church member.[69] For Independents the surrender of congregational autonomy which this necessitated was more significant than the adjustment faced by Particular Baptists. Since the seventeenth century the latter had possessed some form of associational structure, however rudimentary. But for the majority of Independents the county associations of the 1780s and 1790s were a new departure.

Despite these changes the principle of independency continued to receive attention. It enjoyed repeated commendation as the scriptural ideal; the gathered church of true believers. Yet this advocacy has to be understood in context as support for an ecclesiastical model sharply contrasting with the open, parochial structure of the despised Church of England. Furthermore the independence being extolled was by no means a reiteration of the exclusive polity of the middle eighteenth century. Many of the Dissenters most deeply committed to itinerancy, especially those familiar with Calvinistic Methodism, showed little interest in matters of polity. As with David Bogue of Gosport it could be said of them that they adhered to independency 'as the only safe retreat [they] knew from greater evils'.[70] The new organizations formed to promote itinerant evangelism took pains to emphasize the genuine independence of member churches, and, subject to the inevitable limitations imposed by co-operation, their statements were entirely truthful, for individual congregations did retain immediate sovereignty. Yet the independence they offered bore little resemblance to its eighteenth-century counterpart. The ethos of that earlier principle lingered only among an unrepresentative fringe of high Calvinist congregations.

The development of associations accompanying the spread of village preaching was quite unprecedented. English Particular Baptists had since 1689 maintained a loose regional structure, and by the middle of the eighteenth century Independents had begun to follow their example. But these early attempts at corporate activity were limited, faltering and invariably inward looking. A letter from Richard Alliot, a Congregational minister in Nottingham, written in 1841, mentions an early association involving the churches of that county which lasted from 1720 until 1767, but similar bodies were slow to appear.[71] Ministerial associations were eventually formed in a number of counties including Essex (1768), Hampshire (1781) and Lancashire (1786), but these were of comparatively late origin, only narrowly pre-dating the organizations connected specifically with itinerancy.

The Lancashire association widened its horizons by including lay representatives from the churches, but in every other respect it resembled contemporary ministerial bodies in its concern for mutual fellowship, encouragement and the preservation of sound doctrine. At its formation in Bolton on 7 June 1786 the founders declared their obligation to give advice, consult with member churches concerning their peace and order, and suspend from membership any minister judged guilty of erroneous beliefs or sinful practices.[72] Similar warnings against heterodox ideas are found in the letters of the older Baptist associations, and these also dwell at length upon the Christian standards expected of individual believers and in church and family life. Yet the note of self-preoccupation and defensiveness can be misleading, for, though it is still characteristic of circular letters produced as late as 1800, the minutes of the same associations provide clear evidence that a new concern for evangelism was by that time well established.

From its infancy in the early 1740s Calvinistic Methodism had established a connexional framework similar to that employed by Wesley's followers. With no restrictive legacy of independency to modify, and with a focus of interest devoted more single-mindedly to evangelism, its internal structure from the outset differed markedly from the Dissenting model. The records of the English Calvinistic Methodist Association for 1745–9 reveal the close relationship already existing between church and association: they demonstrate an overriding concern to stimulate and organize itinerant preaching both locally and on a more extensive scale.[73]

The rapid growth of associations among Particular Baptists and Independents after 1795 marked the adoption of a similar objective. Over the next quarter century most English counties witnessed the formation of local unions of churches, or the adaptation of existing ones, and, whatever their earlier purpose may have been, the new preoccupation lay with evangelism and the problems caused by growth. This concern is clearly visible in the creation of the Dorset Missionary and Itinerant Society by a group of local Independent ministers at Warcham in 1795.[74] From the outset the corporate effort of the Dorset churches was directed towards the employment and support of an evangelist to engage in itinerant preaching in 'the destitute parts of the county'. Over the following years Independent churches in many other areas established similar societies. In certain counties, most notably Essex and Hampshire, these evolved more or less directly from the earlier ministerial associations, but in Lancashire the 1786 attempt at union had already failed when William Roby and a group of fellow ministers from the Manchester area gathered to form the precursor of the important Lancashire and Cheshire Congregational Unions.[75]

For various reasons, not least the practical influence of Andrew Fuller and William Carey, priority in the development of an evangelistic outlook in Baptist circles has traditionally been accorded to the association based upon Northamptonshire.[76] Yet a careful examination of the minutes and accounts relating to the 1770s indicates that this assessment may be mistaken. Official support for village preaching does not appear in the records of the Northamptonshire body before 1779, whereas the Western Association had circulated a letter among its member churches as early as May 1775 advertising its new fund, the first object of which was 'to encourage evangelizing, or itinerant preaching, in those places where it might be judged necessary and desirable'.[77]

In spite of this encouragement from the older associations, a number of new organizations appeared at the turn of the century. In 1796 the Essex Baptist Association was constituted at a meeting in Braintree. Within a year it had registered a house at Rayleigh and engaged its first full-time itinerant.[78] Ten years later a similar body was formed for the county of Shropshire as an offshoot of the much older Midland Association.[79] Outwardly, acceptance of the corporate obligation to evangelize appeared more or less complete by the close of the eighteenth century, but a great deal of conservatism and inertia remained at the local level. Some of the older associations showed little sign of activity. In spite of certain notable instances of village preaching and missionary enterprise, the prevailing atmosphere of apathy within the unwieldy Western Association is communicated by the circular letters of the 1790s. This impression is confirmed by a comment made by John Saffery, the energetic minister at Salisbury. Writing in 1798 he observed sadly, 'I fear the removal of our dear Bror Steadman will be a loss to the Society as well as the Neighborhood – Hope to be enabled to do what I can to keep alive Missionary exertions in this quarter, but fear I shall stand almost alone.'[80] Though appreciation of the need for evangelism was growing, the initiative remained with individual ministers and laymen; with activists such as Saffery and Steadman in the Western Association, Samuel Pearce of Birmingham in the midland counties and John Palmer, the architect of the new Shropshire Association.

In some parts of the country societies for the promotion and support of itinerant preaching assumed an undenominational character. The reality and limits of the co-operative spirit may be questioned, but its presence within the growing network of association is undeniable. The appearance of the undenominational societies is difficult to attribute to any common factor beyond the irenic spirit of their founders, though practical considerations undoubtedly played an important role. In 1798 when Charles Whitfield, the Baptist minister at Hamsterley in County Durham, joined Hill, his Independent contemporary at Ravenstonedale in Westmorland, and several other Dissenting ministers and laymen in forming an evangelical association for the four most northerly counties, their inspiration appears to have sprung from the scattered nature of the communities, the difficult terrain and the paucity of their separate resources.[81] By contrast, the Union of Christians formed in Bedfordshire the previous year was a logical outgrowth of a long tradition of tolerance within the county's Dissenting community.

Though the attention given to evangelism after 1780 marks an important change in Dissenting attitudes, earlier concerns were not entirely relinquished. This is clear from both the stated objectives of associations and their use of resources. Earlier associations had employed their limited funds in a variety of ways to assist their poorer members. Small sums had been granted to needy ministers and to their widows and orphans. Where strictly necessary some assistance had been given with the repair of meeting-houses, and struggling congregations had received occasional help with the expense of pulpit supplies. These internal demands in no way lessened as policies were adopted which led to growth. Churches and association meetings became increasingly crowded, but the majority of those attracted were by no means wealthy, and to the range of traditional expenses was added the burden of financing itinerant preaching and providing accommodation for those who wished to listen.

The older bodies were not alone in acknowledging a variety of obligations. Some of the associations created explicitly for evangelism pursued their goal with considerable single-mindedness, but few were wholly oblivious to other needs. Most, like the Lancashire Congregational Union, were prepared to aid weak congregations whose future prospects as local centres for evangelism were judged to be encouraging. In carefully approved cases they were even willing to countenance some degree of financial assistance towards the erection of meeting-houses.[82] Among the older Baptist associations where evangelism had to compete with traditional concerns the resources allocated to village preaching often remained meagre. From 1776 to 1800 the annual collections for the fund administered by the Western Association rose from £24 to £86, but in the same period, where the accounts are sufficiently detailed to allow certainty about the distribution of expenditure, the sums awarded to defray the expenses of itinerancy varied only between five and sixteen guineas.[83]

In recent years a good deal has been made of the undenominational character of the evangelicalism which flourished during the period of the French Revolution. Of particular interest here is the suggestion that this feature extended to itinerant preaching.[84] The spread of itinerancy across the midland and southern counties of England during the course of the 1790s is compared in one study with the initial development of Sunday schools in the northern industrial towns. Both are seen as part of the same phenomenon of undenominational activity.[85] If this is true and the new itinerancy was able to transcend denominational differences, it represented for Dissent a significant departure.

Some of the more enthusiastic champions of itinerancy evinced a relative lack of denominational concern. The most prominent of these was Rowland Hill, the peripatetic minister of Surrey Chapel. In the preface to his *Apology for Sunday Schools* Hill acknowledged the accuracy of the derogatory term 'nondescript' as it had been applied by the Bishop of Rochester to the agents and recipients of itinerant preaching.[86] He clearly conceived of his own position and preaching activities in similar undenominational terms. But he was ever the individualist, and in spite of his ready association with Dissenters he eschewed their principles and cannot, therefore, be considered as a true representative of their position. There is little evidence to suggest that either Hill or any other exponent exerted a decisive influence in favour of the undenominational approach. Any Dissenting movement in that direction probably owed more to practical necessity than to the views and influence of individuals.

Collectively the unions and associations for the encouragement of itinerancy provide only a fragile basis for any strict theory of organized undenominationalism. If a lack of concern for specific denominational issues and the participation of members from a variety of religious bodies are selected as two of the basic criteria, then few if any examples of genuine undenominational itinerancy involving Calvinistic Dissenters can be found. Even the well-known Bedfordshire Union of Christians fails to satisfy the second criterion in spite of the hopes of its founder, Samuel Greatheed, tutor at Newport Pagnell Academy.[87] Apart from the early membership and financial support of George Livius, a Bedford Moravian,[88] and the presence of one or two unidentified individuals, the general activity of the union was left to Independents and Baptists who shared a common Dissenting inheritance and a particularly close relationship in Bedfordshire and the surrounding area. Judged by these rather strict standards no other itinerant association displayed any greater concern for genuine undenominationalism. In most cases union meant no more than limited interdenominational co-operation, as is clear from the title of the Union of Independent and Baptist Ministers in the Western Division of Kent, a society formed in 1798. Eleven years later when the 'undenominational' Sussex Mission reviewed its constitution no doubt remained concerning the practical limits of co-operation. The report noted with disarming honesty: 'The plan of this Society is precisely the same as that adopted by the Surrey Mission. It unites for one common object, baptists, calvinistic methodists, and independents.'[89]

If the definition of undenominationalism is widened to include all co-operative efforts where persons from more than one denomination were involved, a stronger basis is found for agreeing with the assertion of one historian that in the years following the formation of the London Missionary Society in 1795 undenominational itinerancies were established 'over most of the country, except in Suffolk and Essex where the Baptists and Congregationalists acted independently, and except where the Methodist itinerancy was in process of sweeping the board on its own'.[90] Freedom from strict denominational identity was not an entirely new development as the case of Societas Evangelica shows;[91] the uniqueness of the later 1790s derives rather from the number of bodies being created. Even so the extent of their prevalence can be exaggerated, for, in addition to those for Suffolk and Essex, the period from 1795 to 1799 saw the appearance of several other denominational associations at the county level and, most significant of all, the antecedents of the Congregational and Baptist Home Missionary Societies.[92] Moreover, the work of existing bodies should not be forgotten, nor the fact that for those formed after 1800 a strict denominational pattern once more became normal.[93]

There is little reason, therefore, to suggest that undenominationalism was an organizational feature of the new itinerancy. The achievement of a true, practical unity where it could be found was invariably the result of co-operation between like-minded individuals. In 1798 a particularly harmonious example existed in North Buckinghamshire. A contemporary report noted: 'there are various good men who belong to Mr Horne, minister of the Established church at Olney, to Mr Hillyard of the Independent, and to Mr Sutcliff of the Baptist church, who unite in Village Reading'.[94] Similarly in Gloucestershire a retired businessman in the town of Nailsworth erected a preaching room which he intended to be open to all religious denominations. For many years afterwards the local ministers preached there to crowded gatherings.[95]

The failure of undenominationalism at the institutional level stemmed not so much from a lack of goodwill as from the intractable nature of three particular matters of principle. In the strictly theological sphere there was the obvious divide between Calvinist and Arminian opinion. In the area of polity itinerancy demanded a degree of irregularity that was quite impossible for loyal Evangelical Churchmen to countenance. Thirdly, and deriving its force from theology and polity, came the issue of baptism with attendant complications over matters of church membership and communion.

Throughout the period active co-operation between Calvinists and Arminians remained minimal. Some suggestion of Wesleyan participation in the Bedfordshire Union of Christians was made by Samuel Greatheed at that society's inception, but the identity of those involved is not clear from the surviving records.[96] Where Dissenters encountered Methodist activity the attitude adopted was often positive. At Hendon in 1826 the London Itinerant Society decided not to proceed with its own initiative in view of Wesleyan attempts to gain a foothold there.[97] Three years earlier the annual report of the North Bucks Independent Association had mentioned the case of a Methodist local preacher who took his turn in the rota for the week-night services held at Maids Moreton under its own auspices.[98] But close relationships were rare and cases of local antagonism between Wesleyans and Dissenters still arose. The one positive development is that disagreements seem by this time to have issued from evangelistic rivalry rather than ingrained theological prejudice. In the years after 1800 there was nothing to match the bitterness evident in William Roby's description of those who sought to frustrate his itinerant work in the villages near Wigan.[99]

In spite of their common concern for evangelism, most Evangelical clergymen felt unable to join Dissenters in itinerant preaching because of the challenge the practice posed for the episcopal concept of church order. This was especially true of the period after 1795 when, as itinerancy became widespread, the need to demonstrate their loyalty to the Establishment led most Churchmen to avoid all but the most innocuous undenominational activities. Two clerical figures, Rowland Hill and John Eyre, did play a significant part in the development of Dissenting itinerancy, but neither had formal parochial ties, and both showed a greater allegiance to the tradition of Whitefield than to the concerns which dominated their Evangelical contemporaries.[100]

The obstacle presented by baptism was rather more variable. In the Surrey Mission, the Bedfordshire Union of Christians and several other societies paedobaptists and antipaedobaptists combined harmoniously in village evangelism. The checks experienced by the undenominational principle came in these instances from other sources. Though the issue of baptism did not exclude the Baptists from undenominational activity so completely as irregularity in the case of Evangelical Churchmen, it did arise more frequently and led in certain circumstances to marked expression of hostility. Some non-denominational societies uniting Independents and Calvinistic Methodists believed that practical co-operation with those holding antipaedobaptist views presented insuperable difficulties. Thus in 1798 when several Baptists applied to work with the London Itinerant Society, a resolution was passed which said, 'That it is the opinion of this committee that the pedobaptists and antipedobaptists can best serve the general interests of our Lord Jesus Christ by preaching and Teaching among the societies of their own persuasion.'[101] Nor did the passage of time necessarily diminish the problem, for nearly twenty years later an unpleasant incident developed within the ranks of the Village Itinerancy when it was discovered that one of the society's preachers had adopted Baptist sentiments.[102] But the issue of baptism was more than a factor determining the composition of certain societies. It was also a cause of the appearance in many counties of separate Baptist and Independent associations with the consequent loss of efficiency and duplication of effort.

Lest the concept of an undenominational ingredient be totally rejected, the presence of a unique spirit of co-operation during the Napoleonic era has to be acknowledged. A genuine undenominational temper appeared based upon a shared evangelical concern to promulgate the essentials of the gospel. In earlier years enlightened individuals had chosen, like Joanna Turner of Trowbridge, to ignore the prevailing climate of theological hostility between Calvinists and Arminians, and had displayed the same positive approach.[103] But it was not until the mid-1790s that this irenical spirit became predominant. Contemporary comments make it clear that the change was recognized at the time. Apart from David Bogue's famous pronouncement concerning the 'funeral of bigotry', other remarks can be found expressing a similar mixture of exultation and surprise at the spread of evangelical zeal among Christians regardless of denomination.[104] The substance of the new spirit is found in the ideas with which village preaching was preoccupied: the central elements of Christian teaching which united paedobaptist and antipaedobaptist, Churchman and Dissenter, and which in some cases even managed to span the deep division between Arminians and Calvinists. In his commentary on the Bible, Thomas Scott, Rector of Aston Sandford in Buckinghamshire, endorsed the tolerant and inclusive character of ideal itinerant preaching: 'They who engage in it should go upon broad scriptural grounds, and dwell chiefly upon those grand essentials of religion, in which pious men of different persuasions are agreed.'[105]

It is instructive to apply Scott's definition to specific cases of itinerancy. A good example is the work undertaken from 1798 onwards in the northern parts of Devon and Somerset by the Baptist ministers from Bampton and Stogumber. Their efforts received financial encouragement from the Baptist Society, but the initial phase of preaching appears to have followed the pattern envisaged by Scott, with groups of converts meeting regularly for prayer and only a minimal emphasis upon sectarian features.[106] This situation continued for at least two years, until in the autumn of 1801 conventional categories were re-established when one of the itinerants reported the baptism of three inhabitants of Tivington near Minehead and voiced his hopes regarding the eventual formation of a Baptist church in that locality.[107]

The least ambiguous indicator of change is found in the statistics of the movement; in the sharp increase in activity after 1780 which contributed to the new sense of progress and which visibly enhanced Dissenting self-confidence. Eighteenth-century membership figures are not the easiest to use. Their incompleteness gives their use as a growth index a degree of uncertainty which makes careful interpretation necessary. Some earlier historians have been aware of this. Ivimey, in quoting the estimate of Particular Baptist numerical strength made by J. C. Ryland in 1753, suggested that his figure of 4,930 members for the congregations located in England required a 33 per cent increase to allow for deficiency, and a further augmentation of 66 per cent for those who attended as 'hearers'. He pointed out that even at the revised level a considerable decline had taken place since the Revolution of 1688.[108]

In the absence of complete membership statistics some impression of the overall pattern of growth can be obtained from the official returns relating to the registration of places of worship between 1688 and 1852.[109] The figures, which cover both England and Wales, show that the number of Congregational and Baptist registrations recorded dropped from 122 in the ten years from 1701–10 to a nadir of 62 in the period 1731–40. Thereafter the figures rose steadily until the 1790s when they increased in one decade by 161 per cent, from 340 to 888. The total continued to grow from 1800 onwards, but rather more slowly, reaching an eventual peak of 1,017 in the decade which ended in 1820.[110] A similar pattern is found when the statistics for the number of extant congregations given in the surveys by Evans (1716), Ryland (1753), Thompson (1773), and Bogue and Bennett (1808) are combined.[111] All available figures indicate a period of steady growth after 1740, with the most rapid expansion taking place during the final decade of the eighteenth century.

The crucial variable underlying this transformation has been identified as recruitment.[112] In practical terms, apart from the influence of the Sunday school movement which grew rapidly in Dissenting circles after 1790, this increase in the attraction of new members can only be attributed to organized itinerant preaching. The latter development coincided exactly with the numerical increase, developing as it did during the 1790s and over the following two decades. The early organization of village preaching had been confined to the work of the Calvinistic Methodist connexions, the rudimentary financial support given by Baptist regional associations covering the West of England and Northamptonshire, and the activity of the non-denominational Societas Evangelica, but between 1790 and 1799 at least thirty-one societies were created or adapted, and the construction of an institutional framework for evangelism was completed over the next twenty years by the appearance of a similar number.[113]

Many records of this expansion still survive, but while they provide valuable details, they do not permit a systematic assessment of the financial and human resources committed to itinerancy or the exact geographical coverage achieved by the movement. Both minute books and printed sources omit important factual details, and the problem of incompleteness is accentuated by the varying effectiveness with which societies approached their task. With no allowance being made for discrepancies, omissions or differing objectives, an examination of five societies formed in the later 1790s shows in 1801 an aggregate itinerant effort amounting to four paid full-time evangelists, twenty-two ministers and identifiable laymen and, for one of the associations, an additional unstated number of village preachers.[114] These personnel and a financial outlay of £650 enabled the five societies to maintain preaching on either a regular or an occasional basis in 170 places extending from Suffolk westward to Devon and northward as far as Cumberland.[115] When the work of at least twenty-one similar bodies is taken into consideration together with the many local initiatives that were unsupported by any external organization, the growth of Dissenting itinerancy during the later 1790s and its probable impact upon existing churches and associations, not to mention society at large, can be appreciated.

This interpretation, the idea of significant change and expansion, is treated cautiously in Richard Carwardine's study of religious revivalism in Britain and America. In both countries, the author argues, itinerant evangelism was employed, yet English Dissent did not experience the periods of 'extraordinary "ingathering" or revival' seen in America. In England the itinerant evangelist was essentially a traditional, pastoral figure acting with greater enthusiasm and in a less restricted capacity than his forebears. By contrast his New World counterpart, the revivalist preacher, embodied different characteristics and employed novel techniques.[116]

English religious developments may have followed traditional lines but the opponents of evangelical Dissent clearly believed that a significant transformation had occurred and that a new and aggressive evangelism was threatening the Establishment.[117] At Salisbury the brief but heated pamph-let controversy that erupted in 1798 followed an expression of concern by the bishop at the increase in village preaching in the diocese, with all that development implied for mischief among the lower classes.[118] Polemical outbursts of this nature were sporadic but the anxiety felt by those who supported the Establishment remained, re-emerging in one final challenge in May 1811 when Lord Sidmouth introduced into the Upper House of Parliament an abortive bill designed to curb itinerant preachers.[119] The very intensity of this reaction demonstrates that he and his fellow objectors, at least, recognized an essential difference between contemporary Dissent and its eighteenth-century predecessor.

3 · Preachers and sponsors

WHERE eighteenth- and early nineteenth-century itinerancy is recognized as a distinct phenomenon, it is invariably associated with laymen of humble origin. Contemporary critics represented the situation in similar terms, adding disparaging remarks concerning the educational deficiency of the preachers, the ill-assorted nature of their secular occupations, and their corresponding lack of suitability for any form of Christian leadership. Yet careful examination of the documentary evidence suggests that the images of lay dominance and of the inappropriateness of the personnel employed are at the best inadequate, and at the worst wholly misleading.

Encouraged by the increasing social tension of the 1790s the general Establishment attitude towards itinerants had by the turn of the century become uncompromisingly negative. Warning his clergy about the 'conventicles' springing up on every side, Bishop Samuel Horsley observed, 'The pastor is often, in appearance at least, an illiterate peasant or mechanic.'[1] Although the educational criticism did not constitute the main point of Horsley's argument, it was a reiterated theme of contemporary polemic and was developed, for example, by Robert Woodward, Vicar of Harrold, who had experienced in his own village the activity of preachers connected with the Bedfordshire Union of Christians.[2] 'Though some of the dissenting teachers are men of education', he admitted, 'yet it is well known that many who take upon themselves to be preachers of the Gospel are uneducated.' '[They are] destitute of Greek learning, the language in which the New Testament was originally written.' 'Brought up to trades, they could not have had an opportunity of being prepared for the high and sacred office of a minister.' Describing those who preached at the gathering in his own parish he said, 'at Harrold, a tailor, a mason, a watchmaker, a sievemaker, a woodman, and a schoolmaster by turns, or as they pretend or imagine they have the power or gift of utterance'.[3] Even the Anglican Evangelical leader, William Wilberforce, who was by no means opposed to the more regular forms of Dissent, spoke disapprovingly of a practice prevailing at Salisbury and Bath 'of a number of raw, ignorant lads going out on preaching parties every Sunday'.[4] Nor were the critical comments confined to members of the Establishment, for the more conservative Dissenting commentators like

Walter Wilson deprecated the nondescript character and injudicious zeal that typified the agents of evangelism.[5]

Modern scholarship has perpetuated this emphasis upon the lay aspect of itinerancy, and in doing so has strengthened the impression that it was overwhelmingly a non-clerical phenomenon.[6] Several factors have combined to encourage this view, the most obvious being the matter of the numbers involved, for, whatever qualifications need to be made, it is clear that lay people formed by far the largest sector within the movement. The idea of lay dominance is reinforced by the aura of novelty surrounding the use of untrained church members in a public capacity. As a corollary, the legal and political moves to curb itinerant preaching seem more concerned with the threat of uncontrolled lay activity than with the evangelistic principle involved, however much the latter may have violated traditional ecclesiastical preserves.

Although the notion of lay dominance rests, therefore, upon an apparently factual basis, it is inadequate, for it represents a complex situation in simple terms. Between the traditional Dissenting ministry and that which evolved to serve the process of expansion, the difference lay precisely in the composite structure of the latter with its dependence upon a range of ministerial personnel, extending from those with full-time pastoral responsibilities to tradesmen in wholly secular employment.

The lay contribution involved support as well as a more active role, but precise analysis is not always possible on the basis of surviving records. From the middle of the eighteenth century George Whitefield and John Berridge recognized the value of lay preachers. During the 1760s Berridge itinerated widely through the villages of Cambridgeshire, gathering congregations at a number of places including Waterbeach and Duxford. Thereafter, until his death in 1793, he employed a team of laymen to maintain this village preaching on a regular basis.[7]

The use of lay itinerancy for consolidation conformed to a common and practical pattern of development, though even the exploratory phase of evangelism was at times entrusted to ordinary church members. In some instances the impetus appears to have come entirely from non-clerical sources. At Leyburn in North Yorkshire the foundations for an Independent congregation were laid by a lay preacher who, acting upon his own impulse, began to hold religious meetings in a cottage.[8] More frequently lay evangelism represented the wider interest of a church or a regional association in a specific area. Even where this was the case the practical initiative remained in the hands of the preacher, together with considerable discretion concerning the opportunities and requirements of the particular locality. This independence within a framework of institutional support is illustrated by the journal kept by Thomas Wastfield as a record of his work in part of Wiltshire. During the course of 1797, faced with opposition from the constable of the Swanborough Hundred and with other difficulties, he found it necessary to turn his attention from the villages of the Vale of Pewsey to neighbouring communities in the upper Avon valley, a decision only communicated to the sponsoring society several months later.[9]

From a geographical perspective the use made of lay itinerants was far from uniform. The incomplete state of surviving records prevents any precise comparison between societies, but differences did exist. In the villages of Bedfordshire and in those surrounding Birmingham and Salisbury lay preachers formed a significant proportion of the evangelistic effort,[10] yet in the same period the bodies created for the promotion of itinerancy in Essex adopted a more traditional, ministerial approach. The records of the Essex Baptist Association mention one or two lay preachers, including John Garrington, a schoolmaster from Burnham-on-Crouch, but their attention is focussed upon the county's full-time evangelist whose work was intended to supplement the local preaching of settled ministers. They show, nevertheless, that when a vacancy for the post of county itinerant did occur, the association was prepared to consider applications from men in normal secular employment.[11] The regional basis of most of these societies makes the conclusion almost inescapable that lay involvement was stronger in some areas than in others.

While the encouragement of a broad basis of support for village preaching continued to be restricted in some places to the indirect realms of finance and prayer, there was after 1780 an increasing concern to involve church members more directly. Baptist association letters, such as the one circulated in 1792 by the Northamptonshire churches, envisaged a range of lay activities extending from the mere presence of supporters at village meetings conducted by their ministers, to personal exhortation and the preaching and reading of sermons.[12]

Despite this theoretical welcome for a higher level of lay involvement, the records of Dissenting itinerancy are strangely silent concerning the subject, and yield relatively little information concerning the utilization of personnel and the results achieved. Several reasons for this silence may be suggested, including the lack of prestige attached to lay evangelism, but, whatever the cause, the result is that the scale of lay itinerancy cannot be determined with any degree of accuracy.

The comparative silence maintained in Dissenting circles was not respected by the critics of the movement, whose object was to demonstrate the alarming extent of popular and unrestrained proselytism. Once again the problem of unreliable representation is raised by the concern of these polemicists to depict the situation in the worst possible terms. In certain localities lay evangelism was organized admittedly with almost military precision. At Bedford in 1798 the three meeting-houses were responsible for sending out thirty or more of their members every Sunday afternoon as part of an integrated plan covering between twenty and thirty villages, while the situation at Salisbury allegedly involved an even greater number.[13] In other places a comparable use of lay resources, though probable, cannot be substantiated.[14] Yet it is dangerous to conclude too much from specific examples. Apart from the uneven distribution of Dissent, any generalization tends to conceal the degree of fragmentation that existed within itinerancy.

Whatever is made of the lay contribution, another important ingredient was the activity of settled ministers. Not surprisingly contemporary critics largely ignored this clerical element, preferring to direct the barbs of their invective against the more vulnerable laymen. Yet from the earliest phase of the Evangelical Revival a strong concern for evangelism had been evident within the ranks of the ordained ministry. Whitefield, Grimshaw and Hill, and those with a similar background in Methodism, demonstrated this orientation quite clearly, but among their counterparts within the older Dissenting tradition serious interest in extended evangelism spread only slowly. It was restrained above all by the strong concept of the settled pastorate and its associated responsibilities, an idea cherished by both Baptists and Independents. Some exceptions to this reluctance can be found, for example the preaching of Caleb Warhurst in the Manchester area during the 1750s, but Warhurst's diary reveals the extent to which a sense of pastoral concern pervaded his itinerant ministry as well as his normal duties at Cannon Street Chapel.[15] In spite of one or two untypical individuals, it was not until the closing decade of the century that a significant number of Dissenters began deliberately to promote evangelistic work beyond the sphere of their own pastoral influence.

After 1790 enthusiasm for itinerant evangelism began to spread rapidly, and the attempt to combine effectively both pastoral and evangelistic roles became the standard practice. At the ordination of Richard Pengilly at Newcastle-upon-Tyne in 1807 William Steadman urged the young minister to extend his efforts beyond his church and congregation, and to use all his energy in spreading the Christian message among the large surrounding population.[16] The ordination charge showed no hint of any possible conflict of loyalty between his pastoral and evangelistic responsibilities, although strains undoubtedly occurred. The concern to avoid that kind of dilemma while still ensuring active involvement in itinerancy is reflected in a resolution passed in 1816 by the Lancashire Congregational Union:

that it be recommended to the Ministers in the Union to itinerate personally through their several Districts for a week or fortnight in rotation; preaching every evening in the week except Saturday, and three times on the Lord's day; and that to accommodate them

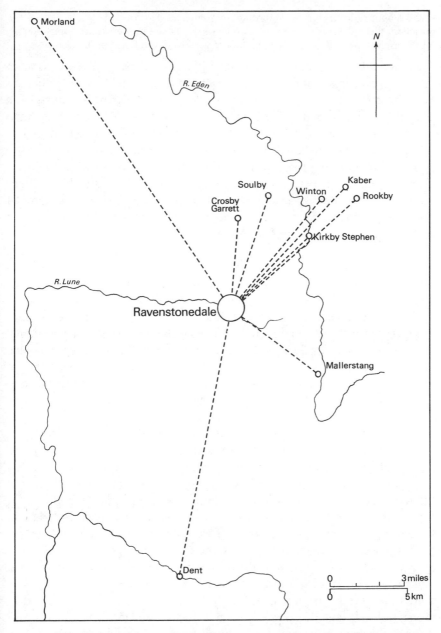

3 Regular local itinerancy radiating from a central base. Westmorland. John Hill of Ravenstonedale (Independent, 1801).

It seems likely, in view of the difficult nature of the terrain, that Hill combined visits to more than one place in the course of a single journey, but no details are given.

Source: Societas Evangelica, minutes. 28 February 1801, DWL New College MS 122/1.

in this labour of love, either a supernumerary minister be provided for each District to preach for them whilst Itinerating, or that their reasonable expenses in providing a supply for themselves, as well as in travelling, be defrayed from the funds of the Society.[17]

Although the adoption of itinerancy by local ministers normally led to an intensive penetration of the home district, some individuals with the benefit of organizational support were able to contemplate lengthier tours. The pattern established by the BMS-sponsored ventures of Saffery, Steadman and Franklin during the summers of 1796 and 1797, was reproduced in subsequent years by the Baptist Society.[18] The rules of this organization permitted support for preaching excursions wholly under its own direction.[19] Over the following decade John Palmer, the minister of the Shrewsbury Baptist church, aided by several others, mounted an intensive programme of village preaching in Shropshire, paying particular attention to the western sector of the county towards Welshpool and Montgomery. Yet he also found time to undertake more extensive tours on behalf of the society, travelling through Central Wales westward to Aberystwyth and Machynlleth.[20] Similarly in 1804 a minister from Chester reported preaching at many places in Worcestershire, Warwickshire and Leicestershire, and for this work received some assistance from the society's funds.[21] Not all national societies were prepared to support such ambitious schemes. The Congregational Society for Spreading the Gospel in England, which from its inception failed to capture the imagination and support of the religious public, found it necessary as early as 1799 to advise an applicant for financial assistance to restrict the extent of his itinerant journeys and to confine his efforts to villages nearer home.[22]

While national societies and county associations were responsible for a proportion of the initiative, the permeation of English rural society was largely left to the local exertions of settled ministers. In their applications for financial assistance some claimed to visit more than twenty villages, but the nine preaching stations in and around the Eden valley mentioned by John Hill of Ravenstonedale in a letter to Societas Evangelica would seem to be a more representative figure.[23] These local itinerancies could, nevertheless, cover considerable distances and occupy a great deal of time and energy when they were linked to stated pastoral duties. The Baptist minister at Horham lived at Stradbroke and from there in 1811 regularly visited five places, two of which, Southwold and Dunwich, were more than twenty miles distant.[24] In some cases this unco-ordinated evangelism seems to have involved a certain duplication of effort, for Dunwich had been visited in 1799 by John Dennant, the Independent minister at Halesworth, although it is quite possible that by 1811 that earlier initiative had come to nothing.[25]

The apologetic tone adopted by those who advocated ministerial itiner-

46

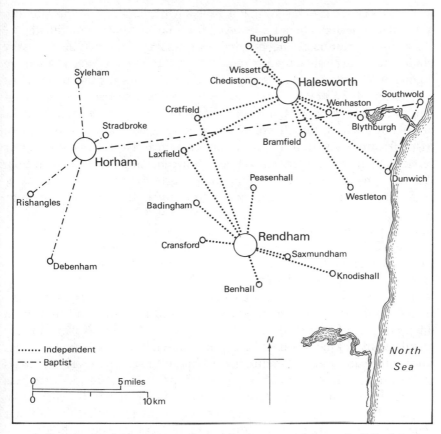

4 Regular local itinerancy radiating from a central base. Suffolk. John Dennant of Halesworth and Richard Wearing of Rendham (Independent, 1799) and Manser of Horham (Baptist, 1811).

The Rendham itinerancy also included an unidentified village named Athington – possibly Athelington, one mile south of Horham.

Sources: Societas Evangelica, minutes. 22 February 1799, DWL. New College MS 122/1; Baptist Society, minutes. 26 April 1811, BMS. MSS.

ancy may well conceal a widespread reluctance on the part of churches to accept any significant level of involvement by their pastors; an attitude arising from the belief that the external interests would inevitably prove inimical to their own prosperity. If this was the general attitude the early minutes of the Essex Congregational Union show that there were exceptions; that some churches shared their ministers' enthusiasm for evangelism. In April 1799 the congregation at Chelmsford offered to spare its minister for two or three Sundays to preach wherever the committee might decide.[26] The Chelmsford offer appears to display an element of disinterested benevolence, but in many

47

other cases congregational sympathy probably depended upon the extent to which the projected itinerancy involved the immediate neighbourhood.

Against the resistance encountered, early apologetics urged the necessity of itinerant evangelism on the ground of Christian duty. As time elapsed the argument turned more to matters of expediency. Gradually the expansionist advantages of the practice came to be appreciated, and annual reports of itinerant societies pointed with increasing frequency to the real benefits derived by the local church which had to be set against any possible loss of pastoral care.[27] Apart from the number of hearers attracted to regular services, there was the general increase in membership which resulted from the visits made to adjacent communities, growth which in some cases represented more than 50 per cent of the total strength. William Roby observed that his own preaching in the streets of Manchester during the summer months had been the principal means of increasing the very small congregation which had confronted him at Cannon Street Chapel when he had first accepted the pastorate in 1795.[28] Nor are rural counterparts to this experience difficult to find. In the Forest of Dean village preaching led to the formation of a Baptist church at Coleford and continued to benefit the new venture to the extent that eight years later its membership had risen from thirteen to one hundred.[29] Similarly at North Shields Robert Imeary calculated that of the fifty members of his church, thirty had come from his work in the surrounding communities.[30] But the assessment was not always so favourable. On at least one occasion the extent of outside activities was thought to pose a possible threat to the harmony and well-being of an existing church. The sponsoring society was quick to remind the minister concerned that he should be careful not to neglect his pastoral duties.[31]

With the rise of a new generation of Dissenting academies strongly inclined towards evangelism the structure of the itinerant ministry in certain areas became further diversified through the activity of theological students. Rarely more than a localized constituent confined to those communities within reach of the academy buildings, it could, nevertheless, prove important to the maintenance of extensive and regular networks of village preaching, and so produce significant results. The evangelistic stimulus provided by theological institutions was in some cases an acknowledged reason for their projection. In 1840 Richard Slate, a Lancashire Congregational minister, lent support to this view by stating that the presence of academies displayed a direct correlation with the growth and prosperity of the various forms of Dissent. As an obvious example he pointed to the flourishing state of trinitarian orthodoxy in Yorkshire where the churches maintained seminaries at Rotherham, Idle and Bradford, the modern successors of institutions dating back to the seventeenth century.[32]

At the majority of academies student itinerant preaching took place on a

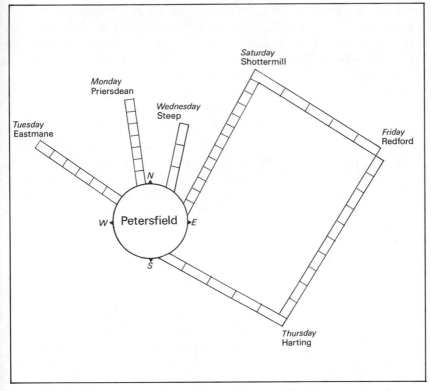

5 Composite itinerancy. Petersfield, Hampshire. The itinerancy plan operated by William Church during his brief employment there as agent of the
Village Itinerancy, 1797.

In the letter Church reported very satisfactory progress 'in my little circuit'. He noted that
he had preached at Priors Dean ['Priersdean'] about six miles distant, and at East Meon
['Eastmane'] where on the most recent visit there were about 100 hearers who behaved
'tolerably well'. He added that he had accomplished Eyre's wishes by having a separate
preaching station for every night of the week and he appended the plan to demonstrate
this. Shottermill lies one and a half miles west of Haslemere.

Source: Itinerancy plan enclosed with letter from William Church to John Eyre, 21
February 1797, DWL New College MS 41/7.

regular basis and formed an integral part of the training offered. It provided
necessary practical experience and useful opportunities for the analysis of
technique. It was also the most effective method of disseminating the
contemporary concern for an approach to ministry which linked the pastoral
element firmly to evangelism. Furthermore, student itinerancy offered the
basis for a sustained and systematic programme of growth, especially in areas
of high population density like the West Riding of Yorkshire where existing
manpower resources were stretched.

Although the standards of these institutions varied, the presence among the itinerants of considerable numbers of men engaged in academic study renders insubstantial any indiscriminate charge of ignorance and lack of training. But some criticisms of that nature related to specific circumstances and cannot, therefore, be so easily dismissed.[33]

The structure of the itinerant ministry became complete with the appearance during the 1790s of the full-time salaried evangelist. Among the earliest examples of this small specialist category were two men stationed at Midhurst and Petersfield by John Eyre in 1796 as agents of the newly formed Village Itinerancy.[34] During the following years similar appointments were made by a number of societies incorporating minor variations in status and mode of employment, but in each case one characteristic remained constant, namely a focus upon evangelism unfettered by stated pastoral duties or the demands of a secular occupation.

Itinerants[35] were in most cases deployed carefully, using their flexibility to overcome the problems created by geographical isolation, demographic pressure and the inadequacy of existing manpower.[36] The more extended forms of itinerancy remained the province of individual ministers or theological students while the professional evangelist was put to work within a defined area, preaching among a group of villages until the nucleus of a new congregation had been gathered. This approach could produce rapid results. The first full-time itinerants for the Essex Baptist Association raised churches at Rayleigh and Thorpe-le-Soken within months of their appointment.[37] But the progress achieved in other localities was considerably less spectacular. The Northern Evangelical Association experienced an unfortunate combination of factors which included difficulty in obtaining suitable personnel, poor organizational oversight and financial uncertainty. Together these rendered the society's efforts entirely nugatory. Between 1799 and 1805 its itinerants worked in South-West Cumberland, the villages surrounding Carlisle, and the vicinity of Milnthorpe in Westmorland, but in none of these places does any permanent congregation appear to have taken root.[38]

The local supervision of itinerancy was in some instances extremely tight. In 1804 the Hampshire Congregational Association resolved, 'That no Itinerant of the County shall on any occasion act from his own views without consulting with the Congregation nearest to the seat of his labours.'[39] This pattern of congregational oversight appears to have persisted in that area, for in 1813, when the association agreed to appoint an itinerant to work in the north of the county, the district committee meeting at Basingstoke decided that the person chosen should reside at Whitchurch and work under the direction of the local Independent minister.[40]

At the opposite extreme occasional examples can be found of free-ranging activity. Societas Evangelica, besides encouraging many settled ministers in local evangelism, also supported William Norris for several years, enabling him to itinerate in a full-time capacity over an extensive but unrecorded circuit in the North Riding of Yorkshire. His correspondence with the society indicates that in 1798 he travelled each week on foot an average of seventy miles preaching eight or nine sermons. Even when he had settled as pastor of the Independent church at Alston and Garrigill, he continued to act as an unofficial itinerant among the Pennine communities of Cumberland, Northumberland and County Durham, making occasional forays into Lincolnshire at the society's request.[41]

Where the work involved the more distant communities, a circumstance for which the professional itinerant was in many ways ideally equipped, close supervision according to the Hampshire model was impossible. Nevertheless some attempt would normally be made to monitor progress and to integrate the more tangible results into the denominational life of the county. Between 1806 and 1813 the Lancashire Congregational Union directed the work of four full-time agents in areas where evangelical Dissent was weak or non-existent. From this activity on the Fylde peninsula and in the vicinity of Southport, Leigh and Burnley, new churches were formed and extensive networks of preaching stations were established, developments which progressively increased the penetration and effectiveness of the original initiative.[42]

Given the importance attached to the raising of churches it was inevitable that the itinerant's role would assume an increasingly pastoral character. The official evangelist rapidly became a normal Dissenting minister, distinguished chiefly by his reliance upon external means of financial support. In a letter to one who enjoyed the patronage of the Cheshire Congregational Union the semi-pastoral nature of the task was openly acknowledged. He was advised that to leave in the face of slight difficulties would be to place in jeopardy the entire future of the infant cause with its dependence upon the person of the evangelist.[43] Attitudes of this kind, together with the obviously pastoral character of preachers like Richard Densham,[44] stationed by the Village Itinerancy at Petersfield until his accidental death in 1802, lend a measure of support to the earlier suggestion concerning the essential difference between religious revival in Britain and revivalism in America.

Nevertheless, the evangelistic content of the work should not be underestimated. In spite of growing pastoral commitments to converts and hearers, most men endeavoured by means of systematic preaching visits to maintain an effective contact with the inhabitants of outlying settlements who displayed no interest in organized religion. The use of paid evangelists enabled Dissent to spread to untried yet well-populated communities such as Marsh Gibbon, Kings Sutton and Charlton on the borders betwen Buckinghamshire, Oxfordshire and Northamptonshire. The North Bucks Independent Association, the local body responsible for evangelizing this area, pointed to an equally neglected group of villages between Oxford and Bicester.[45] Though the latter report was not pursued, the Marsh Gibbon example demonstrates the suitability of the salaried itinerant for an effective and sustained penetration of the remoter villages.

The prevailing climate of economic uncertainty conspired with the restricted financial catchment of most associations to ensure that for many years the number of full-time itinerants remained extremely small. Between 1795 and 1815 few societies employed more than two and only the Lancashire and Cheshire Congregational Unions contrived to support as many as four.[46]

Organizational weakness exacerbated financial stringency, giving the occupation a distinct air of impermanence. Most county evangelists experienced continuity of employment, but a minority were less fortunate, at times being paid off in peremptory fashion. The work of the Northern Evangelical Association is portrayed in its records as a series of false starts interspersed with periodic financial crises. In Essex the Baptist association twice dismissed its itinerant after due notice with no apparent hint of personal misdemeanour or lack of satisfaction.[47] The minutes suggest that on both occasions the reason was temporary and economic in character, but the insecurity engendered by these actions makes it easy to understand why some societies found difficulty in appointing suitable people.

The reasons for the problem of recruitment went beyond the simple matter of security of tenure to more fundamental issues concerning the role and status of the itinerant preacher within the context of Dissent. The category of permanent itinerancy was new and not easily accommodated to a traditional viewpoint. Compared with the respect accorded to the settled pastorate with its emphasis upon learning and careful preparation, the roving evangelist, despite the permanence of the appointment, appeared to occupy an inferior position, a situation not improved by the difficult and arbitrary nature of the work.

Apart from difficulty in filling certain vacancies there is little direct evidence of the low appeal of full-time itinerancy. Yet as early as 1797 William Steadman had suggested that the work called for abilities of a different kind from those required for the normal pastorate.[48] A moment of frustration in the correspondence of Richard Densham illustrates this point, giving an insight into the loneliness and inadequacy the isolated itinerant could feel. Writing to John Eyre he complained, 'My Consciousness of integrity in fulfilling (as far as I can) my engagements in the work committed to my Care by you, renders your dissatisfaction of my efforts exceedingly painful.' Densham's outburst to his sponsor, apparently prompted by a reproof for slackness, eloquently demonstrates not only the physical demands of constant travelling and preaching, but also the effect of a hostile reception and the overwhelming sense of spiritual responsibility for the people of the area.[49]

The most explicit comment upon the changing status of professional itinerancy came from the pen of Robert Burls in 1848 in which he contrasted the honour accorded to the home missionary in his own day with the situation which had prevailed during the early years of the Essex Congregational Union. From 1798 the union had tried repeatedly to secure the services of a full-time evangelist, but its efforts had been frustrated by a combination of factors. The office of itinerant was at that time an innovation among Independents and was consequently held in low esteem. The physical hardship attached to the work was all too often rewarded with ingratitude and indifference.[50] In most cases earlier advocates of itinerancy had been able to face these problems from the security and prestige of a settled pastorate. But for the salaried county evangelist that compensation was lacking: its absence was in no way remedied by an inadequate stipend and only relative freedom from pastoral duties.

In keeping with the individual character of the work, itinerants were recruited from various quarters. The Independent county associations, which employed the greatest number, tended to select their men from the graduates of evangelical seminaries. Thus Job Wilson who worked in Cheshire during the 1790s came from the short-lived academy at Northowram, while his later colleagues Robert Neill and William Silvester joined the newly formed county union fresh from their respective theological courses at Idle and Manchester.[51] The Manchester academy represented William Roby's personal response to the need for trained evangelists in the northern counties. In spite of its short existence six of the seventeen recorded students spent at least part of their subsequent careers in full-time itinerancy.[52] At other times the pattern was reversed. Henry Bean and William Hacking both worked as county evangelists for a number of years before entering different Yorkshire academies to undertake formal training.[53]

In addition to the more conventional institutions, proposals were made from time to time for specialist county seminaries concerned purely with the training of itinerants. Plans were formulated for areas as widely separated as Kent and Northumberland but nothing tangible materialized.[54] The proposed seminaries encountered the same financial limitations that restricted most regional enterprise. But they also undoubtedly suffered from the stigma associated with the very nature of itinerancy. Moreover, some opportunities for training already existed in the evangelical academies. Following the closure of Roby's personal venture in 1808 due to the retirement from business of its chief patron[55] and the pressure of work upon its sole tutor, further attempts were made to revive the idea of a seminary for Lancashire and the neighbouring counties. Though the emphasis upon evangelism was retained, the subsequent foundations lacked Roby's degree of commitment to full-time itinerancy. Not until the period after 1830 did the original intention begin to be fulfilled with the establishment of Home Missionary Society academies at Pickering and at Cotton End near Bedford.

After 1815 the office of salaried itinerant began to assume a greater importance, reflecting contemporary growth in denominational activity.[56] The process began with the stationing of John Jeffery in the Scilly Isles in 1815,[57] but other appointments quickly followed. Between 1820 and 1830 the number of agents employed by the Baptist and Congregational Home Missionary Societies increased ninefold, reaching a total of eighty-nine by the end of the decade.[58]

As numbers grew, signs emerged of a change in the character of the work. In 1826 the Home Missionary Society redeployed one of its agents from the Banbury area, where he had worked for several years, to a preaching centre in Warwickshire, only to replace him almost immediately with another evangelist.[59] A new mobility had entered itinerant consciousness, modifying the established pattern whereby successful evangelism was followed by pastoral settlement. The increased flexibility which resulted indicated a more fundamental development: the acceptance of the home missionary's role as a permanent and independent feature of the Christian ministry. It was this latter change which enabled the historian of the Home Missionary Society to claim that there was in the 1820s no unwillingness on the part of students trained for the ministry to assume the office of itinerant in preference to a settled pastorate.[60]

Dividing the itinerant ministry into formal categories in this way serves to illustrate the diversity involved and the balance between the different components. It has the additional merit of employing distinctions either made or implied by those who were active in the movement. Nevertheless, certain dangers surround the use of any structural model, and it is necessary to examine the relationship between the various elements identified.

The clear distinction between laymen, ministers, students and itinerants requires immediate qualification, for in practice, as the records of a wide cross-section of organizations show, itinerant categories were closely related, and movement by individuals from one to another regularly occurred. In many cases the change itself assumed a formal character following an entirely predictable pattern. Although some evangelistic bodies envisaged prolonged mobility from those they employed, expecting their agents to move to a new locality once the nucleus of a church had been formed,[61] the most common practice, as suggested, was for the itinerant to settle as pastor of the congregation he had gathered. In Essex the evangelistic work of James

Pilkington at Rayleigh and William Bolton at Thorpe-le-Soken developed in that manner to the apparent satisfaction of the county's Baptist association which had provided the inspiration.

Similar progression can be found in the unsponsored preaching of ordinary church members. When a village meeting had developed to the point of permanence and economic viability, the lay preacher who served it, a person recognized by his own church for his qualities of Christian leadership, was in many cases the obvious choice for the pastoral office. At other times successful lay itinerancy was followed by a period of theological training or by employment as a salaried evangelist. In 1820 John Adey, a member of the Independent church at Winslow, commenced a weekly Sunday school in the neighbouring village of Great Horwood, his work quickly developing into a regular preaching commitment in a barn adapted for the purpose. By 1823 Adey had assumed further evangelistic responsibilities for the area, being employed as the official itinerant of the North Bucks Independent Association at a salary of £20 p.a. It seems probable from this low figure that his itinerancy was judged to be compatible with a secular occupation. During the following year the transition was completed when he was ordained as pastor over the congregation he had been responsible for raising.[62]

The available statistics do not permit any accurate assessment of the numbers or proportion involved in this change of status, but the phenomenon was by no means uncommon, the normal progression being towards the settled evangelistic pastorate with its greater satisfaction, respectability and financial security. The dominance of this pattern is merely emphasized by the small number known to have moved in the opposite direction, resigning the oversight of churches for the sake of full-time itinerancy. In 1810 at the request of the Lancashire Congregational Union William Alexander relinquished his pastorate at Prescot in order to work as an itinerant based at Leigh.[63] Two years earlier with no apparent likelihood of comparable organizational support Charles Holmes had left the Baptist church at Wantage to maintain existing preaching commitments to a number of remote communities on the Berkshire Downs.[64] But examples of this kind were rare.

In addition to these local, organic relationships, the character of the itinerant ministry was affected on a wider scale by the changing policy of those responsible for the material support of home mission. The substance of this change, the appearance in the 1820s of increasing numbers of salaried evangelists working for the new denominational societies, has been noted, but it is important to emphasize that the new balance which this created depended upon a conscious movement away from the earlier preoccupation with the settled pastorate. It also required the existence of other suitable conditions. Although the early records of these societies are not available, the rapid multiplication of home missionaries during the 1820s must reflect deliberate policy. This conclusion is reinforced by the historian of the Baptist society who noted in 1897 that the second secretary who held office from 1815 until 1835, 'aimed less at securing stated ministers who should go on evangelizing tours, and more at sustaining missionaries who should give their whole time to the work of breaking up new ground or nursing infant causes'.[65]

Complementing this change in policy there began to appear in the 1820s organizational and economic circumstances more favourable to the spread of full-time itinerancy. Difficulty in procuring suitable personnel may have been a factor contributing to its faltering development, but the problem of finance constituted the major limitation. The deployment of even a small number of paid specialists presupposed a level of material support only possible with the development of a satisfactory denominational structure employing careful financial management and drawing upon a network of local auxiliaries. Even when at the close of the period professional itinerancy had emerged as an important ingredient of evangelism, it was still subject to periods of acute financial strain, as the Home Missionary Society discovered in 1829.[66]

With a certain inevitability the new emphasis upon the professional evangelist coincided with a decline in the already scant attention paid to the work of lay preachers. As late as 1830 despite the absence of accurate statistics laymen probably still constituted the largest category serving itinerancy, but mere numerical strength does not disguise the relegation of their role, a decline in esteem closely connected with the process of institutionalization to which all forms of evangelical spontaneity were being subjected.[67]

The attempt to decide the precise status of individuals prompts a further warning about over-categorization. The rigid approach attributes to itinerancy a degree of organization which bears little resemblance to reality. Prior to 1815 Dissenting evangelism was still at the heroic stage with most visible activity arising from the enterprise of individuals. Though this is obvious in the self-supported work of Charles Whitfield of Hamsterley or Joseph Cockin of Halifax, it is even apparent in situations where the sponsorship and general direction came from outside. A high level of personal responsibility and initiative is revealed, for example, by the letters which passed between Richard Densham in Hampshire and his London-based sponsor, John Eyre. Dissenting evangelism in the 1790s and 1800s carried with it an authentic missionary flavour, especially in counties like Herefordshire and Hampshire where the Evangelical Revival had made little progress. Its manifest individualism does a great deal to explain the diversity which existed and the desultory character of much of the work undertaken.

In practice neither the lay-ministerial distinction nor the place of ordi-nation within itinerancy are capable of easy definition. The relationship between lay preachers, itinerants and settled ministers displays a fluidity which is difficult to categorize however self-evident it may have appeared to contemporary observers. The minutes of one congregation at Haddenham in Buckinghamshire allow a reasonably clear distinction to be drawn between the approval granted to individual members for their part in local village preaching and those cases involving a more general call to the Christian ministry.[68] At other times discrimination is only possible in the light of subsequent developments, as preachers acceded to the wishes of their hearers and accepted pastoral ordination. Even the existence of a secular occupation provides no sure guide in the problem of defining status, for, in the eighteenth century when stipends were very low, ministers were often compelled to support themselves by other means. Thus when William Carey was ordained at Moulton in Northamptonshire he found himself obliged to continue his work as a cobbler, having been promised by the church an annual sum of only £10.[69]

The use of ordination for full-time evangelists creates an additional complication in the assessment of status. Most experienced regular ordi-nation and were in consequence indistinguishable from their fellow ministers except for the absence of pastoral responsibilities. But a minority did not receive this mark of formal recognition. Although the Independent county associations and the Home Missionary Society appear to have been unanimous in their acceptance of the practice, the Essex Baptist Association did not ordain those whom it appointed. Instead the rite was deferred until settlement took place over a particular congregation.[70] The discrepancy appears to have stemmed from a difference in understanding of what the practice signified: on the one hand the concept of conferring ministerial status as Jonathan Scott experienced when he was set apart as a 'presbyter at large'; on the other the recognition of a specific pastoral relationship. Whichever concept prevailed the practical effect was the same, for in all the groups examined the administration of the ordinances, especially the Lord's Supper, was only possible where the itinerant was ordained. Where that did not obtain and the evolution of the preaching station into a properly constituted church had not occurred, the desire of converts to receive communion was normally satisfied with the help of neighbouring ministers. At Tillingham in 1821 the Essex association's itinerant was aided in this manner by John Garrington the Baptist minister at Burnham-on-Crouch.[71]

By now the lay component of itinerancy can be set quite accurately within the wider context of the movement: only the qualitative questions remain unanswered. Contemporary criticism depended heavily upon this area, making much of the unsuitability of lay preachers. Yet in the same way that mere statistics are misleading, the argument based on inability is inadequate for the weight placed upon it. The emphasis on social background merely obscures the serious approach of those involved and the careful process of selection to which they were subjected.

The general character of the more informed social criticism can be judged from earlier illustrations. It is only necessary to add that the most pejorative remarks issued from the lower levels of the clergy; from the very people whose position and credibility were most immediately affected. When a serious attempt is made to evaluate the social and occupational background of lay itinerants the problem of anonymity revives and with it the difficulty of identifying suitably representative individuals. The group for which occupation and status are readily available is small and only a painstaking examination of church books on a wide scale would be likely to add significantly to its number. In many cases even these records do not contain the information required.

Of those who are known the great majority earned their living as self-employed craftsmen or as outworkers, although their ranks were swelled by a smaller but significant number of schoolmasters. Only a handful of the men identified came from the higher social strata: of these five belonged to the merchant and manufacturing class, one person who worked for a short while under the auspices of the Village Itinerancy was entitled to the style of 'Gentleman', while Sir Egerton Leigh represented the sole contribution of the aristocracy. Although it is difficult to judge the representative nature of this cross-section, it does support the modern historical assessment of the social groups to which Nonconformity appealed during this period, and it bears a clear relationship to the facts accompanying the rational argument of Robert Woodward.[72] Some of Woodward's contemporaries were less restrained and the value of their comments as social observations is diminished by the degree of prejudice involved. Little support can be found, for example, for the somewhat extreme assertion made by William Bowen during the course of the Salisbury village preaching controversy that itinerant preachers were 'men, of the most ignorant and uneducated minds, ... capable of expressing only a few broken and incoherent sentences, on the subjects of grace, faith, repentance, salvation, &c.'[73]

While the more moderate critics dealt accurately with the social composition of itinerancy, their treatment of the religious vocation involved and the level of intellectual fitness among the preachers was less satisfactory. Woodward, having admitted the existence of educated itinerants, went on to suggest that for most of them the learning of trades would have precluded the development of suitable intellectual skills. In the absence of sermon records there is little tangible evidence from which to make an informed assessment, but, for a variety of reasons, it seems likely that the picture of ignorance and inability was overdrawn. The journal kept by the schoolmaster, Thomas Wastfield, who was admittedly not entirely typical, reveals a level of ability perfectly adequate for the communication of basic Christian doctrine, while the correspondence of other men who had received no formal training at all displays a similar level of competence. Most preachers must have improved upon the 'few broken and incoherent sentences' mentioned by Bowen or it becomes difficult to understand their popular appeal.

Although formal education may have been lacking, the high proportion of tradesmen involved in village preaching reflects the contemporary thirst within that section of society for knowledge and improvement. The level of self-teaching exemplified by William Carey may have been uncommon even among his peers, but opportunities for educational development did exist and among the advocates of itinerancy there were those who encouraged the process. In County Durham Charles Whitfield, an enthusiastic supporter of evangelism in the northern counties, formed an extensive library for the benefit of his church members at Hamsterley, subsequently underlining his concern for the ordinary Christian's intellectual development in a published sermon entitled *The Obligations to Mental Improvement Stated, and the Use of Books Recommended, Especially to Youth*.[74]

Institutional provision of library facilities for lay preachers seems to have been rather slower to develop. In 1820 it was proposed that the London Itinerant Society should establish a collection of books for the benefit of its agents working in the villages surrounding the metropolis, but it was not until ten years later that £30 was voted for that purpose. By that time each of the society's regular preachers had received a copy of 'Mr Neale's Publication on Antinomianism', while as early as January 1798 twelve copies of Burder's *Village Sermons* had been acquired for general use.[75] Whatever deficiencies there were in the formal education of village preachers, the Dissenting spokesman Robert Hall took exception to vague, indiscriminate charges of illiteracy and ignorant fanaticism. Hall's reply to Bishop Horsley claiming that 'The far greater part are men of good natural sense united to fervent piety' undoubtedly represented the considered Dissenting opinion.[76]

Behind the clerical criticism of lay preachers, half concealed by the allegations of ignorance, lay the conviction that no person who made pretensions to the ministerial office should simultaneously engage in manual employment. Whatever rationalization may have been applied to this prejudice, there is some evidence that Dissenters themselves recognized the deleterious effect produced by the combination of roles. In his memoirs John Clark of Trowbridge recalled how his work as a clothier had given him little time to prepare for local preaching engagements. With obvious regret he wrote, 'I was frequently obliged to go from my counting house directly into the pulpit, and could get no time for previous meditation.'[77] Despite the obvious vigour of this criticism there was no immediate Dissenting response. It was not until 1897 at the centenary of the Bedfordshire Union of Christians that an appeal was made to the writings of Basil of Caesarea and John Chrysostom concerning their approval of the secular occupations of the rural clergy.[78] Double standards were in operation on both sides of the argument since Establishment polemicists conveniently ignored the existcnce of clergymen who were profitably immersed in farming, undoubtedly aided by the convention that their status as landowners did not carry with it the stigma attached to trade.[79]

Clerical attitudes to the control exercised over lay preachers were distinctly ambiguous. On the one hand itinerants were regarded as innocent dupes of organized sedition, while at the other extreme a fear and dislike of unbridled individualism and self-assumed authority ran through many polemical statements. In reality the selection of lay preachers was carefully conducted. At least one trial of preaching ability was normally required, and the subsequent decision took into account factors which included doctrinal views, personal character and previous church standing. The recognition process applied to one member of the Congregational church at Andover in 1817 was entirely typical:

Mr Canon of Abbott's-ann deliver'd an exhortation with which the members in general appear'd highly satisfied, and were led to hope that by his submitting himself to the advice of the Church and Pastor in the exercise of his talent, his services would be render'd useful in the villages.[80]

Church control over preachers did not end with the granting of approval, for those working in neighbouring communities remained subject to normal discipline. At Bethel Independent Chapel, Sheerness a lay preacher was asked to suspend his visits to Minster and Grain for three months during 1826 because of bankruptcy.[81] In the selection of full-time itinerants similar care was taken, with reliance often being placed upon the personal recommendation of noted church leaders. Unless the applicant was known already the association would conduct an interview giving its members at least one opportunity of hearing the candidate preach. Even after the appointment there was in most cases careful ongoing supervision of the itinerancy and its results.

At times the insistence upon church control extended to the point where it threatened to stifle any genuine initiative. In 1808 a lengthy pamphlet appeared addressing itself to the exclusion of two members of an unidentified Particular Baptist church. The author, who was one of the men expelled, indicated that their offence had been to preach in public under the auspices of the London Itinerant Society without first securing a call to the work of the ministry. While admitting that congregational control over the right to preach had been retained by most Particular Baptist churches, he insisted that the 'persecuting principle' of the call had 'generally been suffered to lie dormant' as far as occasional preaching was concerned.[82] The pamphlet established a scriptural basis for an uncompromising rejection of ecclesiastical control; but it also suggested other probable reasons for the exclusion including not only strict denominationalism and an undue emphasis upon the authority of the local church, but also a strongly Calvinist reaction against the itinerants' practice of issuing a general call to repentance.[83] Though these factors may have limited the scope of lay itinerancy, the preoccupation with control also wore a more favourable aspect; it allowed the circulation of publicity giving warning of possible depredations by charlatans and swindlers posing as travelling preachers.

In spite of its detractors lay preaching never enjoyed the dominance alleged, nor did it merit the levels of contempt or suspicion aroused. In so far as it formed a distinct sector of itinerancy, it remained subject to a degree of discipline which renders most contemporary criticism invalid.

Behind its public facade early village preaching depended upon a system of private sponsorship. It was only as the response began to make impossible demands upon personal resources that a more permanent and broadly based means of support had to be developed. The financial and material impetus behind the early phase of itinerancy came to a large extent from the beneficence and paternalism of wealthy individuals. Among the sponsors of eighteenth-century evangelism there was an implicit acceptance of the principle later expounded by Chalmers, that free-trade policies, however applicable to other spheres of human activity, were inadequate for the development of a Christian society, since the desire for Christian teaching bore an inverse relationship to the level of religious need.[84] The wealthier contributors to Dissenting evangelism would not have subscribed to Chalmers' Establishment remedy, but their own massive financial commitment was prompted by the same concern to penetrate those areas of English society where religious apathy prevailed.

In this context the term sponsor is used in preference to patron in order to extend the application beyond the mere provision of financial resources to include those active in the encouragement of itinerant evangelism who were able by their initiative to arrange a secure basis of material support. Even according to this definition individual sponsorship characterized only the early years, being progressively replaced in the opening decade of the nineteenth century by a more permanent organization of national and denominational resources. Yet in its period of greatest prominence a variety of individual support was given, extending from those whose wealth was derived from aristocratic inheritance or advantageous marriage to men whose financial position reflected their own success in industry or commerce.

Patrons of aristrocratic pedigree were never numerous and with the exception of Selina Hastings, the dowager Countess of Huntingdon, tended to be little-known figures. The other members of the circle included such comparative nonentities as Lady Maxwell, the Viscountess Glenorchy and Sir Egerton Leigh. Yet their lack of social prominence should not be allowed to obscure the importance of their contribution, especially to the development of a firm base for Dissenting itinerancy. Their money and support provided the necessary impulse for the establishment of an extensive network of preaching and the training of a generation of ministers inclined towards evangelism.

Unlike the Wesleyans' Contingent Fund, English Calvinistic Methodists possessed no centrally administered financial pool. Consequently chapel building, maintenance and ministry depended upon the giving of each local congregation supplemented by individual generosity. Although much of the money derived from aristocratic sources was used to provide large, expensive chapels (buildings intended as centres for evangelism and therefore quite different in concept from the traditional meeting-house) a concern for itinerant preaching was also prominent.[85] In no case was this more evident than that of the Countess of Huntingdon. From 1768 until her death twenty-three years later she maintained a seminary at Trevecca at which a generation of students were schooled in itinerancy. Sent out on preaching tours they received a degree of material support from their aristocratic sponsor, but surviving letters reveal the parsimonious nature of that patronage and the consequent hardship attached to the task.[86] Despite these personal difficulties the principle of sponsored tours was sound, enabling the influence of Trevecca to spread over a wide area. In the standard biography of Lady Huntingdon the author claims that by 1781 her students 'were ... labouring in almost every county of England, and with very considerable success'.[87] Though her contemporary, Lady Glenorchy, did not initiate a comparable network of itinerant preaching, her legacies included a sum of £5,000 to be applied by Jonathan Scott to theological training: a bequest intended to promote the local counterpart to free-ranging itinerancy, the settled evangelistic pastorate.[88]

Less visible but equally important were clerical sponsors whose interest represented every variety of evangelical Dissent as well as, more surprisingly, the Church of England. It is at this point that sponsorship is used in its widest sense to include the organization of resources, the direction of operations and the encouragement of those involved. Had the definition been made to rest entirely upon the material contribution of the clergy it would have proved inadequate, since the finance necessary for evangelism outstripped the resources of most individuals, even those with the benefit of generous preferment. Yet traces of clerical patronage can be found. As his own activity became curtailed by age and infirmity, John Berridge, the unconventional Vicar of Everton, joined with others to finance the work of two itinerants in Cambridgeshire. His own commitment to the project guaranteed half the annual salary of £40 paid to each man.[89]

In the generation following Berridge some of the most sustained clerical encouragement came from the fringe of the Established Church through the influence of Rowland Hill and John Eyre, whose attitudes had been shaped by their early contacts with Calvinistic Methodism. While there is little to suggest that Eyre's personal contribution extended to monetary support, his initiative in forming the Village Itinerancy in 1796 and in tapping the financial resources of his own congregation at Ram's Chapel in Homerton did much to develop the impetus of the movement.[90] An examination of his correspondence with the early preachers sent out by the society shows that his role extended beyond the provision of money and suitable personnel to that of general superintendence. His words of encouragement, admonition and reproof were reinforced at suitable moments by personal visits of inspection.[91] Eyre's support for home mission, though limited by his premature death, was none the less national in conception, a point under-lined by his part in the founding of the Hackney itinerant academy in 1803.

Clerical sponsorship was by no means the sole prerogative of irregular clergymen cast in the mould of Hill and Eyre. The examples of William Roby and Samuel Bradley, both from Manchester, are sufficient to prove that vigorous ministerial support existed within the Dissenting bodies. Both gave unstinting encouragement to the infant Lancashire Congregational Union, while their churches contributed a large proportion of the money needed for its work within the county.[92]

Although the most obvious examples of sponsorship operated at the national or regional level, some were entirely local in character. The progress of evangelical Calvinism in two areas of Wiltshire owed much to the efforts of a single female sponsor. Born in Trowbridge, Joanna Turner had been influenced by the Calvinistic Methodism she had encountered in Bristol and London, and returning to her native town around 1761 she devoted much of her energy to the organization of regular preaching. Eventually the numbers attending became too large for the premises she was able to provide and the venture culminated in the opening of the Trowbridge Tabernacle in November 1771. Meanwhile her marriage to a substantial local businessman allowed the development of a new area of interest in southern Wiltshire. From 1781 until her death from cancer three years later her attention was directed towards the villages of Tisbury, Hindon and Ebbesborne Wake. Having purchased a house in Tisbury and registered another at Ebbesborne she established regular preaching with the help of students sent out by the Countess of Huntingdon. By her own presence at the meetings and her practice of visiting and holding religious conversation with the inhabitants, Joanna Turner allowed her role as lay sponsor to encompass to some extent that of a female evangelist.[93]

By far the most generous and consistent support came from the business community. From the first explosion of evangelical enthusiasm in the mid-1790s associations recorded their indebtedness to men like Richard Fishwick, director of the Elswick Lead Works at Newcastle-upon-Tyne, and Robert Spear who was prominent in the Manchester cotton trade.[94] As might be expected itinerancy enjoyed the greatest measure of business support in areas adjacent to the principal mercantile and industrial centres, but this limitation was by no means absolute. In 1789 the generosity of George Welch, a London banker, enabled David Bogue to commence a theological seminary at Gosport, while a few years later the Hampshire Independent ministers received an anonymous offer to defray the daily expenses of two preachers appointed to work within their county.[95] Prior to 1790 the field of evangelical philanthropy had been dominated by the prosperous Anglican merchant John Thornton, and although itinerant preaching may not have been the immediate object of his giving, it benefited from his beneficence. In the provision of £200 p.a. for the maintenance of the Newport Pagnell Evangelical Institution during the lifetime of its president, William Bull, and in donations like the one to Henry Philips, the minister of Salisbury Baptist church, enabling him to purchase bibles, tracts and other religious publications for general distribution, the link is quite apparent.[96]

From the mid-1790s Thornton's leadership in the realm of financial sponsorship passed to an Independent named Thomas Wilson. Born in 1764 Wilson had prospered as a London silk merchant. At the age of 34 he was able to retire from business and devote himself entirely to 'promot[ing] the cause of God'. In 1813 his financial capacity was further enlarged following the death of his uncle, a wealthy broad-silk manufacturer, and his generosity to the cause of domestic evangelism increased commensurately. Apart from his interest in the Missionary and Tract Societies and in other evangelical causes his support for itinerant evangelism operated at three distinct levels. In his active membership of the committee of Societas Evangelica there was an obvious concern for the encouragement of individuals in the practice of itinerancy. His efforts towards the recovery of disused chapel buildings and the erection of new ones revealed an understanding of the strategic requirement in some areas for a basic evangelistic infrastructure.[97] But important as these immediate responses may have been, Wilson's primary interest lay with the more pervasive influence that could be achieved by means of a ministerial training which embodied the principle of itinerancy. His service as treasurer of Hoxton Academy was marked by an extraordinary assiduousness and munificence in a forty-nine year term of office which lasted until his death in 1843.[98]

The achievements of personal sponsorship may have been remarkable, but the steadily increasing scale of itinerant activity required more resources than individual generosity could hope to muster. The uncertain factors which governed philanthropy, its dependence upon personal relationships, whims, financial circumstances and even the mere duration of life, all served to intensify this inadequacy and to ensure its ultimate replacement by a more organized and broadly based financial structure. The continuing individualism of Thomas Wilson merely obscures the reality that in the period after 1800 the support of evangelism became a corporate and institutional responsibility.

4 · The academic leaven

Early itinerancy, with its total dependence upon individual initiative, developed unevenly and with little obvious co-ordination. But this phase was short-lived. By 1800 village preaching was becoming a national phenomenon, visible in the remotest rural communities, even in areas unaffected by Methodism. The completeness of this change points to the existence of a common factor; a source of inspiration more universal and capable of exerting more influence than those already identified. Neither the supervision of wealthy sponsors, nor the unifying power of the infant county associations, nor even the example set by early Methodism, are sufficient to explain the rapid expansion of the practice with all it signified for traditional Dissent. Given the prominence of newly ordained ministers among the itinerants, it seems a likely premise that the institutions responsible for their training were also the source of a sustained and systematic impulse towards evangelism. What is necessary, therefore, is to establish and examine their connection with itinerancy.[1]

As suggested earlier, much of the criticism directed at the village preachers by supporters of the Establishment relied upon allegations of ignorance and lack of preparation, defects which reinforced the judgment of social unsuitability. With the ephemeral character of itinerant preaching and the passage of almost two centuries, it is difficult to know if the situation at Salisbury and Bath which attracted the condemnation of Wilberforce represented any more than local imprudence. The impression gained from church and association minutes is that the use of 'raw, ignorant lads' by Calvinistic Dissenters was certainly exceptional. Since the matter was brought to the attention of Wilberforce by William Jay, the conviction that this was untypical is merely strengthened, for Jay, as a product of Cornelius Winter's academy at Marlborough, approved of a theological training whose academic ingredient was firmly related to practical evangelism.[2]

While Establishment opposition concentrated upon the lack of training, drawing apologetic responses from Samuel Clift, William Kingsbury, Robert Hall and the clerical defender of Dissent, 'Clero Mastix',[3] the champions of home mission had to contend with criticism from a much closer source concerning the general principle of ministerial education. Many orthodox congregations, especially among Particular Baptists, showed considerable resistance to any suggestion of formal ministerial preparation.[4] Hence at the start of their work both the Bristol Education Society (the body formed in 1770 to support the Bristol Baptist Academy) and the Northern Education Society (the sister organization which came into being in 1804 with the aim of promoting a similar venture in the North) felt it necessary to deal with prejudice against 'man-made' ministers. In the 'Account of the Constitution of the Bristol Education Society' published in 1770, the usefulness of learning as a preparation for a gospel ministry was commended unequivocally:

It has been suggested by some that LEARNING is designed to perfect the work of the Spirit of God. But this is a mere slander. The only question is, Are we to expect miracles, as in the Apostolic age, to qualify us for the work of the ministry; or, are we to use ordinary means? That we are not to expect miracles all will allow, and, if not, then surely we are to use ordinary means. And so far is this from interfering with the work of the Spirit, that it appears to be the only way in which we may reasonably expect His continued influences; and it seems rather to be tempting the Spirit of God to expect that in an extraordinary, which we are authorized to expect only in an ordinary way.[5]

Some of the older regional associations reserved their support for ministerial education until the early years of the nineteenth century. The Western Association, whose ministerial complement was increasingly composed of men trained at Bristol, did not appeal openly for subscriptions to the Education Society or for the recommendation of suitable candidates before 1804.[6] As late as 1823 John Saffery of Salisbury urged the member churches through the medium of the association letter to set aside their prejudice:

it becomes you to select, not only pious, but educated ministers. The ill-informed and the illiterate shrink from the advantages which they cannot estimate. They imagine that tyranny and self-preference must combine with intellectual acquirements: but conceit and tyranny are the legitimate result of ignorance and folly.[7]

Nor was the task limited to convincing congregations of Particular Baptists. Some Independents shared their distrust of theological education. An account of Hoxton Academy published in 1804 had a discernible apologetic motif directed at those who undervalued academic institutions together with their learning and discipline, and who preferred to depend upon the influences of the divine Spirit. It noted that though the apostles and prophets were taught by God they did not set their faces against human knowledge: many of the early Christian leaders were, like Paul and Timothy, learned men. Similarly, in later centuries the translation of the Scriptures into English was the product of intellectual accomplishment.[8]

Part of the problem stemmed from the character of contemporary theological education. A firm tradition of academic training had long existed, but by the 1770s it was showing signs of decay. Many of the older institutions, having been influenced by Rational Dissent, had ceased to produce ministers with popular appeal. Where the eighteenth-century academies are discussed by historians an element of paradox is found. In one breath they are spoken of as the intellectual counterparts of the universities and as pioneers of future trends in higher education,[9] yet the general picture presented is that of institutions increasingly espousing theological heterodoxy and becoming progressively less capable, therefore, of exercising a serious influence upon the mainstream of orthodox Dissent. The atmosphere of controversy and decline is conveyed by a number of examples but by none more striking than the successor of Doddridge's famous Northampton Academy which, having lost the leadership of Thomas Belsham in 1789 because of his Unitarian beliefs, was dissolved entirely by the Coward trustees nine years later in the face of similar views held by the new principal tutor, John Horsey.[10]

In their attempt to classify the numerous Dissenting institutions most studies of eighteenth-century education have tended to overlook one of the most important developments; the emergence after 1768 of a new generation of evangelical academies. Understandably, interest in the academies has focussed upon the educational aspect, and this approach has caused the particular ethos of the later, evangelical foundations to pass almost unnoticed. Of the twentieth-century historians only Halévy has drawn attention to their distinctive character and hinted at their contribution to the rise of popular evangelicalism during the Napoleonic era.[11]

The phrase 'new academies' does little more than hint at the educational developments which accompanied the spread of evangelicalism. The emphasis of the new institutions was quite different from that of their predecessors. Theologically grounded in moderate, evangelical Calvinism and in consequence displaying a strongly practical bias, the new seminaries (the term itself indicates their divergence from the earlier pattern) afforded regular opportunities for practice in evangelistic preaching and encouraged the growth of personal devotion. Their early development was marked by a fairly relaxed attitude towards intellectual attainment.

Trevecca College, established originally to serve the spiritual needs of the Established Church, provided the inspiration for this new approach to ministerial training. It created what was described at the time by Francis Okeley, Moravian minister at Bedford, as 'a School of the Prophets'.[12] Both in its conception of ministry and in the impetus it gave to the founding of similar institutions Trevecca was seminal. Yet in its original form under the Countess of Huntingdon's direction it gave insufficient priority to the educational aspect. During the spring of 1787 William Roby, later one of the moving spirits behind Independent evangelism in Lancashire, spent six weeks at the college, but left apparently dissatisfied with what it had to offer.[13] In a manuscript outline for a projected autobiography he recorded his disappointment in a few terse comments: 'Trial of preaching before friends at the house of Rev. J.J. Recommended by him to Lady H___ Spring of A__D__1787. Went to the college at T. No advantages there. Various sources of regret in the manner of educating for the Xtian ministry.'[14]

Roby may have been exceptional, having received a good general and classical education at Wigan Grammar School, but the implication concerning the low priority accorded to intellectual attainment at Trevecca is confirmed by other testimony. The standard biography of the Countess of Huntingdon notes that in her desire for preachers who would concentrate on saving souls she was known actively to dissuade her students from learning Greek and Hebrew.[15] Nor was the fault confined to the attenuated nature of the course, for, as resident tutor, John Williams had cause to complain on at least one occasion of the low standard of literacy exhibited by most of the student intake; an ignorance compounded in his opinion by lack of ability.[16] It was possibly the low academic standing of Trevecca that formed the subject of the offensive sarcasm which led to the exclusion of the Calvinist itinerant Rowland Hill from the pulpits of Lady Huntingdon's chapels in 1781.[17]

By his own example George Whitefield had taught English Calvinism to approach the concept of ministry with greater flexibility. Trevecca encouraged that trend. By adapting the existing pattern of theological training, inculcating itinerancy, uniting the role of pastor with that of evangelist and showing comparative disregard for the conventions of ordination, it ensured a continuing state of fluidity. Establishment hostility to these changes was matched by internal resistance from some of the older, orthodox Dissenters. Certain ministers displayed a strong antipathy to the practice of itinerancy, refusing to ordain in consequence except to a stated charge.[18]

In most of the seminaries formed between 1768 and 1830 the influence of Trevecca can be traced, whether mediated through sponsors, tutors, or the members of a governing committee. From the small academies managed by Cornelius Winter and William Roby to the much larger undertakings at Hoxton and Hackney the same fundamental emphasis upon evangelism shaped their development. While the divide between paedobaptists and antipaedobaptists was more significant than one recent study suggests,[19] the interest in itinerancy shown by the long-established Baptist academy at Bristol, and by the new foundations at Bradford and Stepney, owed as much to the demonstrable success of Whitefieldite theological education exemplified in Trevecca, as it did to any personal insight of Baptist leaders such as Andrew Fuller, Hugh and Caleb Evans, and Robert Hall senior.

The Countess of Huntingdon's rather restricted commitment to education casts an unfavourable light upon the whole evangelistic movement, causing it to appear both obscurantist and anti-intellectual. Yet this image does not bear close scrutiny. In the period after 1790 evangelical Dissent displayed an increasing concern for genuine substance in theological education. Many believed that vital faith and intellectual development could profitably coexist, exercising a beneficial effect upon the ministry of the Church. Those most prominent in the encouragement and support of itinerant preaching were also the strongest advocates of a proper system of education and training. Leading educators, including William Roby at Manchester, William Vint at Idle, David Bogue at Gosport and William Steadman at Bradford, encouraged itinerancy, creating in the course of their work extensive networks of preaching.[20] But these views were not confined to academy tutors. The activities of Thomas Wilson and Charles Whitfield demonstrate that the belief in the essential harmony between evangelical zeal and sound learning embraced prominent lay people and men employed in routine pastoral engagements. In the wake of his attempt to launch a concerted scheme of village preaching in the northernmost counties of England, Whitfield showed himself to be one of the keenest supporters of the project for founding a Baptist academy at Bradford.[21]

In the attitude of Charles Whitfield, as in that of the other Dissenting leaders, there are occasional glimpses of currents of thought beneath the simple evangelical concern with salvation. A deep conviction existed that what had been entered upon was a rescuing and civilizing mission, conveying urban Christian enlightenment to isolated villagers living in ignorance, darkness and moral degradation. These terms, though strong, were precisely those employed by itinerant evangelists going for the first time into areas like the Fylde peninsula in Lancashire.[22]

In spite of a common evangelical concern the institutions which provided training for this task were not entirely uniform. Though some displayed a broad undenominationalism, the allegiance of others was quite specific. Few totally ignored the denominational persuasion of candidates and attendant matters of polity. Of those that did the most notable was the academy at Newport Pagnell, a foundation planned and financed by John Newton and John Thornton and presided over by the local Independent minister, William Bull. The most prominent members of the 'undenominational' group, the academies at Hoxton, Hackney and Cheshunt, set certain limits to the tolerance they were prepared to show. They did not admit known antipaedo-baptists.[23] Nevertheless, exclusiveness in one direction could well be matched by latitude in another. Long after the Countess of Huntingdon's chapels had been excluded from the Established Church, the college at Cheshunt, the direct successor of Trevecca, continued to demonstrate its own peculiar affinity with Anglicanism by using the liturgical formularies prescribed in the Book of Common Prayer.[24]

The degree of permanence and financial stability varied widely. Small academies of the kind organized by William Roby in the vestry of Mosley Street Chapel, Manchester, between 1803 and 1808, could operate very effectively. Roby's academy functioned for six years, producing in that period seventeen ministers and evangelists, but its existence was entirely dependent upon a single wealthy individual. When its patron retired from business the academy was compelled to close.[25] In a similar manner the seminary at Gosport barely outlived its president, David Bogue, who as the local Independent minister had been its founder and its principal source of inspiration.[26] Such a narrow financial and tutorial base could never guarantee permanence but it did offer certain advantages. Academies formed on this pattern were easy to establish and they were able to avoid some of the heavier financial burdens associated with more enduring foundations.

Those institutions with a wider, county base might have been expected to enjoy greater financial security. The academies at Idle, Bradford, Blackburn, Rotherham and Newport Pagnell contrived to exist on local support for many years, but others experienced times of acute financial crisis, especially during the lean years which followed the Napoleonic Wars. By deriving the greater part of their income from local sources they found themselves exposed to the economic fluctuations of particular industries. In spite of the financial benefit expected to accrue to the Leaf Square Academy in Pendleton from its associated grammar school, the venture collapsed in 1813 after a mere three years of operation.[27] Yet it was clearly recognized that effective evangelization of the populous newly industrial areas often depended upon the proximity of an academy.[28] The villages surrounding Olney and Newport Pagnell in Buckinghamshire, though lacking large-scale industry, demonstrate the effective coverage that could be achieved with a well-established pattern of student itinerancy.[29]

Unlike the smaller provincial academies, Bristol, Hoxton and similar institutions that were able to appeal to Christian liberality on a national scale, enjoyed complete financial security together with the benefits that such stability brought to academic work. But the increased scale of operations did not necessarily produce efficiency. This is evident in the extravagance associated with prestige. An interesting comparison can be drawn between the new Highbury College opened in 1826 and the premises planned four years later by Idle Academy. While the former cost in excess of £19,000, the budget for the latter was restricted to £3,000.[30] The respective student numbers differed less strikingly: Highbury had places for forty men while the equivalent number for Idle was seventeen.

Differences between the new academies were not confined to the external features. Variations can also be detected in the approach to theological training, particularly in the changing balance between the academic and practical elements of courses. Yet the peculiar combination of intellectual and evangelistic interest which characterized these institutions was present in every case to a greater or lesser extent. That combination is clearly visible in the initial plan of the English Evangelic Academy, the antecedent of Hoxton and Highbury. According to its founders the academy aimed to provide its students with 'proper Instructions ... in English Grammar — in the great Doctrines of the Gospel — in the method of framing Discourses — and ... some proper Trials of their Spiritual Gifts, previous to their entering upon public Work' preferably in 'places apparently void of all Gospel Instruction'.[31]

There remained a broad similarity between selection procedures. In addition to the necessary recommendation of home congregations, applicants were normally expected to relate their experience of spiritual regeneration and to attest their doctrinal orthodoxy. The interviewing committee would need to be satisfied concerning their general intellectual and educational fitness, while the short probationary period would often be used to assess their talent for preaching. The requirement for evidence of conversion was one of the hallmarks of the evangelical seminaries. In 1799 the refusal by the trustees of Wymondley Academy to adopt this standard for future entrants caused the young and able John Pye Smith to decline the vacant tutorship.[32] Where applicants appeared to satisfy the basic entrance requirements they were invited for interview. Standards undoubtedly varied but the examination of prospective students was rigorously conducted. The following terse account of an abortive application to Hackney Academy demonstrates that even at this stage admission was no mere formality:

Mr Davies was examined on personal Election Reprobation on the extent of the Atonement and on special and common Grace and it appearing that Mr D's opinions were Baxterian Resolved That he cannot be proposed to the Committee as a Candidate for the Academy.[33]

Village preaching was itself widely regarded as a necessary preliminary to theological training, and in many cases those applying had already demonstrated considerable potential.[34] The desire for more formal preparation was construed not as an attempt to escape from the work, but as indicating a readiness for full-time employment as an itinerating minister or a county evangelist. Yet even previous itinerancy conferred no guarantee of admission to a theological course, as one applicant to Cheshunt discovered in 1806. The trustees decided that apart from a serious health defect there was 'no satisfactory Proof of his Call to the Ministry, notwithstanding [his] preaching about in various places'.[35] Personal inadequacy was not the only reason given for rejection: in some cases existing success as a lay preacher was deemed to outweigh any advantage likely to be gained from a period of formal academic training. In 1822 the examining committee of the Village Itinerancy advised an applicant named John Hawthorn 'to return and continue his labours in his own vicinity' since it appeared to them that he was already 'in a greater sphere of usefulness than he could occupy at least for some time to come in connection with [the] Society'. In giving this advice they specifically disclaimed any intention of casting doubt upon his principles or his abilities.[36]

The formal curriculum varied little from one institution to another. Academy minutes and reports reveal an approach to academic work which emphasized breadth rather than depth of understanding. Most of the small, provincial academies concentrated from necessity in the period before 1800 upon a fairly limited programme, attempting to give their students basic instruction in English grammar and Christian doctrine, an introduction to the writings of the Puritan divines and practice in sermon preparation, together with a working knowledge of the classical languages. According to the description given by William Jay these were the elements that comprised the curriculum at Marlborough and Painswick between 1783 and 1807. The tutor, Cornelius Winter, adopted a somewhat informal manner. With a student body of three or four at the maximum, lectures were replaced by reading and a tutorial or seminar pattern of teaching. In July 1788 when Jay had left the academy, Winter wrote encouraging him to continue his studies, spending time in particular on Latin and Greek.[37] At Newport Pagnell Winter's contemporary, William Bull, showed similar expectations of proficiency in these languages.[38] By 1802 Cheshunt College regarded successful progress in language study as a condition of further attendance. When, after two years of the four-year course, a student named Shepherd was discovered to have no talent for that aspect of the work, he was advised to enter the ministry without delay.[39] Inclusion of the classical languages was not, however, an invariable feature of the earliest institutions, for the plan of the English Evangelic Academy drawn up in 1778 mentions only English grammar.

By the turn of the century a general growth in the range and duration of courses was perceptible. The 1811 report of the Hackney Academy observed that:

The System of education established at this Seminary is that which appears best calculated to furnish young men for an Itinerant Ministry. They are instructed in the english and greek tongues – they pass through a regular course of Theological an[d] Biblical Studies and of Historical and Ecclesiastical Reading and where the mind has been found very expansive and a previous education has been liberal the Latin Classics have been added and the time of continuance protracted.

In earlier years the training offered by Hackney had varied in length according to the demand for preachers experienced by the associated society, the Village Itinerancy. In 1806 a student had settled at Lichfield after only one year at the academy. But within a decade the period of study had lengthened considerably. By then the majority of students left to take part in itinerancy or to settle over a congregation during their third academic year.[40] At the other influential London seminary, the Independent-inspired Hoxton Academy, ministerial candidates were confronted after 1797 by a well-developed curriculum which linked Latin, Greek and Hebrew with a foundation course in English grammar and literature. It went on to supplement the central biblical, ethical and historical elements with practical subjects which included logic and elocution.[41]

The growth in the academic element only in part reflected the passage of time. It owed its impetus to the increasing size of seminaries. With its staff of three tutors the well-established Baptist academy at Bristol had even before the 1790s been able to include in its curriculum the principles of moral and natural philosophy and the essentials of astronomy, as well as the biblical and linguistic subjects offered by all evangelical foundations. By 1795 the Countess of Huntingdon's college at Cheshunt, with thirteen students in residence, was prepared to outline a comprehensive 'plan of education' which extended to elementary mathematics, and which for strictly vocational purposes even envisaged an optional course in French.[42]

Within the principal subject areas some information is available concerning the content of courses.[43] As an introduction to theological study Hackney Academy required its students to read an essay by Isaac Watts entitled *The Harmony of all the Religions*. Elsewhere other recognized works of theology were used in conjunction with the normal programme of teaching. At Cheshunt in 1828 the annual examination was based upon lectures covering 'the priesthood and suretyship of Christ; ... the nature, the necessity, the reality and the perfection of the satisfaction of the Mediator of the everlasting covenant; and ... particular redemption'. It was noted that as part of the course 'The most weighty objections of Socinians and Arminians to these doctrines [had been] answered; and the general invitations of the gospel, its commands and threatenings ... reconciled, and proved to be in harmony with the gracious designs of God.' Nor was theological study confined to the sphere of dogmatics and Christian apologetics. The 1828 Cheshunt report makes it clear that some attempt at critical exegesis was being made using the Greek text of the Acts of the Apostles and appropriate commentaries.

As a natural complement to the grammatical study of Latin, Greek and Hebrew most seminaries paid considerable attention to classical literature. Their records mention the translation from Hebrew of parts of Genesis and the Psalms, as well as similar work with the Greek texts of the New Testament and Septuagint. In addition a number of classical authors were translated including the Latin writers Virgil, Cicero and Horace and the

Greeks Xenophon, Homer and Thucydides. What is less certain is the methodology employed. To what extent did students engage in textual study? Did they merely practise the mechanics of translation? The answer to these questions is uncertain but the latter supposition seems the most likely. There is also the all-important question concerning the level of individual achievement. Most reports rather disappointingly mention only the examiners' satisfaction with the general level of progress.

Historical studies in general received less attention than either dogmatics or homiletics. But they were not completely ignored: the courses offered included lectures on Jewish history and customs and on the principal developments of the Christian era. In 1806 Hackney Academy prescribed Rollin's *Ancient History* as an introductory textbook for students. According to the plan of education the academy's lectures in ecclesiastical history were devised in conjunction with a course of relevant reading. A similar plan for Hoxton Academy issued in 1809 mentions an historical component, but the enigmatic description of the course as 'The connection of sacred with profane history' gives little indication of its content.

Inevitably the preoccupation with evangelism lent particular emphasis to practical theology. Every seminary afforded weekly opportunities to students for sermon preparation, delivery and analysis under professional guidance.[44] As academic preparation for ministry became more demanding practical training developed commensurately. At Hoxton Henry Burder introduced students to a consideration of style and delivery in a course entitled 'Belles Lettres with a special regard to pulpit composition and Elocution'. The Hackney curriculum listed set books designed to develop the art of sermon preparation and preaching. As a basis for the study of logic it prescribed Isaac Watts' *Improvement of the Mind*, while that was supplemented by Edward Williams's contemporary publication, *The Christian Preacher*. The latter work, a collection of discourses by eminent divines, provided students with practical advice concerning the discipline of preaching. Its inclusion in the course was designed to accompany the regular critical examination of printed sermons.

In the fifty years between 1780 and 1830 the larger evangelical academies pursued the twin goals of greater respectability and improved academic standards. The latter should not be confused with the appearance of more impressive curricula and the increasing length of courses, though these factors do suggest a more rigorous approach to education. The problem confronting any analysis of standards lies in the strong element of subjectivity within educational assessment and the consequent difficulty of quantifying supposed changes.

Despite this problem certain differences are apparent. Nowhere are these more obvious than in the development of Trevecca College. After the somewhat equivocal approach to academic work which marked the Countess of Huntingdon's lifetime, the Apostolic Society in its new home at Cheshunt College adopted a far more substantial and consistent pattern of ministerial education. The initial concern of the trustees for reasonable standards, evident in their search for a well-qualified clergyman to act as resident tutor,[45] continued in the form of regular external examinations in theology and language study, and in a willingness to terminate the courses of students who failed to make sufficient progress.

As the logical counterpart to the rising standards facing students there was a parallel tendency to require higher qualifications of those who taught. When Cornelius Winter opened his Marlborough academy in 1783 he had himself experienced less than two years of rudimentary instruction as a child at a London charity school. His considerable erudition was the fruit of years of diligent self-teaching.[46] Robert Simpson, the able first president of Hoxton Academy, had by comparison pursued a proper course of theological instruction at James Scott's academy at Heckmondwike.[47] But with the appointment of John Hooper as assistant tutor in 1808 fresh from his studies at Glasgow University, closely followed a year later by a second graduate, Henry Burder, Hoxton established the pace for the leading seminaries by showing respect for the rising standards of education expected both from settled evangelical ministers and itinerants.[48]

Together with the appointment of tutors possessing higher academic qualifications, the larger and more enduring foundations continued to widen and formalize their curriculum. As they raised their basic educational requirements, courses of preliminary education for new entrants became necessary. Increasingly, prospective students were sent for short preparatory courses to approved ministers such as Walter Scott of Rowell, John Thornton of Billericay, John Sutcliff of Olney and Samuel Kilpin at Leominster.[49] Even with careful sifting some applicants failed to reach an acceptable standard. In 1813 John Thornton notified the Hoxton committee that a candidate who had been studying with him had been unable to 'bend with sufficient intenseness to the dead Languages', and that he had, therefore, accepted an invitation to itinerate for the Essex Congregational Union.[50]

When the positive signs of academic development have been considered, it is necessary to sound a note of caution. Contrary indicators can be found which, though they concern only the evangelical academies, conflict with the unqualified representation of Dissenting scholarship as the equivalent of that offered by the English universities. Drawing upon his considerable experience as student and tutor at the Baptist academy in Bristol, Joseph Hughes made a surprisingly critical comment, suggesting that as a theological seminary it was deficient both 'in system and in stimulants'.[51] A similarly sour note was sounded by Hughes' contemporaries, David Bogue and James Bennett, in their *History of Dissenters*. As part of their survey of the state of ministerial education, they observed that in the reaction against heterodox Dissent, with its strongly academic emphasis, most of the evangelical institutions had veered to the opposite extreme, offering only 'a half education' in their concern to guard against a loss of spiritual vitality. They warned of the danger of producing a generation of ignorant, lazy and shallow ministers.[52]

Whatever the truth of these suggestions the need to present a good public image was taken seriously. In addition to a yearly examination most academies required their senior students to preach or read prepared papers at the annual meeting of subscribers. These discourses covered such topics as 'The Evidences of the truth of Christianity, arising from Miracles' and 'Faith in Jesus Christ considered as a duty'.[53] As a final seal of approval some institutions awarded testimonials to outgoing students.[54] These were not intended simply as a comment upon academic performance, but took into consideration character and conduct.

Important though intellectual accomplishment was, the primary objective remained the supply of able and enthusiastic men trained in the practical skills of evangelism. Earlier academies had not ignored the practical element, but the new emphasis upon student itinerancy was an important development. Evangelistic preaching characterized the new academies. It sets them apart from their contemporaries more effectively than any analysis of theological belief.

While the formal aspect of sermon preparation was included in the academic programme, every student was required to take part in regular public preaching. The external activity fell into two discrete categories: pulpit supplies were made available to existing congregations with no pastoral oversight, and direct evangelism was undertaken in places where gospel preaching was untried, or where no church had yet been formed. This distinction is outlined succinctly in a paragraph from the Hackney report for 1811:

It must not be forgotten that the primary object of some institutions for the education of pious men for the Ministry is to supply destitute Churches your principal design is to raise new ones whilst they are laudibly aiming to streng[t]hen the stakes of Zion we are as anxiously endeavouring to lengthen her cords. In making a remark of this kind no one we are persuaded will charge us with invidious comparisons since our objects are distinct we cannot act as jealous rivals but ought to act as zealous co-operators in forwarding the same cause by different means. The one may break up the fallow Ground the other may scatter the precious seed, the one may lay the foundation the other the superstructure.

Despite the avowal concerning the importance of both aspects this analysis over-simplifies the situation. In the case of the Bristol Academy the annual reports convey a strong impression of consolidation compared with the expansionist concern evident in the records of similar institutions in the

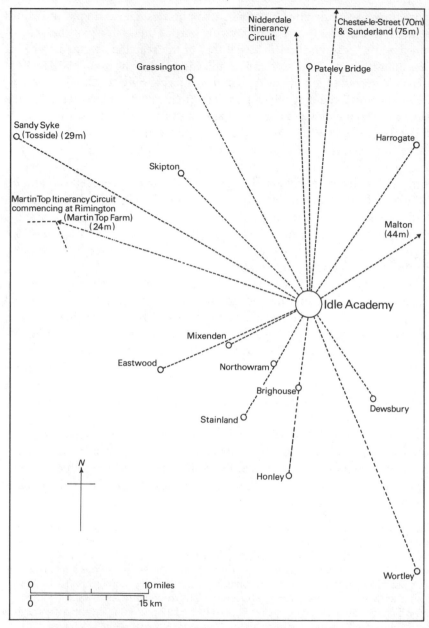

6   Regular local itinerancy radiating from a central base. Yorkshire. Idle Academy student itinerancy network, 1810–15.

Some of the places listed were visited more frequently than others. Several preaching stations such as the one at Grassington received student itinerants for only a limited period before becoming self-supporting Dissenting churches with resident ministers.

Source: Idle Academy, reports 1810–15.

Bradford area. Yet from indirect sources, including biographies and contemporary periodicals, it can be demonstrated that throughout the period of this study Bristol students actively promoted itinerant evangelism.[55] Equally the Bradford academies, in spite of being committed to genuine expansion, found it necessary to deploy a large proportion of their student resources in existing churches. Generally, a combination of both roles was adopted. From the student's point of view this was ideal, for most future opportunities for itinerancy would occur locally within the context of a settled pastorate.

In reality the location, age and size of an institution were more responsible for the balance struck between consolidation and expansion than any conscious aims. Until the appearance of the Northern Education Society in 1804 the Bristol Academy was the only permanent source of trained personnel suitable for Particular Baptist churches. Consequently the efforts of the academy were directed in large measure towards the needs of existing congregations, especially those in the pre-industrial market and textile communities of the West Country. By contrast the Baptist and Independent academies at Bradford and Idle were new institutions in an area of comparative Dissenting weakness. They faced the challenge of an expanding industrial population and the growth of entirely new settlements. In that situation the need to concentrate upon overt evangelism was obvious. Yet, as the records of the Bradford academies reveal, the policy of expansion rapidly succumbed to its own success. As local meetings of Christians developed into a network of churches, so the burden of ensuring an adequate ministry grew and the evangelistic impetus visibly slackened.

Despite these conflicting demands most students experienced a variety of practical work during their training. In order to achieve this academies were often closely associated with other organizations. Two of the London seminaries, those at Hoxton and Hackney, were able to deploy their men throughout the country using their own particular links with Societas Evangelica and the Village Itinerancy.[56] As the examples of Newport Pagnell and Olney demonstrate, the impact of student itinerancy was felt most strongly in the immediate neighbourhood, but longer journeys were regularly undertaken. At Idle under the presidency of William Vint considerable effort was expended providing systematic pulpit supplies. These covered not only the existing Independent churches in the Bradford area but also congregations as far afield as Skipton and Honley.[57] Often congregational life had reached a low ebb and the student preachers found themselves with a natural opportunity for evangelism. Attention was also given to the more remote rural communities. In 1811 at the request of two or three inhabitants of Grassington in Wharfedale, students from Idle began a weekly preaching visit to the village. Until a church was formed the following year this necessitated a sixty-mile journey on foot.[58] In similar fashion the men from

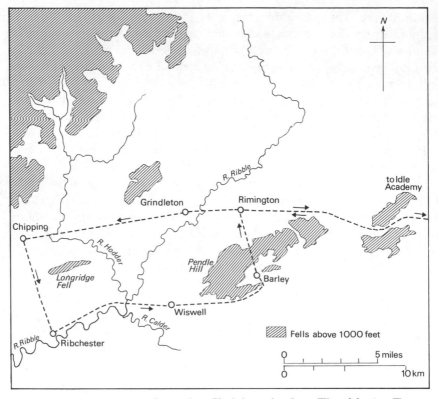

7 Circuit itinerancy. Lancashire-Yorkshire border. The Martin Top
Itinerancy.

Responsibility for the Martin Top Itinerancy was shared between the Independents in the
West Riding and those connected with the Lancashire Congregational Union. According
to T. Whitehead, *History of the Dales Congregational Churches* (Bradford, 1930), pp. 332–3
it enjoyed the services of 'some of the best lay preachers in Yorkshire'. He describes the
operation of the circuit as follows: 'They generally stayed two Sabbaths, the first Sabbath
they preached at Martin Top Farm [Rimington], on Monday at Grindleton, Tuesday at
Chipping, Wednesday at Ribchester, Thursday at Winwell [Wiswell], Friday at John
Singleton's at Barley, and finished the labours of the week by preaching again at Martin
Top Farm.'

Cheshunt College maintained preaching during the early 1820s at more than
a dozen places, some as much as sixteen miles distant. Nearer centres such as
Stanstead Abbotts and Hertford were served every week, but the preaching
station at Woolwich necessarily received only a monthly visit.[59]

Academy-based evangelism constituted only one aspect of student itinerancy. Several institutions regularly provided personnel for more distant
work. At times this involved the classic itinerant style with its constant
movement, but more commonly a student would work for a while within a

given locality. Using the former pattern Idle Academy for many years helped to service a preaching circuit in the Ribble valley among the isolated communities of the Lancashire–Yorkshire border. The Martin Top Itinerancy, as it came to be known, was organized by the academy in conjunction with the Itinerant Society for the West Riding of Yorkshire. Covering approximately thirty miles, it took those involved away from their studies for more than a week, preaching at farmhouses and cottages between Newby and Ribchester.[60] The combination of local and distant preaching seen at Idle made considerable demands upon those involved. Amos Blackburn, who entered the academy in 1818 at the age of seventeen wrote: 'It is three months since I commenced preaching the Gospel, in which time I have preached between 40 and 50 times, which is more than three times a week, and have walked 500 miles for that purpose'.[61]

The itinerant effort of the Yorkshire students, though involving greater than average distances due to the sparsely populated nature of the surrounding countryside, was repeated by men from other academies in various parts of the country. During the six week summer vacation Hackney sent its residents to many places including Hull and Liskeard to gain evangelistic experience under local direction.[62] A further form of extended student itinerancy was noted earlier in connection with the Cornish preaching mission of 1797 supported by the Baptist Missionary Society. Franklin, the student involved, was preparing for the Baptist ministry at the Bristol Academy. He was accompanied by an experienced minister, William Steadman of Broughton in Hampshire, though the pairing offered little in the way of practical supervision. During the eight weeks spent in Cornwall the two men met only occasionally, preferring to maximize the effectiveness of the tour by preaching simultaneously in adjacent parts of the county.[63]

Apart from the more obvious forms of itinerancy students were also used to contact a number of isolated social groups. Brief references appear in academy minutes and reports, but no particular venture receives more than passing attention. The centenary history of the Bedfordshire Union of Christians notes that during the Napoleonic Wars a student from William Bull's academy at Newport Pagnell was sent to preach to French prisoners of war interned at Norman Cross in Huntingdonshire, but no further details of this work are given, not even an indication as to whether the individual chosen was able to converse in French.[64] Similarly in connection with criminal punishment the enigmatic term 'hulks' appears on a list of preaching stations supplied by Hackney Academy in 1806. The reference is to the colonies of prisoners kept in miserable conditions on rotting ships' hulks moored on the River Thames, though once again few other details are available.[65] Scarcely more fortunate were those who endured the degradation of indoor relief. They also received student attention. In its list of weekly supplies the 1804 report for Hoxton Academy noted that 'The students [were] in the constant practice of pointing out the way of Salvation to poor people in various workhouses.' Among even more unusual preaching venues was an undenominational floating chapel for seamen established in 1818. From its inception students from the academies at Homerton and Hoxton offered their services, and at least one visit was made by men from the more distant college at Cheshunt.[66]

In spite of the didactic intentions underlying student evangelism there is little evidence of a systematic appraisal of the work undertaken. Only at Gosport does the general concern for religious expansion appear to have been linked to a careful training programme. There the tutor, David Bogue, employed a newly formed village congregation as a preaching laboratory. New students were required to commence their public preaching at this place where they would attend in pairs, one to conduct the service, the other to listen. The latter would produce a critique of the preacher's performance for constructive examination the following morning. Bogue's biographer noted that so well did he handle this exercise that any potential unpleasantness between the students was avoided.[67]

Although student preaching may have functioned at Gosport as harmoniously and efficiently as suggested, in most academies practical training posed serious problems for the academic curriculum. External preaching commitments conflicted with the requirement for study. The interruptions caused by frequent sermon preparation and lengthy weekend journeys prompted repeated complaints in academy minutes and reports.

At least two different approaches to the problem can be detected. At its foundation in 1778 the English Evangelic Academy had stipulated that no first year student was to preach in public without the tutors' express permission.[68] Nineteen years later under the new name of Hoxton Academy it found it necessary to restate its attitude to student preaching. The new regulations showed some development in so far that they provided the framework for a graded scale of public activity. While first year men were confined to preaching in local poor houses, and those in the second year were restricted to places that would enable them to leave after midday on Saturday and to return before noon on Monday, third year students with the prior permission of tutor and committee could be absent for periods of up to one month to serve the needs of 'destitute' congregations. In 1809, following the extension of the course from three to four years, the restriction on external ·preaching was applied to the second year also, but at every stage prohibition seems to have been prompted by nothing more sinister than the desire to secure for the student a period of uninterrupted study.[69]

By contrast, students at Idle were from the outset committed to a heavy programme of itinerancy. The early minutes of the academy had recorded a decision to prohibit external preaching during the first half of the four-year course.[70] But, as successive reports noted, William Vint felt unable to refuse the importunate requests for preachers which poured in from the many leaderless congregations in the northern counties. The 1810–12 report warned that the two-year introductory period had become a dead letter and that harm was being done by the neglect of studies. Five years later little had changed, for the report for 1817 observed that weekend after weekend students cheerfully put down their books in order to travel far and wide. It calculated that in the course of the previous twelve months the fifteen residents of the academy had walked a total of 17,400 miles; an average of twenty-two miles per person per week.

Whereas Hoxton had responded to the problem by introducing rules designed to restrict premature preaching, Vint issued successive appeals for money to enable Idle to expand its way out of the situation: to increase its intake to the point where the spate of requests could be satisfied while still allowing for an initial period of non-participation.[71] The difference in approach reflects a fundamental distinction between the character of the two institutions. As the principal of a provincial seminary Vint felt a heavy responsibility for the health of the local Christian community, and in his thinking the acknowledged pressure upon students was clearly secondary to the needs of destitute congregations. Hoxton felt able to rise above such local exigencies. For the good of the Church at large it calmly pursued the objective of training a generation of ministers who would be intellectually capable as well as keenly evangelistic. This analysis is confirmed by the disproportionate influence subsequently exercised in Independent circles by those who received their training at Hoxton.

In some situations the conflict of interests did not arise. Like Bogue at Gosport, Cornelius Winter achieved a satisfactory balance between the practical and theoretical elements of training in his academy at Marlborough. From the start of their course the students were expected to preach in the surrounding towns and villages in a pattern which complemented the rather informal academic programme. So positive is William Jay's description of this amalgam that it is difficult to avoid the conclusion that the problems elsewhere were caused by factors not present in the uncomplicated Wiltshire situation.[72] Where tensions did exist they seem to have been provoked by the increasing importance attached to the academic element. It may also be the case that the problem was exacerbated by the general growth in the size of seminaries, especially where students were engaged in preaching beyond the immediate locality and close personal supervision by tutors was no longer possible.

Besides protecting the initial period of study, most academies opposed those congregations which encouraged students to leave precipitately. Premature withdrawal from courses was increasingly frowned upon, so that by the second decade of the nineteenth century even those institutions which had displayed an initial flexibility were insisting upon the completion of a fixed period of attendance. In 1816 Idle Academy emphasized the serious consequences resulting from the attenuation of studies, and the following year it gave tangible expression to that conviction by refusing to give approval to two out of the three applications it received.[73]

The use of the term leaven to illustrate the connection between the academies and itinerancy is particularly apt. It suggests the importance of the relationship without denying its ultimate ambiguity; a discrepancy rooted in the attempt to combine academic study with aggressive evangelism.

It can be argued that the importance of the academies within the overall process of growth derives principally from their role as catalysts. By selecting students on the basis of evangelistic interest and experience as well as a reasonable level of intellectual ability, and by linking regular practical work with the formal programme of study, they produced a stream of men fully trained yet familiar with the practice of itinerancy. Between 1791 and 1800 sixty-seven emerged from Hoxton Academy alone.[74] The commitment to evangelism which this represented is more difficult to assess, though it can be judged to some extent by those who entered full-time itinerancy direct from college. Of even greater significance were the many who, having entered the pastoral ministry, used their congregation as a base from which to establish regular contacts with neighbouring communities.[75] The extent of their impact is seen most clearly in local records. In one church minute book after another the appointment of a minister from one of the new institutions is marked by a revitalization of church life and the appearance of an expansionist outlook. In addition to domestic influences there was also a small but significant number of students who turned their attention to overseas missions.[76] With their accessibility to candidates of limited means and humble social background the academies provided the most effective method of channelling the growing concern for self-improvement into the service of itinerancy.

Their importance was not limited to indirect influence. The example of Idle demonstrates the contribution that academies were able to make to pioneering evangelism. To a movement dependent upon individual initiative they brought cohesiveness and an organization capable of overcoming many of the most common limitations. For some three decades before the home missionary societies became a significant force, the academies provided a rudimentary national framework for itinerant preaching.

The academies not only increased the pace of itinerancy, they also enhanced its quality. But even as they sought to refine and improve upon the simple preaching which characterized the early phase of revival, they began to show a less favourable aspect. As a leaven they appear to have been increasingly harmful. Whereas in the early days they had encouraged itinerancy, so they began to disseminate among their students the very attitudes responsible for undermining that development. Outwardly only the changing emphasis between the academic and practical elements of seminary courses gave any indication of the likely outcome.

As in similar cases involving the institutionalization of religious revival precise analysis of the change is difficult. Part of the genius of those institutions which encouraged itinerancy during its formative period lay in the balance struck between academic work and the weekly experience of evangelism. Neither the frequent interruption of studies caused by preaching expeditions, nor the informality of the smaller, rural academies, served to destroy this equilibrium, yet its delicacy guaranteed its early disappearance. By the third decade of the nineteenth century the atmosphere had subtly changed. Records from these later years provide evidence of a growing preoccupation with status and respectability and a corresponding increase in formality. Viewed in that light Benjamin Cracknell's earlier insistence upon training as the means of deflating personal pride seems more than a little ironic.[77]

During the evolutionary phase the role of the academy as a stimulus to evangelism was repeatedly stated, but as time elapsed this early view gave way to an attitude which valued education for its own sake. Both the English Evangelic Academy and its counterpart at Hackney sprang from the desire to train laymen for more effective evangelism. The scale of activity was at first rather limited, with the former establishment operating between 1779 and 1782 on a part-time basis with lectures on only three days of the week,[78] but this quickly changed. In many contemporary institutions a basic pattern can be traced. Rising academic standards were accompanied by the extension of course length, the progression of increasing numbers of students to university and the appointment of additional and better qualified tutors at greatly enhanced salary levels. These changes tended to separate tutors from the pastoral ministry, forming them into a new professional caste. They also fostered a generation of new, imposing but alarmingly expensive buildings, some of the expense admittedly being occasioned by the need to accommodate greatly increased student numbers. For the students these developments were matched by a general rise in entrance requirements.

At Hoxton the involvement with university courses began in December 1803 when the committee agreed to allow a student, who had been preaching at Aberdeen during the summer vacation, to remain there for the purpose of study until the following April. It also agreed to pay his expenses. In reaching that decision the Hoxton committee had sought the advice of John Ryland whose Bristol academy had for some years encouraged its most able men to undertake further study in Scotland using the financial assistance of Dr Ward's Trust. After the initial step in 1803 the academy's links with the formal university programme were strengthened: the resources of the early eighteenth-century fund established by Dr Williams were made available for the support of two Hoxton students at Glasgow University.[79]

This seal of academic respectability was finally matched in visual terms by the new edifice erected on the imposing site at Highbury donated by the treasurer, Thomas Wilson, Jr.[80] In a period when many academies acquired purpose-built premises, the final cost of the building, even allowing for post-Napoleonic inflation, guaranteed magnificence. Whatever comparisons may be drawn with other contemporary institutions, the new structure on Highbury Hill was far removed from the single rented room at No. 81 Gracechurch Street in the City of London where the academy had commenced its work almost fifty years earlier.

The growing insistence upon initial training courses covering the basic educational skills may have promoted efficiency, but it also hinted at the emergence of a two-tier ministry in which the pastoral and evangelistic roles, closely related since the time of Whitefield, were once again becoming separated. The letter from John Thornton quoted earlier conveys a sense of the inferior requirements attached to an itinerant ministry, and as such it characterizes the initial stage of the separation. The process reached its climax in the period after 1830, following the establishment of Home Missionary Society academies at Pickering and Cotton End.

The increasing emphasis upon the need for well-qualified men in the pastoral ministry was justified in academy reports by reference to rising educational standards among the population at large.[81] While this argument embodied a measure of reality, other more direct causes lay behind the heightened state of educational awareness. Among these were the accomplishment of the immediate evangelistic task within the vicinity of most academies, and the growing demand by increasingly prosperous churches for well-educated and respectable ministers. Pressure of the latter kind conspired with changing patterns of employment to alienate many of the working-class contacts established in the less conventional climate of the 1790s.

In the transitional period covered by this study the evangelical academies with their peculiar combination of the academic and the practical were able to exert a powerful stimulus for change within the conservative realm of eighteenth-century Dissent. But as time elapsed it became apparent that they themselves were not immutable. From an early indifference towards intellectual attainment they moved to a more traditional academic stance, losing much of their taste for aggressive evangelism. At the same time they drifted towards a reassertion of the separate nature of the ministerial office, having at one time inculcated the opposite belief. Whatever these changes meant for their own development, there can be no doubt that their leadership of the growth process belonged to the early part of the transitional period, to the years between 1780 and 1800. Thereafter that role passed to newer agencies both at the local and national levels: the county associations and the denominational home missionary societies.

Two contrasting interpretations have thus been offered: on the one hand the idea that the evangelical academies constituted the primary agents of Dissenting expansion through their early encouragement of itinerancy, being even more significant in that respect than either the county associations or the specialist itinerant societies; on the other the suggestion that by 1830 they had begun to inhibit further expansion. Viewed against the entire fifty-year period they demonstrate a reversal of attitudes; a process in which the academic aspect of ministerial training took increasing precedence over the original, evangelical purpose. For the reasons discussed a healthy balance between these elements proved difficult to maintain. Nevertheless, the leadership of itinerancy exercised by the academies coincided with the brief period when they were in relative equilibrium.

5 · Organization and infrastructure

THE ADOPTION of a wider concept of ministry had raised few problems of principle for late eighteenth-century Dissenters, and this proved to be equally true of the working arrangements necessary for concerted itinerancy. By 1810 the principal features were well in evidence, their evolution being determined by the need to promote evangelism under varying circumstances and in the context of fluctuating and uncertain resources. Not every mode of operation proved in practice to be beneficial. Indeed there is ample evidence to suggest that whatever success was ultimately experienced was achieved in spite of certain inherent weaknesses.

For those engaging in evangelism the matter of organization was immediate and inescapable. Individual and collective effort could assume a spontaneous and unco-ordinated character of the type readily attributable to the unpredictable movement of the Holy Spirit, or it could submit to varying degrees of supervision designed to ensure that the energies available would be applied as effectively as possible to the opportunities presented by a given area. The formation of societies for the financial support of village preaching represented the first stage in this process, but as the records of a number of bodies show there was often an unwillingness to remain content with the mere material benefits of union. They display a determination to exploit more fully the newly discovered organizational potential.

In 1800 the recently formed Essex Congregational Union adopted a statistically based plan for the systematic evangelization of the entire county. The plan, drawn up by Isaac Taylor, Independent minister at Colchester, included a map indicating 'those places where the gospel is truly preached by any denomination, either statedly or occasionally, with the schools, &c. supported by this Union, or any means of religious instruction'.[1] Five years later the Baptist Society embarked on a more ambitious national survey designed to assess the distribution of 'gospel' preaching.[2] The enquiry was undoubtedly intended to improve the utilization of its resources, but, as in the case of a similar questionnaire circulated by the Village Itinerancy in November 1827, the eventual use made of the findings is difficult to assess. By its constitution the latter body was obliged to ensure that its energies remained focussed upon evangelism, and it was that

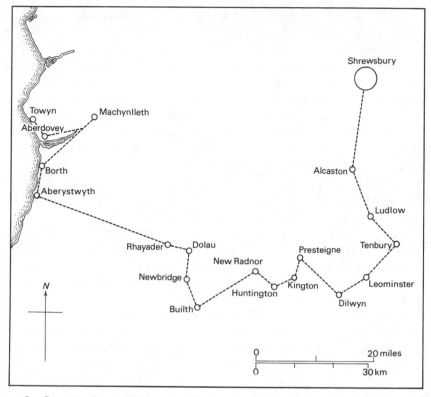

8   Occasional evangelistic tours. Border counties and Central Wales preaching tour undertaken by John Palmer, minister of the Baptist church at Shrewsbury, Summer 1799.

Unfortunately the information concerning the details of this tour is defective. The precise route is not indicated, certain places listed cannot be identified and are, therefore, omitted, and there is a suggestion that preaching also took place at other unspecified locations. The minutes give no help with the accurate dating of the tour, nor do they mention Palmer's return journey to Shrewsbury.

Source: Baptist Society, minutes. 24 October 1799, BMS. MSS.

requirement which prompted the 1827 circular letter to request information from dependent congregations concerning the state of local itinerancy.[3]

   Societies with more limited territorial objectives had less need to conduct such enquiries. Instead they endeavoured by means of methodical application of resources to achieve significant levels of penetration within their area of responsibility. Some impression of the coverage possible using a systematic approach, especially within the geographical limits of a county, can be illustrated from the 1829 report of the undenominational Surrey Mission. Of the one hundred villages mentioned almost a quarter were covered by the work of the society, while resident Evangelical clergymen accounted for a further 10 per cent. Only 40 per cent of the total lacked any form of evangelical activity.[4]

Whatever success stemmed from the policy of research, evangelistic penetration took different forms, the pattern of itinerancy varying according to locality. By the early years of the nineteenth century the spread of the practice ensured that the recipient communities covered a wide spectrum of rural society from compact villages in the midland counties to scattered moorland settlements in northern England. During the earliest phase of activity the most obvious pattern was that of random preaching tours and visits mounted by individuals. These 'occasional' efforts offered a means of exploring the potential of a given area and of reconciling the demands of evangelism with more regular commitments.

From early in the 1770s students preparing for the ministry at Trevecca under the patronage of the Countess of Huntingdon established the precedent for this work by undertaking lengthy itineraries through the surrounding counties.[5] Some twenty years later in the first flush of Dissenting fervour the early exploratory tours of Cornwall by Baptist preachers stimulated similar effort elsewhere, most notably in the northern parts of Devon and Somerset and in the Welsh border counties. In the course of a five-week journey into Central Wales in 1799 John Palmer covered more than two hundred miles. Many of the places listed in the report of the tour as preaching stops were more than ten miles apart.[6] The occasional nature of these expeditions appears to have been particularly suited to hilly areas where travelling was slow and where distances between communities were greater than they were in the more densely settled lowland counties.

As itinerant evangelism became an established feature of Dissenting life so these tentative probings hardened into more regular patterns of visitation. With ministers and laymen showing increasing concern to extend their contact with surrounding communities the approach most commonly adopted was that of self-contained visits radiating from a centre to a number of outlying preaching stations. Full-time itinerants frequently employed this method of regular visitation, travelling outwards from their base to a different village every week-night.[7] The system had considerable merits. In most cases the distances involved were fairly short and were comfortably within the scope of the time available. The use of a central base allowed ministers to employ lay assistance wherever suitable help existed. Outlying preaching stations received regular ministry and supervision and the process of conversion and of the integration of new converts was thereby facilitated. To some extent the process was self-perpetuating, for in the same way that town churches attracted worshippers from neighbouring communities, the new village meetings tapped the population of their own hinterland, thus considerably extending the potential for the evangelistic penetration of a given area.[8]

By 1830 the Independent churches in North Buckinghamshire had achieved an impressive coverage of the communities located within the territory bounded by Towcester, Olney, Bletchley and Bicester. Their network of itinerancy represented an influence which left few if any localities completely unaffected.[9] Yet the operation of an intensive programme of weekly visits made great demands on time and effort. Lest there should develop any inclination towards irregularity, one society encouraged those whom it helped financially to fix set times for village services.[10] As a practice this had the additional advantages of ensuring maximum attendance and leading naturally towards the formation of permanent congregations.

Although the regular, self-contained visit may have suited the compact lowland community where distance was not a serious factor, it did not represent the best solution for areas with scattered populations. Consequently a third form of itinerancy appeared with the development of circuits such as the one in the Ribble valley whose servicing was a responsibility shared by the Independent associations for the West Riding and for Lancashire.[11] Essentially itinerancy circuits were a less extensive and more regular version of the earlier occasional tours. The relative isolation of the small agricultural communities which constituted the Martin Top circuit, as with that of a similar group in Nidderdale, made regular visits by settled pastors or lay preachers all but impossible. Continuity of supply required a level of energy and manpower which only an institution like Idle Academy was able to offer.

Circuits could, nevertheless, be dependent upon less broadly based support. In the northern part of Devon and Somerset the experimental summer itinerancies of 1798 and 1799 undertaken by the Baptist ministers of Bampton and Stogumber hardened into a more permanent arrangement which was sustained for a number of years in spite of the problems occasioned by remoteness and by the demands of regular pastoral commitments. Not even the inclemency of winter constituted a sufficient deterrent. Early in 1800, during what was normally observed as the off-season for itinerancy even under more favourable lowland conditions, Norman, the minister at Bampton, informed his sponsors of a recent preaching journey he had undertaken to Porlock, severe wintry weather notwithstanding.[12]

While sparse population may have been an important factor in the evolution of itinerancy circuits, evidence of a shift towards a more normal form of Dissenting ministry soon appeared. Within three years the two West Country itinerants were anticipating the appearance of a permanent congregation in at least one of their centres.[13] Similarly with the Lancashire circuit the numbers gathering at Martin Top Farm increased to the point where,

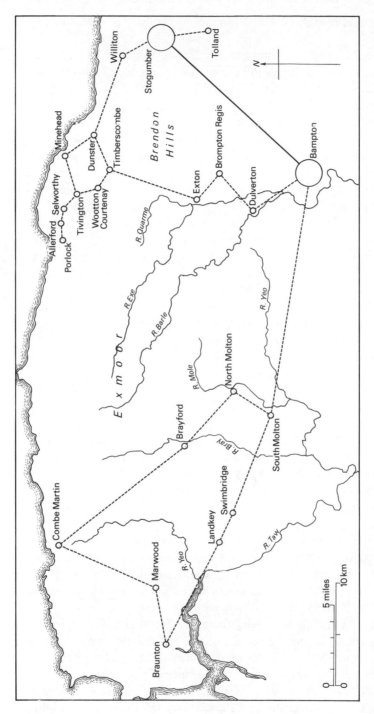

9   Circuit itinerancy. North Devon and Somerset. Preaching circuit served by Norman and Humphrey, Baptist ministers at Bampton and Stogumber, 1801.

The initial exploratory preaching tours by Norman and Humphrey during the summers of 1798 and 1799 had by this time hardened into an established itinerancy covering the places indicated at regular intervals. The frequency of visits varied and the precise route is not known, nor the extent to which the two men worked and travelled together. Some places mentioned such as Cumshead and Sandford have not been identified.

following the formation of a church and the erection of a building during 1816–17, pastoral oversight was eventually acquired three years later on a shared basis with Newton and Wymondhouses.[14]

A further pattern of evangelism emerged as attempts were made in various places to use the facilities offered by abandoned eighteenth-century meeting-houses. Their congregations had dwindled in a sterile theological climate or they had simply succumbed to the constant pressures of illness, death and fluctuating economic circumstances. At a time when preaching accommodation could be difficult to obtain, it required little imagination to realize the potential of these memorials to earlier piety. In areas as widely separated as Surrey and the West Riding of Yorkshire a proportion of the effort expended by theological institutions and itinerant societies was channelled into the revivification of decayed Dissenting causes, especially where an obvious strategic advantage was seen to exist.[15] In spite of the visual continuity with the past, congregations established in this way belonged firmly to the new wave of evangelism, sharing its attitudes and activities and, above all, experiencing the ministry of men imbued with the principles of itinerancy and growth.

Institutional activity, however important it may have been in this respect, could claim no monopoly of the process. Thomas Wilson, the wealthy Independent who acted as treasurer for Hoxton Academy, pursued his own personal programme of recovery, using the buildings he acquired as bases for exploratory evangelism. Typical of these were the disused Presbyterian meeting-houses at Guildford and King's Lynn which he reopened in 1802–3. The ruinous state of the meeting-house at Guildford made demolition and rebuilding necessary at a personal cost of some £700, but by contrast the premises at Lynn merely required a regular ministry, and this he was able to supply using theological students drawn from the academy at Hoxton. The buildings seem to have constituted the only tangible link with the past. In a similar case at Epsom three years later Wilson noted: 'formerly very genteel people attended — many in their carriages. But how was the fine gold changed!' Other severely weakened eighteenth-century congregations, though not requiring so complete a resurrection, invited and received a transformation almost as dramatic. At Chalfont in Buckinghamshire only a handful of worshippers remained by 1812 to mark the close of a forty-year pastorate, yet within three years the attention of Wilson's students had produced a thriving church with all the customary signs of evangelical busyness.[16]

These four methods of itinerancy may have formed the public image of organized evangelism, but they were by no means wholly responsible for the expansion of evangelical Dissent. A number of important auxiliaries aided their work, among the most prominent of which was the Sunday and week-night school movement. Apart from the teaching of reading and writing, the elementary instruction which these schools provided served the wider concern for evangelism by creating familiarity with the biblical narrative. The links between the early Sunday schools and evangelistic activity have been recognized by modern scholarship,[17] but the connection was acknowledged at the time by societies involved in itinerancy. In 1816 the Cheshire Congregational Union recorded its own debt to the Sunday school movement in the following unequivocal terms:

We cannot help expressing our thanks to those persons who have been active in establishing and promoting Sunday Schools in different villages connected with the UNION. It is unnecessary to intimate to our Itinerant Brethren, that this is essentially connected with the success of our cause: the solicitude with which they watch over their interest, — the diligence with which they promote their instruction, — and the prayers they offer for their prosperity, are a sufficient proof that a conviction of their importance has been deeply impressed on their minds. We think it must have gratified every reader, who is interested in the formation of moral character, to find that our schools are all in a prosperous state. The instruction of the rising generation is an essential part of our plan; and that it is viewed in this light by our Itinerants and other Teachers, the progress of the children is a sufficient evidence.[18]

In a youthful society where children accounted for at least 45 per cent of the population this concern for basic education is understandable.[19] The establishment of Sunday schools for village children was regarded as the natural concomitant of the preaching directed at the adult audience. By channelling the evangelistic impulse into an appropriate and acceptable form, the schools prepared the rising generation for a positive response to adult preaching.

But, as the Cheshire Union extract indicates, a wider moral and civilizing purpose can also be detected, one with which the teaching of useful skills accorded well. From the outset the Village Itinerancy adopted a plan for evening schools organized in conjunction with its preaching circuits, and in spite of the general reluctance at the time to go beyond reading, a report for 1806 declared that in several of the schools writing had been added to the curriculum.[20] In due course week-night classes extended the range of subjects to sewing and arithmetic, while a basic education began to be available to an older age group through the formation of adult schools.[21]

Occasionally a more pragmatic note crept into society reports with a hint that schools were being used deliberately as the means of preparing the ground for direct evangelism. The practical example of John Adey's weekly teaching at Great Horwood, a development which led rapidly to the appearance of regular adult meetings for preaching and conversion, could be multiplied many times, but overt declarations of policy involving the idea of deliberate preparation were usually avoided in the face of strong Establishment opposition to all forms of irregular activity. It was not until 1848 that those connected with the Essex Congregational Union felt able openly to acknowledge considerations of strategy. In that year, speaking of the early aims of the union, its first historian admitted:

Schools for religious instruction were amongst its primary objects; and the first projected was at Wivenhoe. Others followed. Preaching the Gospel soon attended the teaching of children to read. It would seem, on account of the existing prejudices, that it was easier, in most cases, to commence with a school, than with preaching.[22]

If Sunday and week-night schools were an important adjunct to itinerancy, so also was the printed word, especially literature of the popular and ephemeral kind. In many cases the distribution of religious tracts formed a distinct activity, yet a close connection did exist. Village preachers frequently took a supply of reading matter with them to the places they visited, and the minutes of a number of societies record the provision of appropriate material as a normal facet of the work. The Baptist Society regularly supplied those ministers whom it assisted financially with bundles of tracts, and at an early stage, before the formation of the Tract Society, the committee even expressed its willingness to support John Palmer of Shrewsbury in the production of a suitable printed address for distribution among his rural audiences.[23]

Similarly the minutes of the north-western district of the Bedfordshire Union of Christians give a complete account of titles circulated during September 1804 in conjunction with the normal programme of village meetings. Most of the twenty-three tracts listed were published by the Tract Society and covered such subjects as swearing, attendance at public worship, illness, Sunday schools, parental duties, family worship and Sunday drilling, as well as the more predictable elements of faith and the overriding concern with the regeneration of the individual.[24]

The distinction between itinerant preaching and evangelism based upon the distribution of religious tracts was a fine one, as a local plan for the latter activity illustrates. The plan which was adopted at Bridport in July 1809 laid down the following guidelines:

The surrounding villages to be drawn out into separate journies, each containing about three or four villages. Our distributors to itinerate as regularly as shall be possible, to their respective rounds; visit each of the cottages, leave a Tract, and endeavour to awaken the inhabitants to a concern for their best interests by appropriate conversation.[25]

In practice, as the plan reveals, both forms of evangelism employed itinerancy, both used printed tracts and both involved the spoken communication of the gospel.

Although the relevance of education and religious literature to a sustained programme of popular preaching is not difficult to discern, the evolution of local charitable aid is a different matter. Here any connection beyond the occidental involvement of the same individuals seems rather tenuous. Yet support for a number of schemes involving social assistance can be found. From Petersfield Richard Densham reported the collection of £5 as a result of a charity sermon he had preached on behalf of the Winchester Hospital. This initiative was taken in response to an appeal by the local bishop.[26] Other practical assistance with the problems of poverty and illness assumed a more permanent form. In 1811 the committee of the London Itinerant Society adopted a plan designed to encourage the children in its schools to attend regularly. The plan envisaged the annual provision of a free pair of shoes for each child, the cost, estimated at £30, being met from the poor fund and from the society's general resources.[27]

More helpful in understanding the motives behind such gratuitous kindness are the remarks made by the North Bucks Independent Association commending a newly commenced lying-in charity at Kings Sutton, a scheme which offered amongst other things a supply of clean linen for mothers during their confinement. The association urged the essential usefulness of the venture which embraced both Church people and Dissenters, and clearly regarded it as an excellent exercise in public relations:

This society will be useful in two respects, – it will leave an impression upon the minds of the poor, that their temporal comforts, as well as their spiritual interests are considered, – and it will have a tendency to lower prejudice, by bringing church people into association with us in doing good.[28]

Evidently those engaged in evangelism felt a need to broaden the basis of their work and to be seen to have not only a concern for the theory of the gospel but also for its practice. It was necessary to exhibit the virtue of an active social conscience in ways that would appeal to their critics as well as their supporters.

Viewed in its entirety Dissenting evangelism depended upon a number of agencies. In every district responsibility for its promotion and support and for the ancillary activities was shared in varying proportions between the local congregation, the county association, the national society and the new educational phenomenon, the evangelical seminary. The image presented to the public was invariably one of harmony; one which emphasized the compatibility of the various components. Yet on occasion cracks appeared in the facade.

Normally county associations and national home missionary societies co-operated at the local level with no outward sign of jealousy. During the 1820s the relationship between the North Bucks Independent Association and the Home Missionary Society was particularly cordial, the national body being able with its greater resources to appoint and maintain preachers in those communities least accessible to the predominantly church-based evangelism of the local society. In other areas, including Lancashire, county associations with a strong base and satisfactory resources regarded the appearance of the new, national organization with considerable distrust. While describing the Home Missionary Society as 'that excellent institution', the Lancashire ministers and churches in 1825 firmly rebuffed an overture proposing a union for the sake of more effective evangelism within the county.[29]

Part of the problem lay with the image of local inadequacy created by John Hyatt in the founding resolution of the national society.[30] Provincial pride did not take kindly to his negative assessment of local achievement. In Dorset as in Lancashire the local Independent churches resented what they saw as a thinly disguised attempt at a take-over. The minutes for 9 April 1828, recorded a firm declaration of their intention to resist empire-building: 'At this meeting a proposal by the Secretary and Committee of the Home Missionary Society to unite our Association with them was unanimously and respectfully negatived.'[31] Even the historian of the national body found himself compelled to acknowledge the existence of some dissent at its formation in 1819.[32]

Whatever rivalry existed between the various agents of evangelism, all faced a common difficulty in the perennial struggle to maintain an adequate level of financial support. No amount of planning and organization could act as a substitute for the stability and purpose imparted to a programme of village preaching by properly financed full-time itinerants, together with provision for the hiring of premises, the distribution of literature and the settlement of other related expenses. In a sermon preached at Bedford in October 1797, recommending the idea of an evangelistic union of 'real Christians' within the county, Samuel Greatheed dismissed any suggestion of financial shortage providing every member gave in direct proportion to their prosperity. From the Church of the apostle Paul's day, which had counted all its resources as belonging to God and, therefore, as available for mission, he argued that a similar attitude would ensure more than enough money for every conceivable item of expenditure, whether for home or overseas mission. He believed that adequate allowances could be paid to itinerants, missionaries and settled ministers, whilst still leaving sufficient support for their widows, for the Christian education of the young and for the renting or building of meeting places.[33] Greatheed had no hesitation in pointing to the rapid growth of the Missionary Society as evidence of the potential of Christian generosity, but subsequent difficulties in the field of domestic itinerancy would seem to indicate that his optimism belonged to the general euphoria exhibited by evangelicalism in the late 1790s; a mood which took too little account of everyday reality.

In practice itinerant societies were soon to discover that expenditure, unless carefully controlled, would rapidly exceed income, and that the consequent financial difficulties would seriously reduce the anticipated scale of operations. Some societies from the outset found it impossible to achieve a sufficiently broad base of support. Despite a generous donation of £30 from its treasurer, Richard Fishwick Esq., the Northern Evangelical Association found itself in a parlous economic state after only five years in existence, a situation which probably contributed to its ineffectual performance.[34] Similarly the early demise of the Congregational Society for Spreading the Gospel in England was directly related to its failure to stimulate adequate giving.[35] In the years following 1807 even so long-established a body as Societas Evangelica was compelled to restrict the assistance it was able to give settled ministers towards the expenses of local preaching.[36]

The problem concerning finance stemmed from a variety of causes. Though many villagers were prepared to respond favourably to the visits of travelling preachers, few demonstrated a similar willingness or ability to meet their expenses. There were, inevitably, limits in this regard both to private generosity and to the giving of the wealthier congregations whether in London or in the provinces. The restricted donorship could hardly be expected to bear the cost of an entire national network of evangelism. Almost all itinerant societies were compelled to seek local contributions at the earliest possible stage. There was, moreover, a distinct trend towards rising expenditure. As the simplicity of the initial enterprise of the 1780s and 1790s disappeared, societies encountered ever more numerous appeals for assistance with the expense of building and with the high cost of providing adequate salaries for full-time evangelists. As if these factors were not enough, domestic evangelism constituted only one commitment among several. In spite of Samuel Greatheed's heady optimism there were signs to suggest that in the period of inflation, economic stagnation and cyclical unemployment which followed the Napoleonic Wars, Dissenting resources were quite inadequate for the demands placed upon them.

In the face of financial insecurity the help available from individual bodies varied considerably. Two London-based societies illustrate the extent of the policy divergence. While Societas Evangelica made it their normal custom to grant only a standard sum of £5 p.a. to itinerating ministers, paying no regard to abnormal levels of expenditure, the Village Itinerancy engaged in a more comprehensive pattern of assistance.[37] Its records note a variety of categories ranging from direct support for itinerancy to the costs associated with the maintenance of a growing network of chapels. Increasingly the funds available appear to have been applied in ways that seem remote from the simplicity of the original, evangelistic purpose. The most striking example of this deviation occurred in connection with the preparation of trust deeds for the society's various properties. In 1828 the substantial figure of £1,000 was recorded as the interim fee paid to John Wilks for his legal services in this connection.[38] Money was, nevertheless, still made available for evangelism. In 1830, in addition to a grant of £10 to the minister at Boxford in Suffolk, enabling him to purchase a pony and thereby continue his visits to eight preaching stations, the committee voted £20 for the North East Cambridge Christian Instruction Society to assist with their work in twenty villages in the Newmarket area.[39]

Other societies, though not attaining the degree of diversity shown by the Village Itinerancy, did endeavour to be more flexible than Societas Evangelica. In the case of the Baptist Society this involved granting travelling expenses for extended tours amounting to as much as £20. In addition the society agreed in 1798 to pay a fixed allowance of two guineas per month to those ministers such as Saffery and Steadman who had been engaged to itinerate on its behalf.[40] In spite of the impression given by the Village Itinerancy, the funds of most evangelistic bodies were dispensed either in the form of travelling expenses or in the direct payment of itinerants' salaries. The balance sheet of the North Bucks Independent Association for 1822 indicates a typical pattern of expenditure: of a total of £95 all but £20 was accounted for by the salaries of itinerant personnel. The remainder included the rent of preaching stations, as well as committee expenses, stationery, and the costs connected with holding the twice yearly general meetings. Even the latter were responsible for stimulating the flow of money.[41] The older Baptist associations showed a more diverse pattern of outgoings, but in their case the reason lay in their earlier evolution and in their concern for consolidation as well as growth.

Among the early patterns of financial policy one of the most persistent was the concern to avoid any idea of a permanent allowance for itinerancy. Apart from the salaries of a handful of recognized itinerants, most societies refunded only the most necessary expenses, and even then were not above asking applicants to restrict their journeys or checking to ensure that they were not in receipt of parallel benefits from other sources.[42] The confined and occasional nature of this financial assistance probably acted as a disincentive, but the influence and achievement of laymen and ministers co-operating in what amounted to largely unsupported local enterprise should not be underestimated, especially in the period prior to the 1820s when the full-time evangelist was a rare phenomenon.

The financial restraint exercised by Societas Evangelica and by the short-lived Congregational Society points to the difficulty of securing adequate resources, even with an operational base in the capital and the attendant access to funds by means of benefit sermons and private donations. The latter were advantages denied to the majority of regional organizations. In Manchester the generosity of Robert Spear permitted the brief appearance of William Roby's academy, but outside London and the prosperous industrial centres of Lancashire and Yorkshire uncommitted wealth was rare. Most societies depended wholly upon the limited potential of the local churches, eliciting individual promises of 'a penny a week' and employing such devices as sales of work and association collections.[43]

To minimize the strain new congregations were expected as early as possible to take an active part in financing their own development. The difficulty with that policy lay in its implementation. The economic restraint encountered by so much itinerant preaching sprang from the overwhelming poverty of the recipients, and from their attendant inability or reluctance to make an effective contribution. Repeatedly this poverty was emphasized in correspondence seeking continuing financial assistance from the Village Itinerancy and other, similar bodies.[44] The artisan composition of Dissent during this period would seem at first sight to contradict this evidence,[45] yet artisan status was deceptive. While it represented the skilled sector of the working class, it was a broad category in which by the 1820s some of the most popular trades were experiencing severe economic decline.

Though detailed enquiry would be necessary to explain the financial restrictions operating upon particular congregations, a possible explanation for the slowness to attain independence may be found in the distinction between internal economic stability and the capacity for financing an external ministry. Left to its own devices a marginal congregation may have been able to survive, but it would have found it impossible to have covered the cost of an extended programme of evangelism from outside without a substantial infusion of external aid.

Itinerant preachers were themselves drawn unwittingly into the process of stimulating finance. Besides affording evidence of their attention to duty, their periodic reports on the progress of their work appeared to sponsoring bodies to hold publicity potential. Yet little of the original material, either in the form of journals or correspondence from preachers in the field, was ever used, and as a result little has survived. The details were preserved at second hand by itinerant society minute books and by annual printed reports, but in summaries remarkable only for their brevity, blandness and monotonous uniformity. If the previous year's field-work was presented to annual meetings of subscribers in anything resembling the stereotyped format and predictable expressions of pious optimism found in these reports, it is hard to believe that the exercise served any purpose except to dampen enthusiasm. Home mission inevitably lacked the glamour of its overseas counterpart, but that deficiency was merely compounded by the failure to produce stimulating publicity. Amid the mass of second-hand reports only the few surviving primary sources, including the letters sent by Richard Densham to John Eyre and the outwardly insignificant diary kept by an itinerating Wiltshire schoolmaster, convey any sense of the difficulties and excitement experienced. The appeal of the latter is that of the unselfconscious participant writing not for publicity but for the information of the sponsor.

Apart from the difficulty of financial provision Dissenting itinerancy faced several other weaknesses. Among the most obvious was its high level of dependence upon the individual. With no connexional organization providing a spur to action the initiative within the world of late eighteenth-century Dissent rested entirely with the members of each local congregation. The scarcity of committed itinerants during the 1790s, which led John Saffery to lament the departure of William Steadman, may have represented a transitory phase, but even the later, complex growth of village meetings in areas as deeply affected by itinerancy as Bedfordshire cannot conceal a continuing dependence upon the preacher as an individual. Congregational approval may have been necessary in the selection of members deemed to possess a suitable talent for preaching, but the responsibility for breaking new ground and for maintaining existing preaching stations remained with those appointed to the task.

Within the records of itinerancy the vulnerability caused by this reliance upon the individual has been suppressed, masked by the many successful examples where personal enterprise and persistence led to the establishment of viable congregations. Considerable personal effort was certainly expended at times to ensure the continuity of preaching even under difficult circumstances. During the winter months of 1798 on days when Thomas Wastfield, the schoolmaster from Imber, was prevented from visiting his preaching circuit in the upper Avon valley, he sent as substitute his assistant Henry Tinhams.[46] Equally, failures were inevitable. Just as itinerant societies were prepared to abandon unpromising localities, so individual preachers for various reasons terminated their visits to particular communities.[47]

As itinerancy developed other factors appeared which served to mitigate the worst effects of individualism. From an early stage the growth of associations ensured that village preaching increasingly took place within the context of corporate planning, staffing and support. Similarly the new evangelical seminaries produced a succession of pastors who, in their uniform conviction concerning the priority of evangelism, endeavoured to enlist the support of the whole congregation. The manifest change in the tenor of so many church minute books in the period after 1780 indicates the extent of their success, an impression confirmed by the increasing number of references in society minutes and reports to group involvement in village meetings.[48] These and other developments, while not removing the problem altogether, did much to make itinerant preaching more resilient.

A second weakness revealed by many society reports sprang from the unremitting demand for visible results. Itinerant evangelism required constant evidence of its own value. To some extent this quest for reassurance stemmed from the relatively intangible nature of the evangelistic process. Until permanent congregations had evolved neither preachers nor sponsors had much to show for their outlay, and it was necessary, therefore, to demonstrate that progress was continuing. Naturally the sense of advance tended to diminish with the passage of time, and at times this fact was faced quite openly. In 1809 the Essex Congregational Union observed:

It is true we have now no report of any thing particularly *new* or *extraordinary* to communicate to you: nor indeed is it to be expected that every year should furnish us with materials of this description; for the first effects of the breaking up of fallow ground are more conspicuous and surprising than those of its after cultivation.[49]

While the inevitability of the loss of novelty was acknowledged by a few societies, most continued to pepper their annual reports with the usual summaries of work in progress. These statements with their abbreviation and paucity of detail were both perfunctory and sterile, and in due course the reports became little more than balance sheets reporting the scale of the societies' activities.

The need to attract the capricious support of potential subscribers in the face of the more exotic attraction of overseas missions led to the use of vivid and emotive imagery. The practical sympathy of the Christian public was directed towards those 'lost souls' who given the current state of things could only anticipate the 'unfathomable abyss' and 'endless damnation'.[50] As the counterpart of this lurid, though undoubtedly sincere, view of a world perishing for want of the gospel, those who received financial support were regularly encouraged to extend their visits to previously untried localities.[51] This raises a question concerning the fate of existing preaching stations. In the cause of extension were these commitments neglected, abandoned entirely, or merely entrusted to the continuing care of lay preachers? Little information is available, though the sheer scale of activity could certainly encourage neglect. In the course of one seven-year period, prompted by financial inducements from Societas Evangelica, Thomas Hillyard, Independent minister at Olney, reported preaching in no less than twenty-one separate villages.[52]

The desire for evidence of progress raised an associated problem; namely, whether or not to persist in the face of a poor or slow response. In practice the solution varied. Some societies pursued a policy of fairly rapid relinquishment. In the case of the Essex Baptist Association work was abandoned at a number of centres originally selected for full-time itinerancy including Bures, Wakering, Grays and Bradwell.[53] But elsewhere a more patient approach prevailed. At Bretherton, in the area administered by the Lancashire Congregational Union, preaching had been tried as early as 1788 by William Roby, and from 1801 it had been supplied by the union on a regular basis. Yet it was not until 1820 that the progress was sufficient to allow the erection of a building and the formation of a church.[54] Nor were Lancashire Congregationalists alone in pursuing a policy of patient perseverance. The *Baptist Magazine* for 1810 attributed the ultimate success of evangelism at Beaulieu to the virtues of quiet persistence and flexibility. The article concluded:

If in our attempts to introduce the gospel in a popular place, we have been unsuccessful in one part, let us try another. The gospel could not be introduced to the town, but its environs received it, and now many come from the town to hear it. A number of immortal souls should not be given up without sufficient trial; a wise general will not raise the siege because one part of the town is invulnerable.[55]

Nevertheless, questions of strategy were prompted by the use made of preaching resources, and at times prolonged attention to an unresponsive community could appear unwise. Thus it was that in September 1800 Richard Densham communicated his misgivings to John Eyre concerning the prospects at Haslemere. He proposed in vain that their attention should be transferred to the villages of East and West Meon. In the event subsequent developments demonstrated the soundness of his judgment.[56]

While a poor numerical response may have clouded the sense of progress in specific localities, the failure of many preaching stations to mature and become financially self-supporting jeopardized the health of the entire movement. Their failure to develop tied up resources needed for expansion elsewhere. Yet the fault was by no means universal. As the first exploratory visits sponsored by the Essex Baptist Association had led within a few months to the formation of entirely independent churches, so in other areas similar ventures produced equally rapid results. At Burnley a small Congregational church was constituted in September 1808 after a brief spell of preaching by George Partington, a former student at William Roby's academy. At its inception it had already achieved partial financial independence by undertaking to contribute £34 p.a. to the funds of the county union.[57] Though a transitional measure of self-sufficiency was normally expected at an early stage, the period of partial dependence was often protracted. At times the congregational contribution amounted to very little. Having ignored the early advice of its itinerant to abandon the work at Haslemere, the Village Itinerancy spent the next thirty years endeavouring to coax an adequate material response from that unpromising congregation. In the end the committee found it necessary in April 1830 to refuse any further aid.[58]

The case of Haslemere may have been extreme, but the problem was a common one. In Cheshire it became sufficiently endemic for the county union to point out in 1814 that its overall programme of evangelism was being seriously impaired:

much more yet remains to be accomplished in the county. The harvest truly is plenteous, but the labourers are comparatively few; and we are well aware that many corners of this vineyard would be more successfully cultivated, if the number of ministers were increased. This cannot be effected, without greater effort in those places in which the word has been preached for some length of time. Their concern should be to lessen the burthen of the Union — to procure and support stated ministers for themselves, and set the itinerants at liberty.

The statement emphasized the healthy condition of the union's finances. What was needed was for the funds available to be applied exclusively to the support of genuine itinerancy and the infant congregations which resulted.[59] Over the following years some progress in this direction was achieved. By 1820 the prolonged support for the congregation at Tattenhall had given way to full independence, while new itinerancies appeared at Gatley and within the semi-urban manufacturing environment of Hyde.[60] Yet the effort expended continued to appear wholly disproportionate to the need. Against the background of general population growth the 1829 report issued by the Cheshire Union specified seven places in Wirral alone as obvious locations for itinerants were the resources to become available. It was clear by then that the problem of non-development would never be solved by exhortation alone. While the preaching stations at Hyde, Gatley and Sandbach had at length achieved independence, other equally long-established congregations at Middlewich, Over and Malpas were still receiving a significant level of external support.[61]

At the outset organization had seemed to offer itinerancy the twin advantages of permanence and effectiveness. In practice it had encouraged superficiality and immobility: the one through the constant demand for visible results; the other because of the prolonged concentration of resources in certain localities. New and serious obstacles had arisen in the path of the very success which the process of organization had appeared to guarantee.

6 · Support and opposition

THE LATTER PART of the 1790s was not an auspicious time for the birth of a new, popular movement. With political sensitivity strained to its limits by the developments in France, the rapid spread of Dissenting itinerancy was bound to provoke a reaction. Aggressive utterances by leading Establishment figures were accompanied by disturbing rumours of impending legislation designed to restrict the existing limited range of religious freedoms. Yet, as the Methodists had discovered earlier in the century, effective opposition arose most readily at the local level. In the absence of decisive action on the part of national authorities, individuals with local influence found themselves organizing the resistance. Immediate practical measures to check Dissenting expansion were initiated not by government but by local landowners, parsons and magistrates capitalizing on the more aggressive elements within the populace. While this opposition is too important to ignore, there is never any suggestion that it constituted more than a temporary setback to the progress of evangelical Dissent.

Although negative attitudes provide the most interesting subjects for analysis, their presence cannot obscure the favourable response with which people from all sections of society greeted the evangelists. Not only were sizeable audiences ready to gather at short notice, in the open air and at unattractive times of the day, but items of correspondence and itinerants' reports mention groups of villagers who were prepared to accompany the preachers from one preaching station to another. Having encountered this kind of response in North Devon and Somerset during the summer of 1802 a local minister reported it to his sponsoring body with obvious delight. In his letter to the Baptist Society he wrote, 'They follow the preaching of the Word for Miles ... It is truly pleasing to see old and young Flock from Village to Village to hear the Word of Life and Salvation.'[1]

Though some encounters afforded less cause for satisfaction the occasional failure did not represent a serious setback. The reports compiled by village preachers show that popular enthusiasm for itinerancy far outweighed any adverse behaviour. Yet audience size did not by itself indicate the degree of popular interest for catchment populations varied greatly. At Callon Green, an unidentified settlement in the West Midlands, John Palmer of Shrewsbury reported preaching in 1800 to only a handful of hearers. By contrast during the following year a contemporary was able to record an attentive audience of 300 in the street at North Molton.[2]

Examples of popular hostility do not by themselves prove the existence of a widespread or deep-seated reaction against evangelism. The pattern of development in even the most notable cases of opposition was for animosity to diminish steadily in the face of persistent effort. When Richard Densham, the Hampshire agent of the Village Itinerancy, began to preach at Rogate in July 1800 he experienced total rejection by the inhabitants, a reaction confirmed by the hail of dust, rotten eggs, insults and threats of even greater physical violence that he was forced to endure. Yet, as he persisted with his visits the more riotous elements in the crowd began to lose interest or were shamed into silence, until at his third attempt he was able to report to his sponsor a quiet and orderly hearing. Densham had encountered more serious and protracted opposition elsewhere in the county, but concerning the Petersfield area he felt able to comment in October 1800 upon the noticeable decline in anti-Methodist prejudice which had taken place since his arrival three years earlier.[3]

If the popular attitude was largely favourable, at least in the longer term, some influential support was also forthcoming. The majority of parish clergymen may have resented the intrusion of itinerants or have chosen to remain aloof, but occasional examples can be found of a more encouraging response. In June 1798 Densham notified John Eyre that at East Meon, where he had preached in the street on Sunday afternoons to 500 people, the officiating clergyman had twice attended and that those occasions had been marked by good behaviour and attentiveness.[4] In a similar vein, though at a more exalted level, the Bishop of Hereford was reported in 1802 as having expressed approval of Dissenting attempts to disseminate religious instruction within his diocese. Having described Herefordshire as the most heathen part of England his words were taken to imply the county's need of whatever religious attention might be available.[5]

Among those charged with the local administration of justice some practised a conspicuous impartiality to the obvious benefit of Dissent. The persistent disturbance of registered premises produced many appeals from those who organized itinerancy, and though some magistrates treated these applications with contemptuous disregard, others fulfilled their statutory obligations. In 1824 in response to a request by Thomas Skeene, Independent minister at Wendover, Sir John Dashwood King took firm action to prevent further nuisance being caused by a group of rowdy youths. The offenders had been in the habit of disrupting the Friday evening preaching visits made by members of Skeene's congregation to the neighbouring hamlet of Little Wendover.[6]

Even clerical magistrates were at times prepared to set aside their scruples and support the rights of the itinerant. Four years after the Wendover incident the newly appointed evangelist of the North Bucks Independent Association appealed successfully to a local magistrate, the Rev. Dr Brown of Launton, for help in quelling disruptive elements who were making preaching difficult in the villages around his base at Marsh Gibbon. Brown issued a warrant for the arrest of those responsible, but at the itinerant's request discharged them, having imposed a fine to cover the cost of making public their apology, and exacted a promise not to repeat the offence.[7]

Yet, in spite of wide popular support and the existence of favourable attitudes among some of the more influential members of society, opponents of itinerancy were numerous. Opposition could even be found within the ranks of Dissent, where critical voices were raised against the trend towards disorderly and innovatory practices.[8] In his *Apology for Village Preachers* William Kingsbury endeavoured to answer the most important of these objections. Against those who urged the disreputable character of village preaching he argued the concern of Jesus for the poor and despised, and the significance of itinerants as those who were prepared to take seriously the apostle Paul, becoming 'fools for Christ's sake'. He conceded that contemporary itinerancy was contrary to normal Dissenting practice, but suggested that such an admission should be the cause of shame rather than pride, the more so as their forebears had employed a similar approach to evangelism. Kingsbury developed his argument by denying that a programme of preaching activity in the villages contravened any divinely instituted church order or necessarily jeopardized preaching and pastoral care within existing churches.[9]

General objections of this nature were widely raised among the more conservative sections of Calvinistic Dissent, but specific opposition centred upon two groups which represented quite different logical developments within eighteenth-century theology: those from the Presbyterian tradition who had moved from doctrinal orthodoxy to embrace a rationalist, Unitarian position, and others who had extended the Calvinist system with remorseless logic to its predestinarian and antinomian limits.

From the outset evangelical Calvinism and Unitarianism displayed a strong and mutual antipathy. In 1790 controversy erupted at Wigan when a group of Presbyterian ministers established a Sunday evening lecture designed 'to knock Calvinism on the head'. William Roby, who was then minister of the Countess of Huntingdon's chapel in Wigan and a regular itinerant in that part of Lancashire, responded vigorously with a firmly reasoned doctrinal tract entitled *A Short Treatise on the Absolute Necessity of the Satisfaction of Christ, or The Dangerous Tendency of Socinianism considered*.[10] But at that stage, possessing little popular appeal, Unitarian rivalry was not a serious factor.

The situation began to change as Robert Aspland, David Eaton and other younger leaders began to press for the adoption of evangelical methods, and as Unitarian itinerant preachers, following the example of Richard Wright, began in the first decades of the nineteenth century to disseminate their ideas.[11] The evidence from Bury suggests that some congregations, especially those in Lancashire, were deeply affected by this development. Soon after William Allard settled in the town in 1803 as minister of the Presbyterian [Unitarian] chapel in Bank Street he commenced a series of monthly preaching visits to the neighbouring hamlets of Heap Fold and Moss Side. By 1818 a network of preaching stations had developed served by lay preachers, among them a calico-printer named Edmund Grundy, an erstwhile Calvinist.[12] Relationships between Unitarians and evangelical Calvinists do not appear to have been improved by this approximation in method. In 1814 the Cheshire Congregational Union still made a point of condemning the 'very ungenerous, illiberal and pertinacious opposition' it had experienced from Unitarian sources in its work at Hyde Lane near Stockport.[13]

From another direction entirely, high Calvinists reproached their evangelical contemporaries with accusations of doctrinal laxity. The latter returned the attention with interest, dubbing their accusers 'antinomians' whether that abusive epithet was merited on practical grounds or merely denoted a particular belief. The number of references by itinerant societies to the existence of antinomian and high Calvinist sentiments suggests that these were seen as a far more insidious threat to evangelism than the more readily identifiable Unitarian tendency. In a series of letters in June 1798 Richard Densham described his suspicions to John Eyre concerning the unhealthy influence of one of his colleagues. The preacher in question, whose name was Callen, regularly conducted the worship of the congregation at Haslemere. At one point an allegation of immorality was even made though it could not in Densham's opinion be substantiated. Eventually Callen appears to have been dismissed or redeployed by Eyre, but not before his views had taken root among the worshippers at Haslemere.[14] Where antinomianism is concerned the problem of identification is crucial. On more than one occasion there is reason to suspect that the accusation was used to mask the clash of personalities or the exercise of preference, and that little if any substance lay behind the charge.

Opposition from Unitarian Dissenters was not the only impediment facing Calvinist itinerancy in the North-West: the same area provided reaction and rivalry of a different kind, as evangelists in Manchester and the western parts of Lancashire were soon to discover. On the coastal plain between Lancaster and Liverpool Roman Catholic beliefs were deeply rooted among the indigenous population and constituted a major obstacle to would-be proselytizers. In 1802 the newly appointed county itinerant, George Greatbatch, chose Newburgh near Ormskirk as a convenient centre for the villages which lay between the Ribble and the Mersey. Many of his excursions were made in the company of a friend named Hooton, a tall man who was able to ford rivers carrying the preacher on his back. The size and strength of this companion were of equal importance in quelling opposition, especially in the district around Scarisbrick where violence was not unknown. Potential troublemakers drew back whenever they saw the figure of Hooton standing impressively, club in hand, at the preacher's side.[15]

Despite moments of local tension, Roman Catholic opposition to evangelical Protestantism was in most cases confined to the literary sphere and to criticism of the contemporary practice of circulating the Bible unaccompanied by any commentary.[16] But the limited nature of the opposition did not conceal from bodies like the Lancashire Congregational Union the positive threat of Roman Catholic expansion, and when in 1825 an appeal was made for increased financial support for itinerancy, one of the reasons given was the need 'to institute some energetic check to the increasing efforts made by the friends of Popery in various parts of this county'.[17] Meanwhile, at the national level the monthly *Tract Magazine* published by the Religious Tract Society endeavoured to draw its readers' attention to the active circulation of popular literature designed to inculcate Catholic beliefs and undermine Protestant doctrine.[18]

The challenge from Dissent and from revitalized Catholicism remained insignificant compared with the opposition which stemmed from the Established Church. If Dissenting activity offended Anglican sensibilities, any sign of participation within their own ranks provoked an even sharper reaction. From the 1770s until his death in 1833 Rowland Hill ignored the aversion to itinerancy felt by his fellow Churchmen, but in so doing he sacrificed any hope of preferment and became in all practical respects an ecclesiastical outlaw. Others possessed of a less formidable social pedigree than Hill paid even more dearly for their rashness. In November 1822 Isaac Bridgman lost his curacy at Trinity church in the Forest of Dean. He also had his licence revoked and was forbidden to officiate in any church within the diocese of Gloucester. The situation leading to this severe punishment was complex, involving not only Bridgman's itinerant preaching within the Forest, but also his relationships with Dissenters, with his rector, the Reverend Henry Berkin, and with the provocative figure of Rowland Hill. In the wake of these events he remained in the area as pastor of an independent congregation at Blakeney, where he produced a pamphlet describing the circumstances of his dismissal. The irony of the situation, as Bridgman pointed out, was that his former rector and bishop were both men 'of acknowledged Evangelical sentiments'.[19]

In spite of their initial interest the Evangelicals' enthusiasm for itinerancy had largely evaporated during the 1790s as they found it necessary to demonstrate their loyalty to the Establishment and to proper ecclesiastical order. Their earlier, easy relationship with Dissenters had been complicated by the political and social uncertainty emanating from France. Though some followed the example of Wilberforce in maintaining their traditional regard for orthodox Dissent, others began to distrust its popular appeal.[20] Nevertheless, it would be unduly cynical to follow the example of one recent study and dismiss instances of friendship between parish clergymen and local itinerants as 'hardly typical'.[21] Records kept by those engaged in itinerancy indicate the existence of a widespread and mutual respect between Dissenters and 'pious', Evangelical incumbents.

Dissenting leaders were only too aware of the offensive character of itinerancy, and were in consequence at pains to insist that they had no wish to encourage Anglican irregularity. In an apologetic letter to the Bishop of Salisbury published in August 1798, Samuel Clift defined the substance of their aspirations as the desire to see the parish clergy taking their pastoral and evangelistic responsibilities more seriously; in particular accepting the need to take the message of the Christian gospel to the homes of non-churchgoing parishioners. Clift emphatically denied the charge of encouraging irregularity, and closed the matter declaring, 'we often censure the imprudent zeal of some of that order who have left their parochial connection.'[22]

If itinerancy provoked a varied response, so too the reaction expressed itself in a number of ways. The purpose of this chapter is to examine the immediate, practical barriers erected against the would-be evangelist. But even the description 'practical' can be misleading, for while it implies the active, physical hostility encountered by the itinerant within the local setting, it can also extend to less tangible matters; to such considerations as the negative social influence exerted by individuals and the impact of popular literature.

One of the effects of the rapid expansion of village preaching was that it brought the churches into direct contact with popular culture, and in particular with the profane chap-books containing ballads, songs and tales which were sold at fairs and hawked from door to door.[23] Those engaged in evangelism regarded the whole literary genre with distaste. In their eyes its unwholesome influence was merely exacerbated by the attractive yet inexpensive format employed and by the system of circulation which had developed. A further cause for concern arose from the increasing dissemination of radical political ideas and from the availability of tracts designed to foster popular unbelief. In 1825 the annual circular letter of the Yorkshire and Lancashire Particular Baptist Association warned of the anti-Christian influences at work. But this was a comparatively late pronouncement. As early as the 1790s George Burder, Samuel Greatheed and other leaders of popular evangelism had become aware of the need to offer a Christian alternative.[24]

That alternative, the organized distribution of genuinely popular Christian literature, became a possibility in 1799 with the formation of the Religious Tract Society, a non-denominational venture which attracted wide support. The immediate problem faced by the new body was that of developing a range of material inexpensively priced, written in attractive and simple language and with subject matter sufficiently gripping to interest the basic reader. The society eschewed the fictional approach employed by Hannah More, preferring to use real events, both commonplace and unusual, which possessed an intrinsic poignancy capable of being turned to religious advantage.

In the tract entitled 'The Dying Criminal' the common spectacle of the public execution was pressed to religious use. The imminence of death for the prisoner was designed to remind the reader of the precariousness of life and to persuade him of his own guilt before God. At the outset he was exhorted to learn from the plight of the criminal while there was still time:

He ascends the scaffold, a gazing-stock to thousands, conscious, like you, of a reasonable nature, it may be, in the prime of life, and in the possession of an unimpaired constitution. But O! how dreadfully alive to the doom which awaits him! What remorse prays upon his conscience! What a tempest rages through all his soul! There he stands, on the edge of time; and perhaps while trembling at the prospect of that eternity which guilt has darkened, he is told that the fatal moment is come. You see him drop, the signal — he is convulsed, and dies.

Every heart is appalled; you return, oppressed with sadness, and shaken with horror; imagination continues to be haunted by the dreary spectacle, when the eye is turned away, and beholds it no longer. Is this all? Came you hither merely to gratify curiosity, or to make an experiment on your feelings? Shall nothing be awakened but a certain fearful emotion, which, without rooting up bad principles, or implanting good ones, will, in a few days, slumber again? God forbid! Be persuaded to cherish due reflection, and let the solemn, the terrible occasion on which you are now assembled, teach as well as impress, edify as well as alarm; from those agitated features, those clasped hands, those tremulous accents, those dying struggles, learn wisdom. O that the Object of your pity had himself been wise — he would not have perished thus prematurely. Bring home the affecting subject, and make vice and ruin, this day, your instructors.

Instead of More's highly romanticized account of rustic piety in 'The Shepherd of Salisbury Plain' or the wholly fictional approach of 'Parley the Porter', the reader of Tract Society publications was confronted by such robust characters as Colonel James Gardiner. The colonel, having spent more than a decade as a spirited young army officer, earning in the process the title 'the happy rake', came to experience religious conversion and subsequently applied that new-found faith to the military life until his gallant death at the battle of Prestonpans.[25]

A partial solution to the problem of distributing these tracts was found by exploiting the existing informal secular network. As well as employing lay Christian agents, from 1805 the society produced a series of tracts designed for circulation by the traditional hawkers of popular literature. These publications copied the style of their secular rivals even to the extent of including woodcuts. The society's strategy included a pricing policy designed to secure the vendor's preference on the basis of the superior profit margin its publications offered.[26] Making allowance for the uncritical character of the society's annual reports and the impossibility of achieving precise evaluation of literary influence, it seems that the tracts issued were remarkably successful, even if success is judged merely by circulation figures. In the first eight months alone almost a quarter of a million *Hawkers' Tracts* were issued from the society's central depository.[27]

Where evangelists rather than secular agents became involved in the process of distribution they tended to operate a policy of aggressive substitution, replacing literature which they judged to be undesirable with works of an improving character. Reporting its own application of this policy the Taunton Auxiliary Tract Society in 1824 observed:

With respect to this town and neighbourhood, during the past year, much vile and superstitious trash has been removed from many of the cottages of the poor, which are now furnished with Broad Sheet Tracts; Tracts admirably calculated, under the Divine blessing, to lead those who read them, to think on their ways, and to turn unto the Lord.[28]

One of the targets in this struggle for influence over the mind was the so-called 'Saviour's Letters', documents purporting to offer the removal of specific troubles and illnesses through the agency of Jesus Christ.[29] The objection to the Letters was based on their encouragement of superstition, but evangelicals were equally disposed to include in their 'Index' items which offended on other grounds, most notably any copies of bawdy songs they happened to discover. In one instance the visitor appointed to Prince's Dock in Liverpool managed with some difficulty to persuade the crew of the *Mary*, bound for New Orleans, to exchange a number of secular songsheets for a supply of wholesome religious reading matter.[30]

The problem of secular literature often seemed less urgent than the more immediate forms of opposition. Crowds gathered to disrupt many of the early meetings in 'spontaneous' expressions of popular hostility, demonstrations which at times even threatened personal safety. Other aspects of resistance also appeared, deriving their strength from various sources, but above all from the support of those with social influence: the resident landowner, the clergyman, the farmer, the parish officer. Men of this kind were inclined to regard opposition as both an expedient and a duty. As their occupation varied so did their reaction to itinerancy, in a series of responses ranging from the subtle intimidation of tenants, which sought to withhold suitable preaching accommodation, to the open encouragement of popular violence.

Research concerned with a number of English counties has revealed an interesting correlation between the growth of alternative forms of religion and prevailing patterns of landownership. The evidence suggests that the fewer proprietors there were, the lower was the incidence of Dissent. In one study 119 single landowner parishes produced only three instances of organized Nonconformity.[31] The influence of a resident landowner could provide the crucial factor which decided the success or failure of itinerant preaching. Nowhere was this more true than among the tightly grouped midland communities with their arable economy. The presence or absence of the gentry affected the range of choices available to their inhabitants. Where the squire was not resident social development including religious life followed a more independent line, and it is estimated that in pre-industrial society this may have been the pattern for as many as a fifth of all English village communities.[32]

In some places itinerants found it almost impossible to acquire suitable premises for preaching. In 1804 John Saffery of Salisbury noted that while he had baptized several people from outlying preaching stations, many villages in the area remained inaccessible. All that was possible in these cases was the distribution of religious tracts.[33] The geographical isolation of many villagers coupled with their position as estate workers, dependent for housing and employment upon the goodwill of the landowner, make it easy to appreciate the effective pressure that could be exerted against visiting evangelists. Not that all landowners were disposed to be hostile. Some even valued the work of itinerants and did their best to encourage it. At Harting on the Sussex–Hampshire border Sir Harry Featherstone provided ground for a new chapel in 1827, arranging for it to be placed in trust with the Village Itinerancy at a peppercorn rent of one shilling per annum.[34]

Even where the landowner's attitude was not a problem the antipathy of farmers and parish officials could be equally telling. At an early stage in his itinerancy during the summer of 1797 the Imber schoolmaster, Thomas Wastfield, was threatened by the constable of the Swanborough Hundred.[35] As a result he felt compelled to abandon open air preaching and seek indoor accommodation which could be properly registered. At Wedhampton and Netheravon he experienced difficulty in finding anybody willing to offer their premises and sign the necessary application. When he did succeed at the latter place those who administered parish affairs vented their displeasure upon his incautious host. Being poor and dependent upon parish relief the man was refused any financial help unless he withdrew the proffered facility. Though he resisted this blackmail he soon found himself caught between the hostility of the parish officials and the vindictiveness of the local farmers, with nothing but Wastfield's sympathy to sustain him.[36]

Parish clergymen accounted for a good deal of the practical opposition to itinerancy. Many endeavoured to use their legitimate authority to resist Dissenting encroachments. A small minority resorted to more reprehensible methods. At its most effective the opposition of the clergy reinforced that of the gentry, as the Baptist minister at Diss was to discover when he attempted to preach in the surrounding villages. At Garboldisham he encountered 'some persecutn entirely for the truth's sake from the Clergyman of a neighbouring Parish who not only preached against [him] but influenced the owner of the House to prevent [his] preaching there'. This opposition was not designed to counteract any popular response; indeed the itinerating minister commented upon the prevailing mood of indifference and worldliness which led most people to 'treat religion as if it was scarcely worth opposing'.[37]

In isolated cases clerical opposition lapsed into rabble-rousing. A late example of this led to the trial in 1818 at Salisbury assize court of William Easton, Perpetual Curate at Ansty in Wiltshire, in an action brought by the Protestant Society for the Protection of Religious Liberty.[38] Easton was found guilty with others including the peace officer of inciting a riot against a group of parishioners who had gathered to hear a visiting preacher within the privacy of a properly registered dwelling-house.[39] Other instances of clerical involvement with the mob can be found but it does appear that they were untypical. Most clergymen were content to express their displeasure in less physical ways.

Outbursts of popular anger, however brief, created a difficult climate for evangelism. Yet itinerants made little attempt to conceal the problems caused by crowd behaviour and normally reported incidents in the course of their correspondence. At Barling in Essex hostilities began during the winter of 1806–7 when the village shoemaker took it upon himself to interrupt those who had assembled for worship in an adjoining house. Since these meetings were the responsibility of the county's Baptist association the preacher wrote to that body in February 1807 emphasizing the worsening situation. The letter mentioned that the ringleader enjoyed the favour of certain members of the gentry including one of the local JPs. The shoemaker and his rowdy companions protected themselves against prosecution by avoiding any physical disturbance of the congregation, but the intervening walls gave the worshippers only marginal relief from the full impact of the demonstration. In spite of the itinerant's appeal little could be done in the face of an unsympathetic magistracy. Consequently the interruptions continued unchecked until an occasion when the noise created by the rioters startled the horses of the parish churchwarden and constable and spurred the two officials into action.[40]

Despite the determination to see off intruders the popular reaction to itinerancy was for the most part limited to rowdyism and ridicule. Only on rare occasions did the mood of the crowd turn to violence. No instances of serious or lasting injury were ever recorded, although in 1794 an ugly incident occurred at Woodstock in which James Hinton, the Baptist minister from Oxford, in the company of some of his friends was stoned and beaten with sticks by an angry mob led by a group of Irish military recruits. Writing soon after the event Hinton expressed their sense of good fortune in having escaped without loss of life.[41]

The incidents recorded by the Dissenting Deputies suggest a cyclical pattern of hostility. Beginning at a low level in the 1760s and rising in parallel with the growth of evangelism, the point was reached by the middle 1790s where popular disturbance became a recognizable factor. Physical harassment continued to dog the progress of itinerancy in an unpredictable fashion until the second decade of the nineteenth century, but with the easing of legal restrictions upon Dissenters in 1812, interference in worship became less frequent and subject to more effective control.[42]

This pattern does require some qualification since many local disturbances mentioned in correspondence were never brought to the attention of those who represented the legal interests of Dissent. Of those that were, a proportion was undoubtedly channelled in the years following 1811 towards the new, aggressive champion of Dissenting rights, the Protestant Society. Few of the records of that body now survive, a fact which makes it impossible to evaluate properly the low incidence of disturbance recorded by the Deputies following the 1812 legislation. The only conclusion that can be reached, therefore, is that the initial phase of itinerancy often aroused hostility, a reaction closely associated with the process of expansion and which tended to moderate with the passage of time.

In making use of the evidence afforded by the Deputies there is a need to distinguish between those cases of disturbance which concerned itinerancy, and those where the disruption was directed at existing congregations. Where open air preaching was involved the connection with itinerancy is obvious. During the early phase of expansion most exploratory preaching took place in the open air, and at that stage the behaviour of the rougher elements could be decisive. The degree of popular ferocity encountered at Alresford ensured that preaching could not begin in that town until a room had been procured and properly registered.[43] Without the security of a building preachers found their position extremely vulnerable, and when threats and insults escalated into violence very little protection was available.

The committee of the Deputies with true eighteenth-century conservatism was reluctant to support anyone who encountered trouble out of doors. In 1791 it refused to defend a constable who had arrested a rioter in the act of disrupting street preaching and who subsequently found himself facing legal proceedings. The committee members resolved 'that [it was] not a proper matter for their Interference'.[44] In spite of those complaints which related to the open air, the majority of cases brought to the notice of the Deputies concerned the disturbance of properly registered premises, and since registration applied to existing as well as newly established gatherings, the opposition recorded was not necessarily directed against itinerancy. Only those examples where meetings of a new and non-permanent character can be identified provide any evidence concerning the latter.

A further difficulty is created by the uninformative character of most judicial records. Absence of detail is typical of this period, but at times administrative perfunctoriness seems to indicate an additional factor; a lack of seriousness towards Dissenting interests. The problem of analysis is compounded by the non-survival of some of the most important documents. In practice the information available suggests that most cases referred to the courts were trivial, representing little more than inconvenience. Uncertainty arises only in connection with the more serious incidents where the use of emotive language makes accurate assessment difficult.

Even where Dissenters believed a serious offence had been committed the official response was often dismissive. The violence at Woodstock directed against James Hinton and his companions received neither the attention it deserved from the parish constables, nor any subsequent redress from the Home Secretary. The Duke of Portland displayed a complete lack of sympathy for the Dissenters' sense of grievance. Nor were the provincial courts more encouraging in their treatment of similar cases: offenders were pursued with apparent reluctance by the representatives of authority, offences were invariably treated as misdemeanours rather than felonies, and prosecutions frequently failed to achieve the punishment of those responsible. Recourse to higher legal authority was always possible and applications were made from time to time to the Court of King's Bench. In a case in 1815 where a satisfactory verdict at the quarter sessions appeared unlikely, the Protestant Society was able to obtain a writ of *certiorari*, and thereby to remove the matter from the jurisdiction of the lower court.

Even the most diligent examination of assize and quarter sessions records provides only a fragmentary picture of those cases in which the process of law was set in motion. In most instances indictment rolls offer more information than the rule or order books in which judgments were recorded. The difference may stem from the uneven survival of particular items, but it may also reflect the difficulty of securing an adequate verdict. The minutes of the

Deputies show that by invoking the law Dissenters aimed to prevent further disruption and not to achieve retaliation. In cases involving disturbance the prosecution was normally prepared to accept a public apology accompanied by a promise not to repeat the offence.

An early production of the Religious Tract Society, aimed specifically at 'Disturbers of Public Worship', admitted that the reason so many prosecutions were dropped had to do with the complainants' attitude. It is, the tract insisted,

> because they pity you, and are willing to hope that you do not know what you are opposing, or what is the consequence of breaking the act of parliament. Instead of seeking to punish you, they pray for you, as dying Stephen did for his persecutors, 'Lord, lay not this sin to their charge'. So you see what kind of men you have been seeking to hurt.

The homily concluded with brief extracts from the Toleration Act of William and Mary and the Riot Act passed at the accession of George I. The passages quoted left the would-be reader under no misapprehension concerning the protection afforded by the law to public worship in properly registered premises.[45]

Where the complainants' conditions were satisfied the prosecution was halted and the threat of punishment withdrawn, the only exception being the insistence in certain circumstances upon a donation to charity by way of recompense. In 1805 the disturbance of an indoor meeting at Stoke Gabriel near Brixham was dealt with in this fashion. Faced with the threat of indictment at the following quarter sessions, the ringleader chose instead to make a public apology in the *Sherborn Newspaper*, to pay the expenses of the local Dissenters and to donate £10 to the Exeter Hospital.[46] Prosecution was not always avoided. In one notable case in 1795 four members of a Suffolk mob which had rioted outside a meeting conducted by Arthur Bromiley, an Independent minister from Needham Market, were imprisoned for six months in the county gaol.[47] But the severity of this judgment was unusual: the normal pattern was for cases to be settled informally.

Though the majority of incidents are recorded in only the barest outline, some cases permit a closer examination. The minute book of Beaminster Independent church preserved the details of a case which appeared at Dorchester assize court on 15 March 1800. At the trial the presiding judge returned a guilty verdict against the Reverend M. A. Hopkins, Curate-in-charge at Stoke Abbott, for his part in conniving at the disturbance of local Dissenters. The curate's son had been involved in a number of ugly incidents in 1798 directed against the house in which they met for religious worship. In the absence of contrary evidence the judge refused to allow the case to go before a jury and fined the defendant £10 together with costs amounting to £30.

The meetings at Stoke Abbott had commenced in August 1798 when Elizabeth Legg had allowed John Rogers, the Independent minister at Beaminster, to preach in her house. Rogers had been assisted in this task by one of his deacons, a local linen manufacturer and lay preacher named Richard Hine. But the venture had quickly run into trouble, and in the face of angry, stone-throwing mobs the meetings had been abandoned while legal redress was sought.[48]

The details of this case prompt some interesting observations. In the first place, if the date of the initial visit is correctly assigned to August, there is clear evidence that those responsible were taking the risk of using un-registered premises. According to the records of the Dorset quarter sessions no registration of any building at Stoke Abbott for the purpose of religious worship took place before 2 October 1798. On that date an entry was made in respect of a dwelling-house registered in the name of Richard Legg.[49] There is, secondly, some doubt concerning the legal status of one of the preachers involved; the layman Richard Hine. Under the Toleration Act of 1689 all Dissenting preachers were required to take the oaths of allegiance, supremacy and abjuration, yet the name of Hine does not appear in the quarter sessions order book until Michaelmas 1799. Even then it is impossible to be certain that the entry recording the administration of the oaths to 'Richard Hine of Bridport' has anything to do with the Independent deacon and lay preacher from Beaminster.[50] In January 1799 Rogers applied to the Dissenting Deputies for advice and assistance concerning the punishment of the Stoke Abbott rioters, but met with a typically negative response. The committee informed him that as he did not appear to be a regularly ordained minister of one of the three Dissenting denominations it was unable to intervene.[51]

There is even some doubt regarding the outcome of the legal action initiated against Hopkins, for the extant court records are incomplete, and the summary of proceedings provided by the *Salisbury and Winchester Journal* for Monday 17 March 1800 makes no mention of the case. Having listed the principal judgments of the court the newspaper underlines the social insignificance of the affair by remarking that 'The remaining prisoners were for trivial offences, and were nearly all acquitted.' The silence of the western circuit estreat book concerning the fine allegedly imposed upon Hopkins is more difficult to explain, but that is as nothing compared with the problem raised by the accompanying process book which indicates that the defendant was found not guilty.[52]

With remarkable coincidence two of the more serious cases of disturbance concerned the same individual, the former Hackney Academy student, William Seaton. Trouble first arose for Seaton in 1810 during his period as minister of the Beaumont Chapel at Woodbridge in Suffolk. In the autumn of that year he took part with others in a concerted attempt to introduce gospel preaching to the town of Wickham Market against determined local opposition. Because of the intimidation of those who would otherwise have been disposed to welcome the preachers a house was purchased and adapted for public worship. Groups of opponents by way of response began to attack the house, forcing those who attended the meetings to run the gauntlet of popular violence and abuse. When at length after several complaints the local magistrates still showed no inclination to act and the grand jury had dismissed an action brought at the quarter sessions, an application was made in the Court of King's Bench in February 1811 for 'rules to shew cause why criminal informations should not be issued' against the principal rioters.[53] As a result of this application six offenders were indicted on the charge that they did

maliciously and contemptuously disquiet and disturb the said Congregation so Assembled during the time of divine service in the said Meeting House and unlawfully riotously and routously did Fire off and cause to be fired off and thrown into the said Meeting house and also into the Common Highway there divers squibs and fire works and unlawfully riotously and routously did Assault beat wound and ill treat divers persons of the said Congregation to wit one John Thompson one William Seaton one Benjamin Haker one Jonathan Turner one Isaac Durrant one John Stollery one Richard Lawrence and one Robert Turner and unlawfully riotously and routously did cast and throw Stones dirt Mud Human Dung and other filth at and against the said [persons].[54]

Those indicted represented a range of artisan occupations from collar making to malting, with one member of the group being described as a mariner. The outcome of the case was not noted by the court records, but the *Evangelical Magazine* was able to report in September 1811 that the issue had been settled before it came to trial. The accused, realizing the likelihood of their conviction, had apologized, withdrawn their pleas of not guilty, entered into recognizances to appear in the Court of King's Bench to receive judgment whenever required, promised good behaviour for the meantime and paid 200 guineas by way of compensation, a sum which the prosecutors intended to donate to local charities.[55] Meanwhile, the entire cost of the action, a figure of almost £800, was borne by the Protestant Society with an alacrity which betrayed the presence of ulterior motives. The society clearly regarded the events at Wickham Market as an important test case for the future.[56]

In 1814 William Seaton moved to Andover only to encounter similar opposition in the course of evangelistic visits to the neighbouring village of Abbotts Ann. He first preached there during the spring of 1815 at the request of a local blacksmith who was one of his own church members. The meetings which were held in the smith's house were well attended, but the initial opposition intensified when it became known that Seaton had failed in his attempt to secure a summons from the local magistrates requiring his opponents to keep the peace. Instead he and his companions had received a reproof for conducting popular worship according to forms other than those of the Established Church. In March 1815 those who took part in the weekly preaching visits to Abbotts Ann encountered a sharp increase in hostility, having to struggle on each occasion for the greater part of the homeward journey with masked and armed assailants.

As a result of this physical interference with the preaching party indictments were preferred at the Winchester quarter sessions against at least twenty of the rioters, and following an application by the Protestant Society, the case was removed by *certiorari* to the Court of King's Bench where, eventually, with the expenses approaching £300, the defendants were compelled to apologize and pay £100 towards the costs.[57] In this particular case it had appeared even less likely than usual that recourse to the lower court would give satisfaction to the aggrieved parties, for the chairman of the magistrates, James Burrough Esq., was related to the Rector of Abbotts Ann. His brother, Thomas Burrough, as an active and resident incumbent must have given at least tacit approval to those responsible for the disturbances.[58]

Careful enquiry into the background of a group of thirteen Abbotts Ann rioters provides some indication of the type of person likely to be involved in such incidents. As might be expected the majority were young men in their late teens and twenties. Of the seven whose ages are known, five were between 17 and 19 while the other two at 24 and 28 were slightly older. At least three of the rioters were married at the time of the disturbances: of these one already had three children, while another became the father of an illegitimate child in May 1815 by a single woman from the same parish whom he did not marry. Apart from one person who cannot be traced and another who probably came from the neighbouring parish of Monxton, all were residents of Abbotts Ann. As far as their occupations are concerned the parish registers afford relatively little information. Most of the offenders were described as labourers, a designation applied to the majority of male parishioners. Three were accorded the dignity of specific trades: blacksmith, carpenter and thatcher. Of the seven whose names appear in the marriage register, five appear to have been literate, at least to a degree, for only two were unable to sign their names.[59]

The events at Abbotts Ann and at Ansty three years later marked the demise of the persecuting mentality. The legislation of 1812, designed to remove the worst of the religious disabilities suffered by Dissenters, was accompanied by a general diminution in the level of hostility shown towards itinerancy. Only three cases of disturbance were recorded by the Deputies during the fifteen-year period which ended in 1830, and in each of those tranquillity was swiftly restored.

7 · Criticism and legality

THE COMING of the French Revolution produced in England a wide-spread agitation for political reform; an expression of democratic idealism which struck fear into the heart of the English Establishment. In spite of the moderation and lack of concert shown by those who espoused the radical cause, the alarm felt by Parliament was sufficient for the government of William Pitt to secure the suspension of habeas corpus, and the enactment of repressive legislation prohibiting seditious meetings and assemblies and imposing the severest of penalties upon those found guilty of inciting contempt for monarchy or constitution. Already the quasi-republican senti-ments of Richard Price had earned the unequivocal condemnation of Edmund Burke, and that rebuff had been reinforced in the legislature by the abject failure of Price's co-religionists to secure the repeal of the Test and Corporation Acts. In the years following 1795 the legal position of Protestant Dissenters appeared increasingly precarious as political tension threatened to spill over into the religious field with measures designed to curb the insidious effects of popular preaching.

Although the 1790s saw no new restrictions placed upon religious freedom, itinerant preachers were not unaware of their legal vulnerability at moments of particular political sensitivity. The newly appointed agent of the Essex Baptist Association arrived at Rayleigh in June 1797 to find himself at the centre of a highly charged situation:

Instead of being received with a hearty welcome, he was informed, that, altho' it was desirable to have preaching, it was not the proper time to begin:- because of the mutiny in the fleet at the Nore, opposite Southend, near Rayleigh;- the troops were at Southend to keep off the rebels, and that the whole country was ripe for rebellion. To all these objections, Mr P[ilkington] said, 'I am aware that I am liable to be cast into prison: but if you will leave me alone, I will begin, and leave myself in the hands of the Lord'.[1]

In the event the itinerant's determination to proceed was justified. His preaching within the confines of a house provoked no official hostility. The moment of crisis passed and the nucleus of a permanent congregation was gathered. The situation at Rayleigh emphasized the prevailing atmosphere of tension, but the Nore Mutiny was an exceptional occurrence. In the years prior to 1800 political circumstances appear generally to have exercised little practical restraint on Dissenting evangelism.

If legal restrictions were not immediately forthcoming, that omission was not due to any noticeable restraint on the part of those who criticized itinerancy. Strident voices, especially those with a clerical timbre, began to raise a crescendo of protest against the rising tide of popular evangelical activity. The public hostility of the clergy largely manifested itself through literary polemic, though it tended to assume an impromptu character, with individual writers dealing with the subject of itinerancy as it was brought to their attention or impinged upon their own local interests. Many outbursts of clerical concern were associated with episcopal visitations, a circumstance which did not escape the notice of Dissenting apologists. During the heated exchanges of the Salisbury village preaching controversy, Samuel Clift observed that for some unknown reason many of the clergy were unable to neglect the opportunity offered by a visitation assembly for publicly holding up the Dissenters 'as objects for popular contempt or indignation'.[2]

At the turn of the century a stream of clerical pamphlets attempted to enlist public sympathy against the interlopers. The influence of these ephemeral publications is difficult to assess, but even if they were ineffective in restraining itinerancy, they elicited a literary response which treated their vitriol and unsubstantiated allegations with complete seriousness. Tracts representing both sides of the argument were published in provincial towns as well as the metropolis. While these were often stimulated by local developments, the collection emanating from the Salisbury controversy shows that their contents ranged from the specific issues of the locality to the more general implications of itinerant preaching.

On some occasions polemical tracts of a more general character were circulated by local incumbents for popular consumption. In July 1789 in a letter to Sarah Roper, his future wife, William Roby wrote of the opposition building up against the barn services he had been holding in the neighbouring parish of Ashton-in-Makerfield. He added, 'the Minister of the Parish has begun first by distributing some Pamphlets entitled "An earnest and affectionate Address to the People called Methodists", wherein his Parishioners and others who have followed those whom he calls Methodists are exhorted to forsake all such erroneous enthusiastic Preachers as are followed by the unwary and return to their Church again.' The anonymous tract which Roby mentioned apparently enjoyed the patronage of the Society for Promoting Christian Knowledge.

A decade later Richard Densham discovered that 'some of the Genteel People of Petersfield' were industriously circulating a similar publication; a pamphlet containing 'the most bitter Invectives against the Methodists possible'.[3] Nevertheless, many polemical works were closer in character to Woodward's criticism of the Bedfordshire Union of Christians than they were to the tracts approved by the SPCK. Their origins and distribution were local, giving an air of impermanence to the whole literary genre. The contributions of Bowen, Malham and Bowles merely emphasize the spontaneity involved by demonstrating the clear link that existed between the urge to attack in print and the opportunity provided by specific circumstances.[4]

Though the polemical assault issued from a variety of clerical pens, ranging from the emotive appeal made by High Churchmen to the more restrained and rational style of their Liberal contemporaries, the arguments employed display an essential unity. Proper analysis demands the separation of themes, although that process must be undertaken with caution, recognizing that much of the conviction which affected both writer and reader sprang from their interrelationship.

One of the most serious points of contention between supporters and opponents of itinerancy concerned the matter of authority. Many Churchmen despised the ignorance, the lack of social standing and the apparent absence of preparation which in their eyes characterized the great majority of village preachers. The latter appeared to depend entirely upon self-assumed authority. To John Malham self-appointment represented an incontrovertible disqualification, and he pointed confidently to the severe words of Jesus concerning those who had worked in his name but without his authority.[5]

The slighting tone in which the occupations of the preachers were discussed conveyed an unfavourable impression to onlookers, but the image of quackery was reinforced by more important considerations. The most telling of these centred upon the accusation that village preaching fed the vanity of those engaged upon it, and that those who entered the work did so from a desire for personal aggrandizement.[6] That claim, however false, was difficult to refute.

The obverse of the objection to self-assumed authority is seen in the resentment which supporters of the Establishment displayed towards Dissenting criticism, whether explicit or implied. The committee of the Baptist Society noted in April 1798 that some of the clergy had declared their intention to resist the introduction of itinerant preaching in their particular towns and villages. They believed that 'as they attended to their Duty, no such thing was wanting amongst them'.[7] The real offence to Establishment pride sprang from the inevitable assumption of spiritual superiority by the Dissenting preachers, together with their arrogation of the right to judge the quality of the regular parish ministry. With considerable heat Malham responded to Kingsbury's assertion that village preachers had never interfered where an incumbent was carrying out his duties conscientiously. He pointed out that by saying this, 'they seem[ed] to make themselves judges of the doctrines, as well as the conduct of those Ministers.' Angrily he threw back the accusation of neglect, asking if Dissenters themselves always fulfilled all their preaching engagements.[8]

A second objection to Dissenting activity seized upon its assumptions concerning a pluralist society. Those who entered the lists on the Establishment side attacked what they saw as the sin of schism, presenting it as the inevitable yet undesirable outcome of rampant, enthusiastic sectarianism. By the mid-1790s the threat from Rational Dissent had faded, only to be replaced by the more insidious pressures of evangelism. The new generation of Dissenters in their impeccable orthodoxy, outward respect for the law and political quiescence seemed to be creating an even more subtle schismatic influence through their growing hold upon the lower social classes. It was schism, moreover, which given the prevalence of the Warburtonian ideal impinged upon the authority of the State was well as the Church. Churchmen, suspicious of the good intentions of the peripatetic evangelists, quite naturally treated even the most explicit disavowals of hostility towards the Establishment as being insincere. In an extremely partial sermon delivered in Chichester cathedral three months after the defeat of Lord Sidmouth's bill to curb itinerancy, William Goddard, Rector of Treyford in Sussex, warned of the growing assault upon the Establishment and of the likelihood that the Church of England would soon find itself outnumbered by 'Sectaries'.[9]

Whatever significance was attached to these initial objections, the main preoccupation of the controversialists centred upon the social and political intentions of the itinerants and their alleged desire for subversion. Those who opposed village preaching tended to regard it as a manifestation of a much wider attempt to undermine the entire structure of authority; a plan as secular in its conception as it was religious. When legislative measures for the curtailment of itinerancy were proposed the question at stake was whether or not the government would act to protect the Establishment as a whole. The earlier liberal tendencies of prominent Dissenters made it easy to associate expansionist activities with worrying political ambitions. Polemicists ignored the prevailing mood of political quietism within the evangelical community and chose to present itinerant evangelism as the respectable cover for a nefarious plot with revolutionary aims. In 1798 John Douglas drew the attention of his clergy to the alarming increase in the number of meeting-houses and preachers within the diocese of Salisbury.[10] The following year Francis Wollaston, Rector of Chislehurst, cautioned his parishioners respecting the presence of a group of 'Jacobins' operating under the guise of an itinerant society; the so-called Union Society of Greenwich.[11] Finally, in 1800 Samuel Horsley, Bishop of Rochester, completed the conspiratorial sequence with a warning concerning the growing use of Sunday schools by 'nondescript' preachers and teachers for the purpose of alienating the minds of the young from the Established clergy. As evidence for the existence of sinister intent he pointed to the associational structure designed to finance these activities, and to the significance of the sequence of events. He pointed out that the various undenominational congregations had only appeared since 1795 when the passage of Pitt's Treason and Sedition Acts had made more overt forms of political activity impossible.[12]

Before these speeches are dismissed as scaremongering, it is important to remember that, apart from the troubled political climate at home and abroad and the sense of millennial expectancy which gripped the nation during the later 1790s, there were more substantial grounds for Establishment alarm. Failure of the harvest in 1795 had resulted in famine and social unrest on an abnormal scale. Frustration with the war and the worsening economic situation had led to waves of rioting in many parts of the country including the capital. In Gloucestershire the quarter sessions, besides instituting a programme of relief, had been forced to use the military to control a situation where the poor were being driven to desperate measures. Attacks on houses and property had taken place, flour had been seized illegally from millers, bakers and river barges, and sinister gatherings had produced threats of an armed uprising. By October that year the riots, demonstrations and mounting political activity had alarmed the politicians to such an extent that serious restrictions on public freedoms had seemed inevitable.[13] In the atmosphere which followed it was not difficult to overrate the seditious potential of itinerant preaching, or to misinterpret the contemporary surge in applications for the registration of meeting-houses and for the administration of oaths to would-be preachers under the provisions of the Toleration Act.[14] If certain Anglican leaders realized the debilitated state of the Church of England and the degree of popular estrangement that existed, equally some Dissenters questioned the appropriateness of itinerancy in so highly charged a political climate. Any aggressive evangelical activity, they believed, however well intentioned, could only arouse unnecessary alarm.[15]

In the wake of the political charge the remaining objections appear extremely trivial. There was the inevitable attempt to discredit the agents of village preaching using accusations of dishonesty, financial motivation and a restless desire for innovation. But the attempt to present low moral standards as the logical consequence of humble social status was weakened by a lack of suitable evidence. Only two incidents could be found which provided an element of substance for the charge. The first concerned the conviction of a known itinerant on a charge of bigamy: the other involved a village preacher who had been caught stealing garden produce under cover of darkness.[16] Occasionally the level of argument descended to mere pettiness. During the 1798 controversy at Salisbury one of the disputants, John Malham, went so far as to complain that the large number of village preachers issuing from the city on Sundays meant that often there were no horses available for hire, and that in consequence the country curates found themselves having to trudge through the mire to their parish churches.[17]

While Establishment polemic reflected genuine fear, it was in many cases formulated with strategic considerations in mind. Among its principal objectives was the encouragement of ridicule against those who peddled the new varieties of popular religion. A number of episcopal charges demonstrate, however, that this negative tendency was compensated by a positive concern to revitalize the parochial ministry and to persuade neglectful incumbents to approach their responsibilities with greater seriousness.[18] There was also the hope expressed by one controversialist that by meeting the objections of those to whom the new movement appealed, the wave of defections could be halted and even reversed.[19]

The presence of other, less worthy intentions is more difficult to assess, though the suspicion is certainly possible. One investigation suggests that the purity of the note of alarm sounded by the Salisbury clergy may have been sullied by more venal, careerist considerations. Minor clerical figures like Bowen and Malham took their stand upon matters of principle but their motivation probably owed at least as much to the desire to ingratiate themselves with their Ordinary and to enhance their prospects of ecclesiastical preferment.[20]

In spite of this hypothesis those who found themselves the subject of criticism treated the polemic with complete seriousness, responding to the various accusations with careful, rational argument. The apologetic writings produced by Kingsbury, Clift and Hall provide perfect examples of studied moderation. Meticulously the defenders of itinerancy attempted to dismantle their opponents' arguments, showing by the invalidity of each constitutent point that the overall stance of hostility could not be justified. As might be expected with such experienced controversialists as Robert Hall and Rowland Hill, great faith was placed in the efficacy of reason. In his defence of village preaching Hall carefully outlined the real danger facing religion as he sought to reject the allegation that the fanaticism of the preachers was tending to bring Christianity into contempt:

Enthusiasm is an evil much less to be dreaded than superstition. The latter is a disease of opinion, which may be transmitted with fresh accumulation of error from age to age. It is the spirit of slumber in which whole nations are immersed. Placing religion, which is most foreign to its nature, in depending for acceptance with God on absurd penances or unmeaning ceremonies, it resigns the understanding to ignorance and the heart to insensibility. No generous sentiments, no active virtues, ever issue from superstition.

Superstition is the disease of nations, enthusiasm that of individuals; the former grows more inveterate by time, the latter is cured by it.[21]

The moderate tone in which the argument was conducted did not imply servility or undue complaisance. Even mild apologists like Kingsbury and Clift were quite prepared to correct the exaggerations of their opponents and to offer their comments upon the causes of weakness within the Established

Church. In keeping with his independent and more abrasive personality Rowland Hill did not hesitate to employ a generous measure of sarcasm in his reply to the Bishop of Rochester's inflammatory remarks concerning the activities of nondescript religious teachers. With no attempt to disguise his scorn Hill observed in an open letter accompanying his address to the Sunday School Society that

These *atheistical Jacobinical hypocrites*, who deserve a halter as much as ever his lordship does a better bishopric — so soon as he has proved the charge, and surely there can be no great difficulty, if, as he says, he knows it to be 'a matter of fact': — these abominable infidels in disguise, I say, are receiving Bibles and Testaments from you that they may *disseminate infidelity* by distributing and explaining *the book of revelation*![22]

Within the debate some accusations demanded the most urgent and serious attention. Apologists turned as a matter of priority to deal with the dangerous insinuations of political disloyalty and subversion which had been made by a number of critics. From the outset leaders of popular evangelicalism appreciated the need to declare their own allegiance, whilst urging their followers to avoid any suggestion of political involvement. As early as 1792 when Dr Tatham, Rector of Lincoln College, Oxford, warned of the disaffection towards the government being shown by 'ignorant and itinerant teachers of every denomination', persons whose activities were increasingly evident within the bounds of that city, James Hinton, the local Baptist minister, defended the theological orthodoxy and political loyalty of his fellow Dissenters as well as that of the Methodist community.[23]

The strong Dissenting concern to give no grounds for criticism is seen repeatedly in the apologetic material published during this period. During the brief controversy at Salisbury William Kingsbury warned those engaged in village preaching to ensure that their discourses were centred upon the principal New Testament doctrines and duties and to show constantly that the gospel they preached strengthened 'good order and subordination in society, from the highest to the lowest; and [was] an utter enemy to a rebellious and levelling spirit'.[24] At Warrington during the course of an ordination charge William Roby, having urged upon the ordinand the duty of tireless and unrestricted evangelism, used the example of Jesus and the question of paying taxes to Caesar to warn of the dangers of political entanglement.[25] Nor was this concern limited to individuals, for at least one itinerant society felt it necessary to declare in its initial statement of principles that it was no part of its aims 'to disseminate political opinions, or to canvass the affairs of State'.[26]

As might be expected, the most overt suggestions of disaffection prompted the most vehement and comprehensive denials. The powerful attack upon the agents of popular evangelism delivered by Samuel Horsley before the clergy of the Rochester diocese was subjected to minute examination by

Rowland Hill. Hill was himself an arch-controversialist and proved a capable foil for the belligerent bishop. In his visitation charge Horsley had spoken of the seditious and atheistic aims of the numerous undenominational Sunday schools and conventicles springing up within the diocese, but where, asked Hill, was his evidence for such a statement? The bishop had certainly scorned to hide behind the cloak of anonymity used by those who wrote in similar vein for the *Anti-Jacobin Review*, but in issuing such calumnies he had been 'cruel and unjust' and Hill was determined to expose the falsity of his remarks, at least in so far as they touched upon the activities of the Southwark Sunday schools.

Far from engaging in political teaching the work of the schools was purely religious, centring upon the distribution and teaching of the Scriptures. How was it, he asked, if Horsley knew of the existence of a seditious plot, that he had not made known its details? The Southwark schools never attempted to conceal their conduct or exclude visitors; on the contrary their meetings were open to inspection at any time as the law required. He challenged his opponent and those of like mind to produce '*one single instance* of *one single school*, in which *one single hint* of a political nature ha[d] ever been dropt; excepting as the teachers communicate[d] from the scriptures all due obedience to the powers that [be]'. Nor was there any significance, as the bishop had suggested, in the appearance of the 'nondescript' congregations only since 1795, the year in which the Treason and Sedition Acts had been introduced to deal with the Jacobin threat. The evangelistic impulse belonged to the period before that legislation had been enacted and represented a parallel attempt to counter the influence of atheistic ideas.[27]

If the Sunday schools were innocuous so also were the supporting associations. They were neither secret nor sinister; their membership was open to all who were willing to subscribe, and their supposedly clandestine meetings were widely advertised. Their natural and unexceptionable purpose was the financial support of the Christian schools already established. As far as the political views of individuals were concerned, Hill insisted that he knew of no one associated with the Southwark schools who held republican sentiments. On the contrary, he argued, 'truly pious dissenters and nondescripts' held aloof from politics knowing that mere political revolution could accomplish little without a corresponding internal change; the renewal of the human heart.[28]

In every respect the *Apology for Sunday Schools* advanced a positive view of contemporary evangelism, presenting the characteristic political justification that gospel preaching and teaching were beneficial activities which reinforced social stability. Not only did evangelical teaching support the existing structure of authority and engender subordination, it also acted as the surest means of preserving all that was good in society. Hill even went so far as to suggest that the Church of England would benefit from the services of some of the maligned Sunday school teachers, suitably educated as clergymen! Nor did the undenominational character of the schools signify any intrinsic opposition to the Establishment: their existence simply reflected contemporary religious needs. With considerable perception he pointed out that the schools in no way represented a triumph for Dissent, for real Dissent would always remain a minority phenomenon, and the attraction of the meeting-houses would rapidly fade once the Established Church had recovered its diligence and zeal.[29]

In this tract more than any other the apologist can be seen not merely defending, but rather extending defence to the point of retaliation. Boldly Hill parried the charge which linked undenominational evangelism with underground political activity by launching a counter-accusation against Horsley, that of covert Catholicism. The bishop's charge with its anti-evangelical propaganda could be interpreted, he argued, as part of a popish plot aimed at discrediting Protestantism and achieving the reintroduction of Roman supremacy.[30] Such outspokenness was uncommon. Significantly it came not from Dissent but from the pen of one who, despite being in Anglican orders, enjoyed an unusual degree of independence.

The response to the political objection by no means exhausted the arguments of the apologists. Other approaches were necessary if a complete vindication of village preachers was to be achieved. Every opportunity was taken, therefore, to emphasize that the concern for evangelism depended upon entirely commendable impulses. It was pointed out that in the struggle against vice and unbelief Dissenters made common cause with the Established Church, and that in consequence their efforts ought to be welcomed by Churchmen.[31] In this respect the Baptist Society spoke for all the bodies engaged in itinerancy when it outlined the pressing need for effective countermeasures against the rapid growth of popular irreligion and deism, and committed itself to a programme of village preaching as the most appropriate form of action.[32]

Reinforcing this emphasis upon the exceptional moral and religious needs of the age was a parallel insistence upon evangelism as a Christian duty; an obligation which involved ministers and lay members and which could not be confined to recognized places of worship.[33] To encourage internal support associations emphasized the national significance of the work and its long term effects: only by their efforts, they argued, would Britain truly become 'a land of light'.[34] The positive view was not confined to Dissenters. Apart from Thomas Scott's enthusiasm for itinerancy, a pseudonymous clergyman even earlier had the audacity to enter the Salisbury debate on the Dissenting side.[35]

If itinerant preaching could be justified in this way there still remained the difficult practical matter of schism; the reality that by their presence in communities previously untouched by religious dissent the evangelists created an explicit rivalry with the Established Church and its clergy. To meet this objection a number of defensive replies were formulated. It was suggested by Henry Wansey, a Salisbury clothier, that Dissent thrived precisely where the Church of England was weak and where its parochial responsibilities passed by default to those who were willing to assume them.[36] It is interesting in this connection to observe that modern socio-historical studies by Everitt and Gilbert have demonstrated the essential truth of this argument. They have shown that even in the central and southern heartlands of the Anglican parochial system Dissent was able to expand and thrive within communities and sectors of society in which the Established Church exercised little influence.[37] Although the apologists were correct in linking the process of expansion with the obvious weakness of the Church of England, the growth seen was a direct reflection of the enormous increase in evangelistic effort during the later 1790s. This naturally constituted an area of sensitivity about which they preferred to remain silent.

Repeatedly the apologetics disclaimed any intentional rivalry with the national Church, and strenuous attempts were made to refute the charge of sheep-stealing. Attention was focussed upon the undeniable Christian task of influencing the unconverted. To this end Samuel Clift insisted that far from attempting to entice regular churchgoers from their places of worship, village preachers had encouraged their audiences to support 'zealous' clergymen by their attendance.[38] Yet that very assurance, with its assumption of the right to assess the piety and religious zeal of the parish clergy, was guaranteed to promote rather than placate Establishment hostility.

With equally irenic intentions Clift's fellow Dissenter, William Kingsbury, declared that 'compassion for the best interests of mankind' lay at the heart of itinerant motivation. The evangelists, he claimed, went to the poor and ignorant, to those whose lives were characterized by irreligion and vice. This concept of a disinterested work of rescue probably proved no more palatable to members of the Established Church than the former argument because of the inescapable implications of neglect, but Kingsbury anticipated their scorn, suggesting that the imputation of lesser motives merely reflected the unhappy state of those who saw fit to criticize.[39]

In a final attempt to convince the critics that no rivalry was intended, the impermanency of itinerant evangelism was emphasized. It was presented as a response to the needs of the moment; one, moreover, which Dissenters would be glad to relinquish once they saw evidence of a revival in parish life. What they wished to see were the ordinary clergy performing their visitation and other duties diligently, and preaching the gospel truths enshrined in the articles, homilies and liturgy.[40] The claim to be in sympathy with the formularies of the Established Church was one which was frequently made by those who supported Calvinist itinerancy, and the embarrassment which this was calculated to engender may be reflected in Samuel Horsley's concern to impress upon his clergy the importance of doctrine; of grounding their preaching on a firm theological base.[41]

When all the arguments and counter-arguments have been exhausted there remains the task of evaluation. On both sides exaggerations and misleading statements abound, but they do not diminish the underlying seriousness of the contest. In the course of the debate at Salisbury some disputants sacrificed the essential argument for the sake of such irrelevant issues as the quality of their opponents' grammar. In similar fashion a concern to discredit at any cost is evident in the repeated parallels drawn between the village preachers and the seventeenth-century regicides, and in the unwarranted emphasis placed upon personal misdemeanour. In turn Dissenting apologetics laid the entire blame for village preaching and the antagonism it caused upon the shoulders of the parish clergy, depicting those engaged in itinerancy as the unimpeachable agents of a divinely ordered movement of popular spirituality and religious fervour. If exaggeration and irrelevance weakened the Establishment case, the flaw in the defensive argument lay in its tendency to over-simplify and to minimize the effects of Dissenting activity. Any proper assessment must take this element of distortion into account.

The greatest polemical divergence concerned the political intentions of the preachers; the apparent threat posed by itinerancy to the security of the Established Church. Even if the unequivocal denials of hostility which issued from the apologists did not succeed in allaying the fears of their opponents, the published reports of the various Dissenting bodies demonstrate in retrospect their apolitical stance. Apart from early support for the Anglican-dominated campaign for the abolition of the Slave Trade, the records of the Baptist Western Association yield only one political comment of any consequence; an innocuous statement expressing the opposition of the member churches to military training on the sabbath. The more doubtfully orthodox General Body of Protestant Dissenting Ministers confined itself to effusive expressions of loyalty to Crown and constitution, while the majority of organizations maintained a conspicuous silence on all political matters.[42] By 1800 Rational Dissent had entered a phase of political quiescence. What possible suspicions could have been entertained, therefore, concerning those of orthodox persuasion?

But as perceptive Churchmen began to appreciate, the real threat to the Establishment came not so much from overt political action as from the more subtle social and religious changes encouraged by popular preaching. The many thriving congregations founded by the itinerant evangelists offered an attractive alternative to the established form of religion. The success of itinerancy threatened to rekindle the earlier demand for the amendment of that body of legislation whose very existence was seen by many to guarantee the security of the Church of England.

The other contentious issue too readily dismissed by those who supported itinerancy was the blame incurred by the preachers for their part in promoting schism. In their defence the apologists emphasized the wholly constructive and supplementary nature of contemporary evangelism, but there is some room for legitimate doubt concerning the adequacy of this interpretation. Was it true, as the apologists claimed, that those who gathered to hear the village preachers were also encouraged to attend the regular worship of the parish church; and was itinerancy merely a temporary expedient designed to satisfy a genuine religious need?

There is evidence to suggest that other, more partisan considerations exercised an influence, and that even the central claims made by the defenders were not entirely justified. Against the insistence that the attention of the preachers was directed at those who habitually neglected all forms of religious worship, there has to be set the example of Richard Densham who, seizing his opportunity, preached to the inhabitants of Rogate as they waited in the village churchyard for the start of matins.[43]

While deference was paid to ministers of the Established Church, especially to those of Evangelical persuasion, the expansionist aims of village preaching and the desire to achieve a Dissenting presence were in many cases calculated to foster Anglican displeasure. Although John Malham's unsympathetic account of a parasitic and self-interested preacher persisting in his unwelcome attentions to a community already enjoying adequate service from 'the regular Minister' may be dismissed as High Church rhetoric,[44] there can be no doubt that the simple aims of the evangelist were sometimes complicated by less disinterested motives. Hence at Deddington in Oxfordshire, when the parish church acquired an Evangelical clergyman, the North Bucks Independent Association decided to continue its support for the infant Independent congregation on the grounds of alleged local demand and the impossibility of guaranteeing the religious character of future incumbents.[45]

Despite appearances to the contrary the conflict over the need for village preaching illustrates the irreconcilability of ideas rather than the clash of abrasive personalities. To a High Churchman like Malham the preaching excursions which flourished on every side represented an unthinkable lay intrusion into the sphere of priestly duties; whereas to his opponent, William Kingsbury, the concept of a valid ministry had less to do with ordination than with matters of regeneration, piety and pastoral diligence. Similarly, in sociological terms the controversialists approached the situation from opposing viewpoints. For the ardent champion of the Establishment any concession to unauthorized preaching represented an assault upon the parochial system and upon the theoretical monopoly of religious provision, the traditional prerogative of the Church of England. By contrast his Dissenting counterpart with no suggestion of rivalry could point to numerous communities, especially those of an industrial character, which would lack any kind of religious presence were the task to be left to the parochial ministry. In the light of these deep divisions of opinion it is scarcely surprising that the polemical writers attributed to their opponents the worst possible motives.

Although the publication of their sentiments may have afforded the supporters of the Established Church a degree of satisfaction, there is little evidence to suggest that pamphleteering was more effective in restraining unauthorized evangelism than more direct forms of opposition. Only one means of coercion remained untried; namely, recourse to the authority of the law. The attempt to exploit the restrictive potential of the legal system typified the period from 1800 to 1812. Confronted with a sudden, sharp increase in the registration of meeting-houses and in the administration of the statutory oaths to preachers, magistrates and politicians came to believe that itinerancy broke the spirit if not the letter of the law. It was felt that the Toleration Act, designed to satisfy the religious scruples of Dissenting pastors and congregations, was being openly exploited by vulgar, uneducated men acting with scant regard for traditional forms of supervision.

However alarming popular evangelicalism may have seemed, appropriate means of control were not difficult to conceive. A permanent solution to the problem required a simple political initiative to update existing legislation and to remove areas of uncertainty. The alternative was for the civil and diocesan authorities to exercise their powers of restraint, withholding recognition in cases judged to infringe the surviving penal legislation or to offend against the spirit of the Toleration Act. The quest for a legislative solution took much longer than the intervention of those charged with the local administration of justice. Consequently the attitude adopted by the magistrates had a more immediate bearing upon the practical success of Dissenting evangelism than the activity of the politicians at Westminster.

In the prevailing atmosphere of political tension most sponsors took care to ensure that the preachers they supported complied fully with the existing legislation, and that situations of doubtful legal propriety were avoided. The practice of open air preaching exposed an area of particular uncertainty, and in the face of an increasingly hostile magistracy, some societies felt compelled to restrict the activity of their agents. In August 1800 the committee of Societas Evangelica was informed that a Justice of the Peace had given orders for its itinerant, William Norris, to be arrested while preaching out of doors. The non-implementation of the command had been due entirely to the leniency shown by the constables detailed to apprehend him. The members of the committee were told that the secretary had written to the person concerned advising him not to preach in the open at any place where he had reason to expect the interference of the civil authorities.[46] Two years earlier the London Itinerant Society had taken legal advice on the subject and had received the recommendation 'to preach as little out of doors as possible'.[47]

In spite of these voluntary restrictions there is little reason to think that the more vociferous opponents of itinerant preaching would have been satisfied with self-regulation, however effective it might have been. More definite restraints were thought to be necessary; controls which in the spring of 1800 appeared imminent following the announcement by Michael Angelo Taylor, the Member for Durham, of his intention to bring before Parliament a bill designed to amend the basis for qualification as a Dissenting teacher.[48] The proposed bill, which reflected the views of influential figures including the Prime Minister and Bishop Pretyman of Lincoln, threatened the very existence of itinerancy by granting magistrates discretionary power in the administration of the statutory oaths. Dissenters were not the only group to feel alarmed. Evangelical Churchmen, aware of High Church attitudes to popular evangelism, feared restrictions upon their own activities, and through the person of William Wilberforce, their parliamentary spokesman, pressed the Prime Minister to abandon the measure. For a variety of reasons the expected bill did not materialize[49] and the immediate threat of legal restrictions receded, leaving the problem of restraining itinerancy to the local magistrates. For the next decade it was they rather than the politicians who acted as the most effective brake upon the movement, imposing their own rather arbitrary interpretation of the Toleration Act.

Although the matter of achieving more effective legislation was to lie dormant for the next nine years, considerable tension remained; an atmosphere of uncertainty which derived its substance from unfriendly attitudes at home and ominous legal developments overseas, notably in the Caribbean colony of Jamaica. In December 1802 the Jamaica Assembly, fearing the subversive potential of itinerant preachers working among the black population of the island, enacted legislation designed 'to prevent preaching by persons not duly qualified by law'. This measure effectively banned religious dissenters from taking part in any form of public preaching. The law gave complete discretionary power to the magistrates concerning the recognition of preachers. It provided for the arrest as rogues and vagabonds of all unqualified or unauthorized persons addressing assemblies 'of negroes or people of colour' upon the island. Offenders were to experience hard labour and flogging, while those who allowed the use of their premises faced a fine of £100 and imprisonment pending payment of the penalty.[50]

Inevitably English Dissenters and Methodists believed their own interests to be involved, and as appeals for assistance were received from Jamaica, so representations were made to members of the government. These overtures resulted in the Privy Council disallowing the 1802 act as it had done with a similar measure passed in St Vincent.[51] For obvious reasons Jamaican society bore little comparison with that of England, yet the pressure exerted by the Dissenting leaders, Abraham Booth, Andrew Fuller and Robert Hall, in their joint application to the Privy Council Committee for Trade and Plantations, betrayed the distinct fear that the Toleration Act if breached in Jamaica could also be eroded in England. The justification for this pessimism became obvious in June 1809 when the need for new controls over the recognition of Dissenting preachers was suggested by Viscount Sidmouth to his fellow peers.

The fruit of Sidmouth's research into the number of preaching licences granted by the civil authorities appeared on 9 May 1811 when the noble lord rose to propose a measure bearing the deceptively innocuous title: 'A Bill ... to explain and render more effectual certain Acts of the First Year of the Reign of King William and Queen Mary, and of the Nineteenth Year of the Reign of His present Majesty, so far as the same relate to Protestant Dissenting Ministers.'[52] The provisions of the bill made plain Sidmouth's conviction that the statutes conveying religious toleration to Protestant Dissenters were being widely abused, and that a variety of persons of doubtful religious provenance were using the legislation to legitimize their self-appointed and unqualified status and to gain exemptions and privileges to which they were not entitled.

Although the measure as it finally appeared did not completely preclude an itinerant ministry, its insistence that those applying for recognition as preachers should produce an attestation of fitness signed by six 'substantial and reputable householders' of the same congregation or persuasion, was designed to ensure a strict containment of the phenomenon, and to secure its restriction to persons other than the rag, tag and bob-tail of cobblers, tailors, pig-drovers and chimney sweepers mentioned in Sidmouth's introductory comments. The bill made no mention of his earlier desire for a more formal notification of meeting places. Rather, it entrusted their control to the wider consequences of the limitations placed on personnel. But in one respect its opposition was more specific. It confined the privileges of exemption from civil office and military service to recognized ministers. By so doing it underlined its author's conviction that many of the laymen engaged in village preaching were using that avocation as a means of escaping from their normal obligations.

Dissenting opposition to the bill was quite predictable. In May 1810, a year before its publication, a sub-committee of the Deputies had met with Sidmouth and, according to the official account published by that body, had politely but firmly indicated their rejection of the very terms on which his measure was subsequently based.[53] Despite this warning he had persisted in his design and appeared genuinely surprised at the Dissenting and Methodist hostility which greeted its introduction to the Upper House. Confronted with his critics and with a 'mountain' of petitions against the bill, Sidmouth insisted that his contacts with respectable Dissenters had led him to believe that the measure would be welcomed. Various interpretations have been placed upon this discrepancy, ranging from self-deception by the bill's author to complicity on the part of William Smith and the committee of the Deputies. Whichever view is correct Sidmouth did not appreciate the extent to which the generality of Dissenters regarded the recognition of preachers under the Toleration Act as a right rather than a privilege to be granted at the discretion of the magistracy.

Whether the failure of the Deputies to provide effective opposition stemmed from their own elitist disdain for popular evangelism or from a predisposition to the more gentle and persuasive tactics of the eighteenth century, effective leadership of evangelical Dissent passed to a more aggressive body, the nascent Protestant Society for the Protection of Religious Liberty. The new society and the Methodist Committee of Privileges between them collected more than 600 petitions against Sidmouth's bill in the space of forty-eight hours; an 'avalanche' of parchment which created an impressive spectacle within the chamber of the House of Lords.[54]

The petition laid before the House by another long-established organization, the General Body of Protestant Dissenting Ministers, provides clear contemporary comment on the reasons for the opposition. Not only did the proposed legislation threaten existing rights, but it departed from the general spirit in which the Toleration Act had been observed for more than a century. By curbing those who were accustomed to act as occasional preachers, and by limiting the right of congregations freely to choose their own ministers by placing restrictions upon probationers, the projected measure appeared retrogressive. Far from achieving greater toleration and freedom, it envisaged a situation where magistrates would retain discretionary powers, and where, ultimately, those who signed the preacher's application would constitute the effective judges of the man's fitness for the ministry, in spite of being denied an opportunity of testing his ability. Although Sidmouth protested his sincere regard for the principle of religious toleration, the General Body had no compunction in dismissing his measure as a betrayal of trust prompted by the most uncharitable of motives.[55]

The failure of Sidmouth's bill to gain a second reading has received various explanations. Understandably, the victorious parties regarded the favourable outcome as a direct result of the pressure they had brought to bear upon Parliament. Others saw defeat as a reflection of the anachronistic and reactionary nature of the proposed amendments. More recently the emphasis has shifted to the political realism shown by Perceval's government. As with the earlier attempt in 1800 the projected legislation threatened to alienate a sector of the population conspicuous in its loyalty to Crown and constitution. At a time of increasing pressure for Roman Catholic emancipation gratuitous offence to law-abiding Protestant subjects made very little sense. If this interpretation is acceptable it vindicates to some extent the claim made by Dissenters that it was their pressure which had been the deciding factor. Clearly the expediency of not provoking alienation itself implies a recognition of social, economic or political significance.

Despite this unfriendly episode and the tense political atmosphere which accompanied the rapid expansion of itinerant preaching, there is no evidence of any official government hostility towards Dissenting evangelism. Nor was there a deliberate attempt to arouse popular reaction. Parliamentary moves designed to curb itinerancy stemmed not from government but from individuals; from Pretyman, Taylor, and most notably Sidmouth who was out of office during the crucial years 1809 to 1812. While it is likely that the political leaders of the day sympathized privately with the restrictive aims of the 1811 bill,[56] the public policies of Perceval and Liverpool favoured expediency rather than personal preference. Any thought of a national political reaction against itinerancy is, therefore, inappropriate. Only at the county level does the concept of official opposition have any substance. There, within the jurisdiction of the quarter sessions, local magistrates displayed an increasing determination to restrict village preaching by exploiting the ambiguities of the Toleration Act.

Under the terms of the Toleration Act of 1689 Protestant Dissenters were able to avoid the penalties of earlier penal legislation by registering their places of worship either at the quarter sessions or with the appropriate diocesan authorities. The quarter sessions were also empowered to administer the prescribed oaths to those who wished to act in a preaching or teaching capacity. Throughout the eighteenth century a trickle of refusals to implement these provisions, mainly in respect of the registration of premises, had come to the attention of the Dissenting Deputies. In most cases the matter had been successfully resolved. But from the 1790s a new and ominous reluctance to administer the oaths to intending preachers began to appear within the magistracy. The tendency to demur usually centred upon the applicant's lay or student status, or upon his inability to prove a settled pastoral relationship with a particular congregation.

From the limited evidence provided by the Deputies the number of refusals is impossible to ascertain, but contemporary accounts suggest that the isolated cases reported during the 1790s and early 1800s had greatly multiplied by 1810. The unwillingness to recognize preachers and to register places of worship, coupled with the increasing readiness to prosecute under surviving penal statutes, constituted an attack on both the human and material bases of itinerancy. Whatever its inspiration it has to be seen in the context of the various attempts to secure more restrictive legislation. Its effectiveness was reinforced, moreover, by the tendency of those involved to minimize the gravity of the more practical and popular forms of opposition.

The theoretical basis for the new, stricter interpretation of the Toleration Act was thoroughly Warburtonian in character, exemplifying the closest possible alliance of Church and State in the concern shown by the civil magistrates to safeguard the Establishment against spiritual encroachment. Similarly, the attitude to Dissent was perfectly predictable: while freedom should be accorded to those who for reasons of conscience differed from the Established Church, dissent could not be allowed to develop into religious pluralism by means of proselytizing. But to Dissenters the renewed emphasis upon the discretionary element cast a new light upon the Toleration Act. In its account of Lord Sidmouth's bill the contemporary history of the Deputies suggested that the use of the word *licence* in connection with the recognition of preachers was both 'invidious and unwarrantable'. The term did not occur within the relevant legislation, nor were the legal rights conferred by the process of registration and by the taking of oaths in any way discretionary.[57]

The minutes of the Deputies suggest that as late as 1802 any reluctance on the part of magistrates to administer the oaths to intending preachers could be overcome by the mere suggestion of an appeal to the King's Bench for a writ of *mandamus*. In that year the committee successfully persuaded the local Justices to allow a preacher named Burns from Kirk Ella near Hull to qualify in spite of his secular occupation as a farmer. As the decade wore on the magistrates in certain counties, most notably Buckinghamshire, Devon and Suffolk, became less tractable. An increasing number refused to recognize certain categories of preacher.[58] In 1806 the Suffolk quarter sessions sitting at Bury St Edmunds rejected an application from a preacher named Samuel Squirrel unless he could prove that he was the minister of a settled congregation. Although nothing more is recorded by the Deputies concerning this case, the magistrates at Bury St Edmunds refused similar applications from a man named Thomas Squirrel in May 1810 and July and October 1811.[59]

The inability to produce evidence of a relationship with a distinct congregation, the hallmark of the itinerant preacher, presented an ideal opportunity for a strict interpretation of the law. In Suffolk and similar areas of Establishment strength official intransigence was only to be expected. The uncompromising approach adopted was not merely a reflection of the zealous attitude of lay Churchmen; the minutes of the Suffolk quarter sessions make it clear that there as in other counties the local courts relied heavily upon the services of clergymen. The application made by Squirrel in 1810 was laid before a bench of magistrates on which those in holy orders outnumbered their lay colleagues by ten to four.[60] The phenomenon confronting these representatives of the Establishment was no longer the revolutionary Jacobinism apparent during the 1790s, but the impudent and successful activity of religious rivals with all the attendant social implications. At a time of increasing difficulty for the Church of England the growth of itinerancy created conditions in which the employment of restrictions to control religious dissent became impossible to resist.

The new representative body, the Protestant Society, under the leadership of John Wilks had none of the deference to authority shown by the Dissenting Deputies. Nor did it continue the old mannerly belief in the efficacy of quiet rational persuasion. Its response to the behaviour of the county courts was to test the legality of their interpretation of the law by selecting cases for reference to the higher authority of the Court of King's Bench. In October 1811 Wilks reported to the society that he had attended the quarter sessions at Bury St Edmunds to support applications by Leonard Ellington, the teacher of a congregation at Mildenhall, and Thomas Squirrel, a lay preacher, but both had been rejected. The case of Ellington had been refused only because a certificate signed by his congregation had not been produced. While the matter of Squirrel was deferred, the case of Ellington was taken by the society to the higher court where 'a rule to shew cause' was duly forthcoming, the rule being made absolute the following Easter Term.[61]

Since Ellington exercised pastoral responsibility for a particular congregation further test cases were judged to be necessary in order to produce a decision relating to those categories of preacher which lay at the heart of the controversy; men who were training for the ministry and others whose preaching took place on an itinerant and occasional basis. The cases selected by Wilks involved Thomas Brittan of Bristol, at that time a student at Hoxton Academy, and a currier from Dursley named John Packer, who 'had preached for several years at different congregations in Gloucestershire'. In due course the applications of both men were refused by the Gloucestershire magistrates, whereupon the process of appeal was set in motion. By taking this action Wilks hoped to secure a *mandamus* that would overturn the decision of the quarter sessions and establish an important precedent.[62]

The crucial decision came on Tuesday 5 May 1812 when the Lord Chief Justice, Lord Ellenborough, gave judgment in both cases. To the extent that the leaders of the Protestant Society had applied for a writ of *mandamus* compelling the magistrates to administer the oaths, they were successful, for the writ was granted, but Ellenborough made it perfectly clear that the issue was by no means settled. In his judgment he outlined the grounds for further refusal and the subsequent procedure for an appeal to the higher courts. His judgment invited further expensive litigation with the clear implication that if the matter were adroitly handled the appellants' case would ultimately fail.[63] Ellenborough's hostility towards the Dissenting case and the negative tone of his speech were only too apparent and both Dissenters and Wesleyans were quick to react. Within two or three days of the judgment Spencer Perceval received separate requests from the Protestant Society, the Deputies and the Wesleyans for parliamentary action to re-establish the earlier, milder interpretation of the Toleration Act in so far as it concerned the recognition of preachers.

As early as January 1812 it had become known that magistrates in more than thirty counties were refusing to administer the oaths to men whose 'preten[ce] to holy orders' was judged to be inadequate.[64] Some kind of action had been necessary to resolve the situation, and by the time that Ellenborough was ready with his verdict Perceval had already expressed his willingness to promote or support a parliamentary measure designed to break the legal impasse.[65] Not even his untimely assassination on 11 May was able to arrest the process, for his successor, Lord Liverpool, wasted little time in espousing the cause of toleration.

Liverpool's concern to revive the former, liberal interpretation of the Toleration Act derived its force from the same pragmatic considerations which had influenced Perceval, and which had led even earlier to the abandonment of Taylor's proposals. In the presence of insistent demands from Irish Catholicism there seemed little point in needlessly alienating any section of Protestant opinion. Although the developments at county level appeared unpromising, there were by the spring of 1812 a number of factors which favoured the progress of religious liberty, not least the reaction created by the defeat of Lord Sidmouth's bill. The additional measures of toleration outlined in Parliament by Lord Castlereagh on 10 July were the direct result of that reaction. With their provision for the repeal of the purely religious parts of the hated Stuart legislation,[66] the mandatory administration of the oaths to preachers and new rules governing their exemption from civil and military duties, they represented all the immediate objectives of the Dissenting and Methodist leadership. With only one significant change the bill progressed rapidly to the statute-book.

With its revision of existing legislation the 1812 act consolidated the gains made by religious toleration. Though it did not abolish the penalties for meeting in unregistered premises or for preaching by unrecognized persons, it removed the principal sources of grievance and relaxed the remaining restrictions. At the heart of magisterial opposition and the small but disturbing number of prosecutions lay the Conventicle Act of 1670 with its stipulations concerning unauthorized religious gatherings. The 1812 act quietly effaced this memorial to the religious intolerance of the Restoration.

A similar decisiveness marked the approach adopted to the revival of discretionary powers. The new act was unambiguous, leaving those responsible for its implementation with no doubt that when any preacher, lay or ordained, itinerant or settled, offered himself for recognition, it was their duty to administer the oaths and grant the appropriate certificate. With its enactment, the tolerant spirit of the eighteenth century was re-established, but on a more secure legal footing. Moreover, with the creation of the Protestant Society the principle of religious toleration had been furnished with a guardian more effective than its predecessor. Only in one respect did the 1812 act fail to accomplish desired objectives, namely, in its refusal to exempt occasional and lay preachers from the burdens of civil and military duty. The decision to exclude the largest section of itinerant personnel from these privileges was a sop to conservative opinion in the House of Lords.

At the close of July 1812 Dissenters found themselves once more facing only private hostility. The closest approach to concerted opposition had been the refusal to recognize preachers or to register premises, but the grounds for that action had been removed by the new act. Far from permitting the restriction of itinerancy, the law now conferred extensive protection upon the itinerant preacher and rendered serious opposition all but impossible.

8 · Developments and trends

ITINERANCY challenged isolationism and brought to an end traditional quiescence but the transformation did not end there. It was soon apparent that the new activism was no more immune to change than earlier attitudes. As English society began to emerge from the difficulties of the Napoleonic era evangelical activity showed signs of settling down. During the second and third decades of the nineteenth century the freedom enjoyed by the early itinerants succumbed to a process of institutionalization. Evangelism came increasingly to be regarded as a denominational rather than local responsibility, and in spite of certain positive developments, the 1820s witnessed the first signs of formalism and stagnation, twin forces which in time sapped the recruiting power of Victorian Nonconformity.[1]

When English Dissent first embraced itinerancy it entered a period of steady expansion. In order to stimulate interest organizers assiduously cultivated the religious public, emphasizing the numbers of preachers and hearers involved in the movement. They published full details of the places visited and the network of regular preaching stations established; they publicized the work of numerous itinerant societies, noting their growth in size and scale of operations and analysing their cost effectiveness. Unlimited progress appeared axiomatic: it was assumed by every enthusiastic observer. From the 1790s to the 1820s a mood of optimism gripped the majority of evangelical publications. Growth on such a scale was quite unprecedented. It merited and received extensive coverage in the religious periodical literature of the day. Reports were published annually by most itinerant societies, while their contents were given an even wider circulation by the ubiquitous *Evangelical Magazine*. Month after month domestic news was dominated by reports of chapel openings; buildings whose origins lay in the work of a generation of itinerant preachers. The question raised by these reports is one of interpretation. To what extent did the progress they depicted represent genuine expansion?

It may have been possible to measure the dynamics of the Dissenting community in a number of ways, but the evidence which made the greatest impression upon the opponents of itinerancy was the increase in meeting-house registrations and in the number of preachers applying for recognition. Routine administrative awareness combined with political sensitivity to produce alarums of the kind sounded by John Douglas, Bishop of Salisbury, in 1798. The local character of these warnings did not conceal their broader significance. In pointing to the large number of qualified preachers recorded during the previous year the bishop offered confirmation of a wider, national trend. In the same year the London diocesan authorities recorded a worrying surge of 60 per cent in the figures for meeting-houses, and the registers in almost every diocese provided evidence of a similar increase in activity. In the event the grounds for Establishment alarm were not substantial: the high level of expansion seen in 1798 was not sustained and subsequent registration peaks were considerably lower.[2]

The most significant conclusion to be drawn from the London figures, and from the national statistics compiled by Parliament at the request of Lord Sidmouth, is that the increase, however large and distinct it may have seemed when judged by traditional standards, remained within the bounds of comprehension. It involved nothing more remarkable than a doubling or tripling of existing activity. Even the factor of two or three which operated in most instances probably exaggerated the true rate of growth, since the act of registering a place of worship paid no regard to the question of permanence. It was by no means uncommon for a series of meeting places in the same village to be registered within a short space of time, successive entries often bearing the names of the same applicants. In Smethwick during one five-year period, from 1812 to 1816, three separate houses were used by the growing congregation of Independents.[3] Elsewhere factors other than growth determined the need for re-registration. Registered premises frequently ceased to be available. At times dispossession was brought about by nothing more sinister than a change of ownership; in other instances congregations found themselves facing the perennial problem of landlord hostility.

Adequate financial support depended upon effective publicity and that in turn required reliable information and the maintenance of accurate records. It should be possible, therefore, using the statistics preserved in minutes and reports of area associations to form a general picture of religious activity and of the principal changes arising from it. Yet the figures available require a great deal of circumspection. To draw national conclusions from local evidence is to invite methodological criticism, especially if some of the necessary information is lacking. The true significance of local details lies in their ability to confirm or contradict national trends.

Confronted with an ecclesiastical polity based upon autonomy and an eighteenth-century emphasis upon the importance of total identification with the local church, the natural temptation is to seize upon membership as the most obvious indicator of evangelistic growth. Yet several factors conspire to rob this category of its usefulness. The majority of Independent county associations did not appear until the early years of the nineteenth century, and even then their minutes and annual printed reports devoted little attention to the matter of church membership. Only the older Baptist organizations, the Midland, Northamptonshire and Western regional associations, afford a continuous record dating from the 1780s and so provide a basis from which to judge the impact of the new movement.[4] Fortunately for the historian, the annual circular letters produced by these bodies incorporate brief statistical summaries which record the leading components of growth and decline; the yearly totals for baptism, transfer, restoration, exclusion and death. In addition most of the letters conclude with a note giving the yearly increase or decrease in total membership experienced by the associated churches.

Even from this source the use of statistics is not without its difficulties. A considerable number of the flimsy circular letters are missing from the principal collections. The gaps are particularly serious in the case of the Midland Association. Moreover, inconsistencies of presentation abound: many record the net increase or decrease in associational membership yet provide no information concerning the total strength of the member churches, or even in some cases the number of churches within the association. Allowance must also be made for the element of distortion caused by a rate of mortality which is very high by modern standards.

While none of these points casts doubt upon the essential accuracy of the information published, the inability to contruct a systematic comparison between the figures for the annual increase or decrease in church membership and the total strength of member congregations removes much of its value. The growth of regional associations by means of a slow but steady incorporation of unattached congregations merely conspires to conceal still further any process of genuine expansion. By 1823 the Western Association numbered 78 member churches, an increase of 44 since 1780. The expansion had come about by a combination of factors: by internal growth, the absorption of existing congregations and the effects of a developing programme of evangelism. In spite of this the 1823 circular letter remarked that there were still 'many churches in the seven western counties not connected with [the] Association, nor indeed with any other'. In the light of these complications it is impossible to avoid the conclusion that church membership does not offer a satisfactory basis for a statistical assessment of village preaching.

It is difficult to devise a useful alternative. The nearest approach to a true index of evangelistic growth is probably to be found in the figures for recorded baptisms. Without ignoring the importance of internal growth there is good reason for suggesting that the increasing numbers of baptisms bore a direct relationship to the systematic expansion of village preaching and the conversions resulting from it.

Yet the baptism of mature converts does not provide an infallible guide to evangelistic growth even if the imperfections of the statistical record can be discounted. It merely provides the least unreliable indicator; the only one which leads to sensible conclusions. Its inadequacy stems from the element of choice associated with the administration of the ordinance. The records kept by Particular Baptists suggest that only a minority of those converted through itinerant preaching proceeded to baptism. Many contented themselves with regular attendance at open air or cottage meetings, later becoming adherents at the local meeting-house rather than full members of the congregation. Many village preachers lacked ordination and were, therefore, unable to administer the ordinances. Indeed, the essence of early itinerancy was the concern to convert rather than create church members. Baptism and church membership were of secondary importance: they were, moreover, inextricably connected, a point which provided a further disincentive to many converts. The one was not administered where the other was not anticipated. In practice many of those who responded to village preaching were unwilling to identify themselves formally with religious dissent. They preferred to maintain their independence as part of the large sector of uncommitted worshippers to be found in any nineteenth-century congregation.

Any assessment of this more nebulous area requires a shift from the intangible realm of statistics to the physical evidence afforded by bricks and mortar. From the point at which the initial tendency to meet out of doors began to give way to indoor gatherings under the influence of the English climate, some impression of the scale of the convert community can be gained from the size of the buildings erected to meet the increasing appetite for public worship. This factor will be discussed later in greater detail.

While the baptism of converts reflects deliberate and mature choice, it remains a volatile guide to the success of village preaching. Annual figures were often subject to sudden, sharp fluctuations caused by a variety of personal factors with no obvious external stimuli. Yet they represent the best indicator of growth available, for there is undoubtedly a correlation to be found between the incidence of baptism and the general level of evangelistic activity. From the extant baptismal figures for the Midland, Northamptonshire and Western associations it is possible to construct a series of graphs using an index based upon the average number of baptisms per church per annum.[5] In spite of certain deficiencies the resulting growth curves point to a number of useful conclusions.

The figures for all three associations demonstrate conclusively that the introduction of village preaching (from as early as 1775 in the Northamptonshire and Western areas) was not accompanied by any spectacular increase in the formal size of member churches. For each of the associations the index of baptisms shows a steady upward trend, but the increase is spread over three or four decades rather than concentrated into a shorter period. Although the statistics for the Midland Association present the simplest picture, the conclusions that can be drawn in respect of that body are less reliable than those relating to its sister organizations because of the large gaps which exist in its records. Some baptismal indices for the three associations relating to the years before 1817 point to rates of growth five times higher than those experienced in 1780. Yet the factor of five is misleading for it represents only the optimum rate of expansion. Growth was rarely constant, and for much of the period annual increases were of far more modest proportions.

Not only were average growth rates unspectacular but annual variations between associations were often minute. The records for the Northamptonshire and Western associations show a divergence of less than 2.0 baptisms per church per annum for thirty-two of the fifty years following 1780. In any consideration of the baptismal index it is important to remember that the figures are extremely small. The entire range of the index lies between 1.5 and 8.3 baptisms per church. With figures of such an order it is difficult under any circumstances to speak of spectacular growth.

Although the index figures for the three associations are marked by sudden, sharp and inexplicable fluctuations (variations which probably reflect no more than the vagaries of individual choice) they also reveal distinct trends of growth and decline. Those for the Northamptonshire and Western associations show a steady fall following the high point of recruitment reached in 1815–16. The figures show that the slide was eventually arrested by a smaller wave of expansion which took effect between 1828 and 1830. During the same period the statistics for the Midland Association demonstrate a similar, but less pronounced, downward tendency.

Viewed in entirety the baptismal records suggest that the most rapid church growth occurred between 1795 and 1798 and from 1805 to 1817. The Midland and Western associations reported their highest rates in 1816, the Northamptonshire body one year earlier. These maxima coincide with the events surrounding the end of the Napoleonic era, the successful conclusion of war and the painful transition to a peacetime economy, but the causality which seems to be implied is difficult to prove for there was no noticeable slackening in evangelistic effort.

To judge by evidence provided by the Midland Association the majority of local congregations followed a common pattern of growth. The circular letters for 1817 and 1824 reveal a fairly uniform expansion when the calculation is based upon the figures for church membership. Of the twenty-one churches mentioned in both letters only seven experienced any decrease and in only two of these did numbers decline significantly. As a group the twenty-one congregations enjoyed an average increase in membership of 27 per cent over the seven year period.

This image of quiet but steady growth agrees with the registration statistics mentioned earlier and supports contemporary analysis. As early as 1798 John Rippon's *Baptist Annual Register* attributed expansion to the beneficial effects of village preaching. Writing of the Salisbury church the editor said:

Salisbury — John Saffery. From the association of 1796, to that of 1797, twenty six members were added to this church; and in the next year 1798, nineteen more, — Nine of the former number were from the surrounding villages, into which the gospel had lately been introduced.[6]

Other leaders paid similar tributes to the importance of itinerant preaching as a means of augmenting church membership.[7] In 1823 the North Bucks Independent Association, a society distinguished by its systematic approach to record keeping, expressed delight at the success of evangelism. During its first five years of activity not one of the original churches had suffered a decline in membership. Most had experienced a gradual increase in strength; in some cases the gain had been rapid. A total of 191 new members had been added to the churches, a net increase of 111 after allowing for deaths and removals. This figure represented the addition of more than twelve new members for each of the founder congregations. By 1823 the sixteen member churches were supporting regular evangelism in thirty-nine localities. But in spite of this initial success the process of expansion appears to have reached a plateau. Six years later the number of congregations had increased by only one, while the number of villages exposed to visitation had declined marginally to thirty-seven.[8]

From these examples it appears that the statistical evidence supports the earlier contention that the English Dissenting Revival followed traditional lines. For all its preparedness to abandon the restrictive attitudes of the past, there was little sign of that dramatic growth which characterized the equivalent bodies in America. This is certainly the case in so far as it is possible to judge from the figures for formal membership.

At this point an obvious question arises. How can the changes associated with itinerancy be regarded as the signs of a true metamorphosis if the increase in baptisms and church membership involved only a doubling or tripling of existing levels? In spite of the limitations of the formal increase many contemporaries, critics and supporters alike, emphasized the magnitude of the response to itinerant evangelism. The level of Establishment alarm has already been noted. At the opposite extreme evangelical journals and society reports displayed undisguised pleasure at the growth of public interest in religious worship throughout the country. Whereas the older

Baptist associations published the annual changes in their statistics of membership with no specific reference to the results of evangelism, their Independent counterparts and other societies formed explicitly to promote village preaching dwelt on the detailed progress of itinerancy, recording the expansion of evangelistic activity and the increasing size of congregations as well as the more formal gains in membership.

In 1806 the annual general meeting of the Baptist Society was informed that John Palmer of Shrewsbury had included in his regular preaching circuit two places where large congregations augured well for the future. The report added that other work in the area undertaken by some of his own church members offered equally encouraging prospects. Similarly Charles Holmes, having commenced preaching in a derelict barn at Baydon in Wiltshire, had experienced such an increase in the number of hearers that he felt it incumbent upon him to try to erect a meeting-house. Concerning the neighbouring village of Aldbourne where he preached in an overcrowded dwelling-house he informed the society that 'the last time he was there many of the Poor Men who had been laboring hard all the Day were obliged to stand all the time betwixt the Forms on which others sat.'[9]

Society reports in the first and second decades of the nineteenth century were preoccupied with the theme of expansion and the size of evangelistic gatherings. From Church Minshull in 1811 the Cheshire Congregational Union reported both increasing numbers and further opportunities for evangelism within the district.[10] Ten years later its counterpart in North Buckinghamshire noted in a comprehensive survey of local evangelism that one Independent minister preached regularly in five hamlets to groups which varied in size from twenty to eighty persons.[11]

Although there is ample evidence of a strong surge of religious activity from the middle 1790s and of related developments in the sphere of physical accommodation, the exhortatory motive behind these reports should not be ignored. Year after year with monotonous predictability 'pleasing prospects of usefulness' and similar vague expressions of religious optimism were allowed to pepper the reports submitted by itinerants, their use clearly designed to stimulate the necessary public enthusiasm. It was also the case that economic uncertainty and the added glamour of overseas missions produced a considerable temptation to massage results and to seize upon the most appealing statistics.

Yet religious activity there was in abundance. The crucial issue is the precise nature of the public response. To what extent did village preaching become a popular movement and how did this popularity manifest itself in ecclesiastical terms? If the true impact of itinerant preaching did not reveal itself in the formal statistics of membership and new congregations, how is it to be assessed? The answer to these questions lies in the distinction drawn by contemporary records between 'members' and 'hearers'. Whereas the majority of Baptist associations persisted in their traditional focus upon church membership, most societies and periodicals emphasized the social and geographical coverage achieved by evangelical preaching. Thus in a note concerning the village preaching organized by the Independent church at Olney the *Congregational Magazine* for 1819 observed:

The following places now enjoy the advantage of these periodical services:

Ravenstone	congregation about		100
Lavendon	"	"	100
Weston Underwood	"	"	40
Clifton	"	"	40
Warrington	"	"	40

Two years later the same journal reporting the annual meetings of the Essex Congregational Union noted: 'there are upwards of forty stations for village preaching, supported by this Union, at which more than 5000 persons hear the Gospel every Sabbath.'[12]

The attraction of this general audience represented the itinerants' most significant contribution to Dissenting strength and influence in the longer term. As far as established congregations were concerned the increase in the membership roll was dwarfed in the majority of cases by the numbers of adherents who swelled the meetings Sunday by Sunday. The sheer press of bodies necessitated an almost continuous programme of building alteration and extension. The discrepancy between membership and adherence was if anything even greater in the outlying villages. There entire audiences were composed of adherents with the exception of a handful of individuals who had chosen to identify themselves with the congregation responsible for initiating the cause.

Some idea of the ratio of hearers to members can be gained from figures published in connection with the opening of premises or the formation of churches. At Torpoint in 1818 the 200 hearers outnumbered the 30 members by almost 7:1, whereas the proportion reported for a chapel at Gold Hill in Buckinghamshire was rather smaller at 200:50. Other comparative figures include 310$^+$:41 at Wendover in 1821 and 116:34 at Brampton, Cumberland the following year.[13] As early as 1797 the *Evangelical Magazine* recorded the opening of a Baptist meeting-house at Westbury Leigh, Wiltshire, which had accommodation for almost 1,000 worshippers.[14] Despite the prominence of Westbury as one of the traditional centres of Dissent, it is inconceivable that such a large building was erected with the needs of the formal membership primarily in mind.

Though the details of earlier attendance patterns are not available the exclusive character of eighteenth-century theology placed considerable emphasis upon church membership. It guaranteed that members would form the majority of the worshipping community. All congregations had their share of adherents but these tended to be more closely identified with the church than their nineteenth-century counterparts, the products of a promiscuous scouring of the countryside. Eighteenth-century adherents were in many cases the relatives of church members. Their separate status was merely the indication that they had made no acceptable profession of faith. With such a narrow base and the prevalence of disease and poverty many of the smaller congregations experienced a precarious existence.

The effect of itinerant preaching directed at evangelical conversion rather than the inculcation of specific doctrines or forms of polity was to bring many families with no tradition of Dissenting membership within the ambience of the meeting-house, or chapel as it was increasingly known. Rowland Hill underlined this point in his reply to the accusations of Samuel Horsley. He emphasized that the audiences attracted to itinerant preaching were drawn by the sincerity and vitality of its content and not by the principles of religious dissent.[15] In spite of Hill's reassuring words the weakness of the Church of England continued to encourage a mood of religious restlessness. Popular dissatisfaction led increasing numbers of people into an informal relationship with non-established religion. The early decades of the nineteenth century witnessed the creation of an important constituent of Victorian society, the uncommitted chapel-goer.[16]

As itinerancy began to affect the internal composition of Dissent so it also initiated important geographical changes. The local church found itself at the centre of a steadily widening circle of influence. The process of expansion dominated thinking both at regional and at national level. The earliest national societies displayed a marked variation in strategy. Societas Evangelica and the Baptist Society contented themselves with the payment of expenses, leaving the local minister to decide upon the most suitable locations and to make all necessary arrangements.[17] The Village Itinerancy, by contrast, adopted a more comprehensive role. With its Calvinistic Methodist origins it maintained its own evangelists and linked them in a rudimentary connexional structure, thereby exercising considerable control over the geographical factor. At its founding in 1796 the society's limited resources were wholly devoted to the needs of two locations: the weavers of Spitalfields and a limited rural area on the borders of Hampshire, Sussex and Surrey.[18] But this narrow geographical base soon widened with the opening of the academy at Hackney in 1803 and its ability to produce a steady supply of trained evangelists. Apart from student evangelism the society's direct involvement in itinerancy by the year 1811 included the oversight of ten chapels in the South of England extending westward from London to Sidmouth.[19]

The geographical expansion which affected local and regional societies differed from that of the non-territorial bodies in so far as it concentrated upon the intensive penetration of an area rather than outward extension. Judged by the criterion of density the operations of most area societies provide evidence of expansion in the early years of the nineteenth century. Some organizations grew quite rapidly. From its creation in 1797 with three preaching stations with which to serve the needs of the outer metropolitan area, the London Itinerant Society had expanded by 1800 into fourteen other communities, most of which lay to the south and west of the capital.[20] Although this early growth was not sustained, exploratory preaching continued to be a feature of the society's work. Of the sixteen preaching stations listed in 1832 ten owed their origins to the years after 1800. Most area societies display a similar pattern of development, a process of expansion not necessarily terminated by the evolution of the weekly gatherings into autonomous congregations. In some instances the attainment of independence marked the rebirth of evangelistic initiative. At Great Horwood in 1823 preaching carried out under the auspices of the North Bucks Independent Association led to the formation of a church with its own responsible government, but that in turn resulted in further expansion into the neighbouring villages of Nash, Whaddon, Shenley, Singleborough and Wigwell.[21]

Nevertheless, it would be a mistake to attribute all territorial expansion, including the direction of growth, to an irresistible tide of human effort. The geographical direction of itinerancy owed as much to the tensions of English society as it did to the inclinations of the pioneers. The success of the movement says as much about the inadequacy of the Established Church and the industrial dislocation of the lower classes as it does about the appeal of popular preachers. Not only did the latter defer to Evangelical incumbents, they also failed to make significant progress in communities subject to the traditional supervision of resident squire and parson.

Other factors also shaped the spread of itinerancy. At Alresford the primary check to evangelism came from the unprovoked hostility of the populace.[22] Elsewhere less striking but no less effective barriers were erected by popular apathy, non-availability of accommodation and sheer physical isolation. Rural communities did not have to be in the remote upland areas of the North or the South-West to present problems of access for the intending preacher. One difficult area lay only six or seven miles from the city of Oxford, a neglected and isolated tract of countryside known as Ot Moor. Referring to this area, which was watered by the River Ray and its tributaries, the North Bucks Independent Association observed that the roads were almost impassable during the winter months.[23] While an element of exaggeration coloured some reports, the poor state of communications in certain lowland districts shaped the development of itinerancy as surely as did the distances and general difficulty involved in upland terrain.

The intensifying penetration of the English countryside is illustrated most clearly by the example of Bedfordshire. This small south midland county, already a stronghold of Dissent, was subjected in the years following 1797 to a veritable bombardment of itinerant preaching organized by the local, self-styled Union of Christians. The minutes of the union's north-western district make it clear that the aim of the operation was nothing less than total coverage, at least so far as the distribution of tracts was concerned.[24] A shortage of information makes it impossible to chart the precise progress of individual preaching stations, but as early as 1799 the union was able to claim 'more than 3000 opportunities of evangelical instruction . . . during the [preceding] twelve months [directed at] persons who would not otherwise have had the Gospel preached to them'. The 1799 report named fourteen places which received regular attention and gave a clear implication that some parts of the county, most notably the central area, enjoyed almost total coverage. By 1814 penetration had progressed still further. The association's records noted that financial support alone by then extended to twenty-one preaching stations.[25] Expansion within a given area was limited only by the saturation potential. In Bedfordshire with its long tradition of religious dissent the saturation threshold was high, yet it was there if anywhere that maximum expansion was achieved.

In spite of the unsystematic character of so much itinerant effort and the fragmentary record bequeathed to posterity, stable geographical features can be seen. In the midland, southern and East Anglian counties itinerant preaching was widespread and the infrastructure and effects were well defined. In other areas the reverse was true: in Lincolnshire, parts of the Welsh border and the four most northerly English counties the Dissenting presence was extremely weak and efforts to establish viable itinerancies met with varying degrees of success. Insoluble problems were created by religious indifference, geographical isolation and financial constraint.

In the upland counties of the North scattered Presbyterian, Independent and Baptist congregations continued to maintain a long if precarious existence, but few developed significant networks of itinerancy. Exceptions to this rule were provided by the churches at Ravenstonedale, Alston, Brampton, Kirkby Lonsdale and Hamsterley, but even in these cases the achievements were often limited. The village preaching based at Brampton was probably confined to the pastorate of Robert Ivy and was in the early stages at least heavily dependent upon external finance.[26] The Hamsterley itinerancy, which operated over very difficult terrain, represented the enormous personal energy of the pastor, Charles Whitfield, while its counterpart at Kirkby Lonsdale was able to continue only with protracted support from the Lancashire Congregational Union.[27] Significantly, the body formed to evangelize the northern Pennine communities accomplished very little.[28]

The problems faced by Dissenters in establishing regular visits to remote rural areas were only too apparent. In 1799 a request from a Baptist church in Lincolnshire for assistance with local evangelism elicited the official response that as no minister of that denomination lived nearby nothing could be done.[29] By the same token it was possible as late as the 1830s to find an area as large as Furness with only one Congregational church, and that at a very low ebb.[30] In counties such as Lincolnshire the absence of Dissenting evangelism was compensated by the success of Methodist itinerancy, but in many parts of the North no alternative form of popular evangelicalism existed.

The period between 1790 and 1815 was marked by a preoccupation with rural society. County associations devoted their attention to the hinterlands in preference to the larger centres of population. Even national bodies pursued similar objectives. The Congregational Society revealed its own bias as it asked, 'How many villages are there where the inhabitants even to the present day are without hope and without God in the World [?]'[31] A slight shift in emphasis may have been indicated by the formation of the London Baptist Itinerant Preachers Society in 1809, a body created to serve the needs of the capital, but its appearance aroused the resentment of the Baptist Society, its subsequent development was not recorded and its founders spoke only of their intention to supply preachers to 'congregations near London'. The national body, while appearing to resent the implied criticism of its own inactivity, made no attempt to redirect its energies, even when its title was changed to the Baptist Home Missionary Society.[32] There was in the Napoleonic era little awareness of the developing scale of urban irreligion.

The only genuine understanding came from those caught up in the urban explosion. In 1807 a lone voice summoned the attention of Yorkshire and Lancashire Baptists to the changes which surrounded them. As it warned of the new situation it asked:

Should not the populousness of this country urge those of our churches in these parts, to associate together? This is uncommonly great. Not only are towns and villages enlarging, new villages nearly as populous as towns in other parts of the kingdom springing up; but the whole country is, as it were, overspread with the habitations of immortal beings.[33]

Ten years later an Independent minister named Docker pointed to the growth of irreligion in his own setting. His argument was based upon the general dearth of religious accommodation. The churches in Sheffield could hold only a third of the town's inhabitants yet many sittings remained empty. It required little analytical skill to conclude that relatively few families were regular in attendance at public worship.[34]

Even before Mark Docker referred to the northern industrial context his southern contemporary, James Bennett, had spoken enthusiastically in support of an Independent society established in 1813 for the evangelization of the metropolis. In his concluding remarks Bennett had underlined the crucial change of emphasis that he believed to be necessary:

Let us employ, but not exhaust our strength upon villages, so as to leave the metropolis of the world neglected; as though we thought scores in a corner more precious, than hundreds of thousands in the capital city.[35]

Bennett's words were significant. Although urban objectives had been pursued before, the dominant concern had always been the spiritual welfare of village society.[36]

With the spread of urban awareness came a recognition of the difficulties involved in establishing effective contact with city populations. In Manchester large tents were erected capable of holding up to 800 persons, their flexible construction enabling even larger audiences to be addressed when the sides were raised. Tent missions of this kind made impressive claims concerning their effectiveness in reaching the unchurched sector of the populace and the method was adjudged a great success.[37] Yet in spite of the imaginative element urban mission remained an unattractive option. The balance of effort continued to favour rural evangelism.

Development had an equally pronounced effect upon the internal structures of itinerancy. According to one interpretation the movement passed through three distinct phases as the individualism of the pioneering generation yielded to the rudimentary organization of regional societies and in turn to national networks of evangelism under the control of denominational bodies. The latter were capable of integrated planning and direction. Their ability to mobilize resources gave itinerant evangelism a new sense of permanence and stability.

The simplicity of this analysis is attractive but it glosses over a number of difficulties. The appearance of denominational home missionary societies did not lead to the demise of either regional or individual activity. Both continued to play an important part in expansion. As late as the 1820s the efforts of ordinary church members were still responsible for raising congregations. The reluctance of earlier structures to disappear was matched, moreover, by a tendency for later ones to emerge before their time. Even during the 1790s the Baptist Society and the Congregational Society for Spreading the Gospel in England had begun to promote denominational interests on a national scale. A further complication stems from the varying fortunes of active societies. A number of bodies, including such prominent names as Societas Evangelica and the Congregational Society, began to exhibit signs of decay and in doing so limited any idea of progressive development. But the most serious objection of all arises out of the decline which overtook the earlier spirit of co-operation. As structural development was influenced by that process matters of scale and centralization became almost coincidental.

The impetus for structural change stemmed from the quest for greater efficiency and the growing sense of denominational identity which accompanied the return to peacetime society. The interest in efficiency reflected a concern to minimize constraints created by a narrow financial base and exacerbated by economic recession. Behind these factors lay the stealthy advance of institutionalization exploiting the belief that greater centralization would bring about a more effective use of resources.

By 1830 the shape of the movement had visibly altered. The old emphasis upon free-ranging, outdoor evangelism had been supplanted by a preference for indoor gatherings. During the early stages of expansion outdoor preaching had been undertaken not only as a response to adverse circumstances but as a natural summer activity. Richard Densham illustrated this point in May 1798 when he wrote to his sponsor acknowledging that the season for outdoor preaching had almost come.[38] But the spontaneity of the 1790s had long since disappeared. Village preachers had yielded to the pressures of convenience and formality and with relatively few exceptions had moved their audiences indoors.

Behind the growing formality rival concepts of ministry struggled for pre-eminence as pastoral duties appeared to conflict with the obligations imposed by evangelism. John Angell James, minister of Carr's Lane Chapel, Birmingham, spoke for many when he urged that the roles should remain united. Where a separate responsibility for evangelism existed authority should belong to the recognized pastor.[39] The weakness of this view lay in the tendency for pastoral duty and status to usurp the place of evangelism. At an early stage the committee of the Village Itinerancy displayed some awareness of the problem as it warned the congregation at Sidmouth of the dangers of insisting upon a third chapel service on Sundays. It urged that Sunday afternoons and weekday evenings be used for village preaching, suggesting that evangelism would 'ultimately increase [the] congregation and promote its respectability and prosperity'.[40]

Despite this advice enthusiasm for evangelism was waning. Contemporary correspondence indicates a pattern of retrenchment as ministers withdrew into their pastorates leaving village preaching stations to their own devices, even where there was a measure of external support.[41] Itinerancy outlived the 1820s but its future looked distinctly uncertain. Gone was the dominating concern to make converts: in its place stood the less dramatic but demanding task of ministering to the needs of small, unviable congregations.

The redirection of energies was accompanied by an increasing sense of financial uncertainty, a mood intensified by widespread departure from the strict standards of economy practised in the 1790s. The root of the problem lay in the growing preoccupation with buildings and the mounting burden of debt which their provision and maintenance incurred. The earliest indoor gatherings, though involving the sponsor in certain expenses, required only a modest per capita outlay. But as audiences expanded the problem of accommodation became more acute and expenditure rose alarmingly.

Some societies were more successful than others at keeping their costs in check. In Bedfordshire the Union of Christians was quite exemplary. Its funds were administered sparingly using rented accommodation wherever possible. In 1802 the cost of providing premises amounted to £36.2s.9d., a far smaller sum than the £65.3s.0½d. needed for the reimbursement of travelling expenses. Annual rents rarely exceeded £4 and fitments were usually modest in character. The acquisition of property merited even stricter economy and with that in mind the society noted the expenditure of £50 in 1815 for the purchase of a barn at Hockliffe. While the entry made no mention of alterations the sum expended represented a considerable saving over the cost of erecting a chapel.[42]

In contrast with the caution of the Bedfordshire Union many societies were prepared to sanction building schemes. The earliest constructions differed little from their eighteenth-century predecessors, being small, plain in architecture and relatively inexpensive, but the success of village preaching encouraged a growth in seating capacity and a steady increase in capital expenditure. A typical outlay of £400[+] in 1807 had risen 50 per cent by 1817 and the upward trend continued unabated.[43] But these costs with their attendant economic difficulties fell far short of the sums expended by Thomas Wilson in securing an evangelistic presence in some of the new residential suburbs of London. The first of his suburban chapels, which opened at Paddington in 1813, cost in excess of £7,000.[44]

The construction of specialized premises did more than merely accommodate the increasing numbers attracted by evangelical preaching. It appeared to enhance the very effectiveness of itinerancy. In contrast with the limited tenure which applied to most rented accommodation, purpose-built chapels seemed to offer a permanent and visible focus for evangelism within the community. It is hardly surprising, therefore, to find the infant North Bucks Independent Association attributing the success of village preaching in the Newport Pagnell area to an active programme of chapel construction.[45]

But a sense of permanence and progress cannot entirely explain the obvious enthusiasm for chapel building. Behind the numerous schemes projected lay more mundane financial considerations. In 1817 the Independent minister at Hexham appealed to the Village Itinerancy for assistance with the cost of erecting a chapel at Brampton in Cumberland. His appeal was based upon the argument that only the provision of 350 permanent sittings could guarantee the level of income necessary to retain the services of the current itinerant, Robert Ivy.[46] Similar reasoning was employed elsewhere to support the enlargement of existing premises. In 1821 a minister from Torpoint wrote to the society saying, 'an additional reason in my own breast is, that by taking in this piece of ground the Chapel will be capable of producing something like an Income for a minister in future.'[47]

The practical effects of permanence upon evangelism were less attractive. Any increase in the optimum size of congregations tended to suppress the formation of offshoots, thereby removing one of the most effective means of making contact with new communities. As congregations grew the proportion of members actively employed in itinerant preaching decreased, causing the impact of domestic evangelism upon the church base to decline commensurately.

Gradually the burden of debt created by building schemes began to exercise its own debilitating influence. Evangelism yielded to infrastructure as the latter encroached upon the modest sums needed for the support of itinerant preaching. In 1815 the London Itinerant Society found itself hampered by a debt of almost £300, a sum which reflected the cost of providing permanent accommodation for two of its preaching stations.[48] More obvious damage was done by the decision of the Home Missionary Society a few years later to withdraw its support from a thriving network of village preaching in North Devon. The abrupt curtailment of financial assistance exposed the weakness of local congregations, some of which were struggling to pay off their own chapel debts. It also demonstrated that where itinerancy was forced to compete with more pressing obligations the latter could threaten its very existence.[49]

Few societies remained entirely unaffected by the building boom but some did more than others to resist its insatiable demands. For many years the Bedfordshire Union pursued its undeclared policy of simplicity, reducing to the minimum all forms of structural expenditure. In a rare case at Shefford where a debt was incurred the committee, having paid the interest on the outstanding sum for four years, warned the congregation that it should not rely on the continuance of this favour.[50]

The Village Itinerancy though more explicit was less effective in achieving restraint. In 1817 the committee rather curtly informed an applicant that it did not engage in the building of chapels. Yet the society's policy belied its practice for all too frequently it acceded to requests for financial assistance. In one instance an emergency grant of £50 was promised to a congregation at Monmouth to enable it to purchase the premises it was being compelled to vacate. From an early stage in its development the society discovered that a willingness to assume the responsibilities of chapel trusteeship aroused expectations of material aid. But in spite of making regular grants for building purposes it contrived to support evangelism with undiminished generosity and with little sign of the financial constraint which afflicted similar bodies. For the Village Itinerancy the worst effects of capital expenditure were mitigated by its singular success in attracting substantial legacies.[51]

If building schemes threatened to consume a disproportionate share of resources the general economic climate did nothing to alleviate the problem. The return of peace in 1815 was accompanied by a sharp and protracted recession which bore heavily upon many Dissenting congregations. Although the county associations eschewed political comment their financial records mutely charted the progress of the local economy. As early as 1813 the Lancashire Congregational Union found itself with a deficit that was caused in part by the widespread commercial distress within the county.[52] From similar terse remarks in other quarters it is clear that industrial and commercial stagnation continued to affect churches in many parts of the country until the beginning of the 1820s.[53] At that point a brief improvement was experienced before austerity returned in 1826.

These examples appear to bear out the suggestion that in times of economic depression English Dissent with its limited social catchment was unable to cope with the demands made upon it.[54] While the argument may be true in broad economic terms or in connection with specific localities it is contradicted by the continuing support given by some societies to itinerancy throughout the years of greatest difficulty. Optimistic remarks made by the Cheshire Congregational Union in 1816 and by its counterpart in North Buckinghamshire thirteen years later reveal a determination to support evangelism whatever the circumstances, and this in spite of the fact that itinerancy was the most voluntary of all ecclesiastical activities.[55] The evidence suggests that the relationship between economic distress and evangelism was far from simple.

Financial instability and decline were never far from any congregation. Small independent churches enjoyed a precarious existence at the best of times without additional pressures imposed by crises such as the collapse in 1824 of Philip Ball's bank at Mevagissey.[56] In 1830 the church at Great Horwood found itself compelled to relinquish the short-lived services of its pastor having lost the income of thirty or so members through the unpredictable ravages of migration and death.[57] Even for national bodies shortage of funds became a problem at certain points during the 1820s. Whether the financial crisis stemmed from extravagant building projects, from the marked discrepancy between home and overseas giving, or from the general economic situation is difficult to say.[58] What is clear is that a number of evangelical organizations including the Home Missionary Society found themselves trying to meet increasing financial demands out of inadequate resources.[59] In spite of these difficulties the 1821 report for Idle Academy felt itself justified in regarding the years of post-war depression as a period of surprising evangelical enthusiasm and generosity:

The exhausted state of things, which has succeeded exertions of no common description, may indeed be supposed to have affected all the sources of public liberality; but our grateful surprise must be excited on perceiving, that He who has the hearts of all men in his hands, has in such unfavourable circumstances, created a prevailing disposition to carry forward the designs of preceding years, with undiminished energy, notwithstanding the new but imperious claims of poverty and wretchedness.

Closely linked with the decline in field preaching and the preoccupation with buildings was the emergent cult of respectability. Upwardly mobile Dissenters felt compelled to revive the earlier apologia for itinerancy. Those who now sought to justify the practice did so on grounds of utility. The North Bucks Independent Association made obvious use of the utilitarian argument in 1828 as it described the moral reformation accomplished by gospel preaching in the once 'notorious' community of Charlton. Whatever the reality behind the statement its publication betrayed an obvious desire to clothe the disreputable practice in more acceptable garb.

The welcome accorded to itinerant evangelism in the 1790s had been essentially pragmatic. Village preaching had been synonymous with rapid growth and successful penetration of the countryside, and the attractiveness of this formula had led to the widespread adoption of the practice. Those who disliked itinerancy had been left to reflect upon its disagreeable character powerless to influence the direction of events. But the success of evangelical preaching had contained the seeds of its own downfall. Gradually the self-improvement of the converts and the growing education of the preachers combined to create a powerful sense of respectability, an ideal which dominated Dissent from the 1820s.

The first signs of this new attitude had appeared much earlier. At its preaching station at Barnet in 1798 the Congregational Society had made a conscious attempt to satisfy the desire for personal pews expressed by a number of 'respectable inhabitants of the town'. At that stage the interest shown in their presence seems to have been largely financial; a recognition of the benefit that would accrue to the cause from the letting of seats.[60] More symptomatic of the real change in priorities were the later remarks of a minister who visited the small Oxfordshire village of Blackthorn. His report of the visit drew attention to the shortcomings of the meeting place which the inhabitants were compelled to use. Its meanness appeared to him likely to discourage the attendance of respectable villagers. 'It would be unreasonable', he argued, 'to expect persons, above the very lowest class to enter it, unless influenced by a much greater love to divine truth than is generally felt by those who are unaccustomed to the joyful sound.'[61] By the time his thoughts appeared in print in 1830 his concern for respectability was widely shared.

Meanwhile a similar change of attitudes had overtaken the evangelical academies. In 1809 a subcommittee appointed to examine the premises occupied by the seminary at Hoxton reported that in the current state of overcrowding they were hardly suitable for 'the prosecution of ... literary pursuits'. Nor, it was said, did they afford 'those conveniences that [were] proper and decorous for those who [were] preparing to sustain the important character of the Ministers of the gospel'.[62] By the use of such terms Hoxton betrayed its growing social confidence. In 1826 the academy's standing was enhanced by the opening of the new building on Highbury Hill. The creation of this edifice seemed to provide a fitting monument to the achievements of the previous thirty years. London Congregationalism had at last arrived! Two years earlier the committee which proposed the building showed in its recommendation just how far evangelical Dissent had moved from the unpretentious missionary spirit of the 1790s:

It is due to the number, opulence, and increasing respectability of the religious denomination to which we belong, that their public edifices, and especially Institutions for the education of their future ministers, should be held on the best and most secure tenure; that they should be well adapted to the purposes for which they are designed; and that they should evince in their structure, the esteem in which they are held by those whose spiritual wants they are intended to supply.[63]

In 1831 a previously unsuccessful body known as the General Union of Baptist Ministers and Churches was reconstituted in order to provide a focus for the growing sense of denominational identity felt by English Baptists. The following year amid some controversy its Congregational counterpart was born. The appearance of these bodies at this particular juncture was not coincidental nor was their professed concern for growth in any way remarkable. Both were the products of an age of expansion. The creation of permanent denominational structures revealed for the first time the full extent of the transformation which had taken place since the 1780s. The experience of concerted evangelism had taught a generation of Dissenters to think connexionally and to reject the more extreme notions of congregational autonomy inherited from the eighteenth century. Subsequent historiography has tended to associate the developing interest in denominational union with the strong concern for overseas missions seen in the early years of the nineteenth century, but while it would be unwise to ignore this connection the present study has shown that equal importance should be attached to the experience of five decades of extensive, practical co-operation in the cause of domestic evangelism.

The emergence of denominational union demonstrated in more concise form the difficulties that underlay the development of itinerancy. Both revealed the limitations of institutionalization within the process of growth. The desire for denominational action may have produced a systematic and efficient approach to the organization of evangelism, but there is little reason to suppose that the results were more remarkable than those already achieved through the spontaneous application of local and individual effort.

Conclusion

ALTHOUGH formal categories may be of limited value in an investigation of the dynamic character of early itinerant evangelism, the immediacy and individualism associated with that phenomenon must not be allowed to obscure the underlying developments. Changes in dissenting Protestantism were taking place which were eventually to prompt no less a personage than Lord Sidmouth to issue a warning of dire consequences for the religious life of the nation. Despite the unpromising theological legacy of strict Calvinism, the traditional concept of the settled pastorate and the customary association of itinerancy with the less inhibited traditions of Methodism, village preaching came during the late 1790s to occupy a prominent place both in English Dissent and in the life of the nation at large. It was a development which alarmed parliamentarians and High Churchmen alike and which provoked considerable internal opposition. The remains of mid-century Calvinist introspection combined with the tradition of congregational isolation and a static view of the ministry to create in conservative Dissenting minds, such as that of Walter Wilson, a deep distaste for itinerancy. From this traditional viewpoint the practice was scarcely less disruptive and unpalatable than it was to those who with impotent rage defended the privileges of the parochial Establishment. Yet, however great the shock to contemporary minds, this 'methodistical' practice had by 1810 spread to every English county, fracturing attitudes, values, beliefs and structures. In this process the abandonment of the isolation traditionally associated with congregational polity epitomized the thoroughgoing and irrevocable nature of the changes involved.

Within the Dissenting ministry the point of change was marked by a recasting of the pastoral function to suit contemporary evangelistic needs and by a degree of fluidity in lay-ministerial relations that was remarkable even by the comparatively flexible standards of earlier Hanoverian independency. Yet in spite of the impression created by the statistical prominence of ordinary church members the new itinerant ministry was never dominated by the lay element, but rather by the concept of the evangelistic pastorate within which men like Saffery and Hillyard acted as exemplars and organizers. Moreover, in spite of the state of flux affecting the ministerial office and the apparent abrogation of traditional limitations, careful supervision was maintained over those who took part in village preaching.

While the changes associated with itinerancy may have been less dramatic than those seen in American revivalism, their appearance in the English ecclesiastical context was scarcely less significant. Whatever elements of continuity were to be found there was a real sense in which the adoption of the practice marked for Dissent the transition between two entirely different worlds.

Yet if such a radical break was in progress the more obvious feature of the movement was its undoubted success. The reasons for the striking progress made by Dissent after 1780 range from the essential to the contingent, but if the wider circumstances of the early Industrial Revolution are disregarded, three principal elements can be identified.

In the first place the spread of itinerancy owed its impetus to the new generation of evangelical academies modelled upon Trevecca. Acting as catalysts to the movement they provided a stream of able personnel trained in village preaching and convinced of the need for aggressive evangelism. Nevertheless, in the longer term the same institutions inhibited the very practices they had helped to initiate. Their increasing preoccupation with education for its own sake and their growing concern for respectability conspired very effectively to weaken the earlier evangelistic imperative.

Within itinerancy there was, secondly, an intrinsic flexibility which coped with the problems raised by fluctuating resources and by changing geographical and environmental circumstances. Particular situations presented preachers and organizers with specific local difficulties, but in the normal course of events sufficient scope for adjustment could be found within the four principal patterns of evangelism which evolved. Internal limitations were another matter entirely, for however successfully the practitioners of itinerancy overcame external barriers the effectiveness of their work was all too often impaired by inherent weakness caused by a combination of individualism, demand for visible results, and sloth and prolonged immaturity on the part of newly raised congregations.

The third reason for success was negative in character, and concerned the inconsequential nature of the opposition encountered. In spite of the charged political atmosphere of the period in which the movement came to prominence, and notwithstanding the hostile remarks and actions which emanated from members of the Establishment, effective opposition remained an individual, localized and temporary phenomenon. Whatever popular resistance appeared quickly evaporated, and with the exception of one or two ugly incidents hostility never formed the primary response to itinerant preaching. The most serious check to progress was administered by individuals possessing influence at the local level: clergymen and landowners, and local magistrates who for a brief period prior to 1812 caused considerable disruption through their strict interpretation of the Toleration

Act. For a short while, indeed, during the winter and spring of 1811–12 the combination of these local initiatives did appear to constitute a de facto national policy of obstruction towards Dissenting evangelism. Considered in entirety, however, the opposition, while successful in erecting temporary local barriers, did little to arrest the progress of the movement, and by August 1812 with the demise of Lord Sidmouth's bill and the passage of the 'New Toleration Act' it had achieved the reverse effect, of removing the remaining penal legislation and stimulating the creation of a new and noisy watchdog for Dissenting privileges, the Protestant Society for the Protection of Religious Liberty.

The success of the first phase of itinerancy produced important changes within Dissent. As soon as village preachers began to penetrate new communities and gain a response, an inevitable growth appeared in the number of worshippers. The majority of church records, with their emphasis upon the traditional criterion of membership, reveal only a gradual, if fairly steady, accession of strength. The real evidence of numerical advance is found among the less readily verified statistics for adherence. In that area the rate of growth was striking.

The rapid increase in the number of 'hearers' was important for two reasons. Firstly, by diluting the element of commitment it effected a fundamental change away from the serious character of eighteenth-century Dissent with its strongly doctrinal emphasis. Secondly, it accomplished a transformation in more tangible, numerical terms, causing the rate of expansion to outstrip even that of the general population. The older Dissenting bodies consequently became in due course an important constituent of nineteenth-century Nonconformity; a development which was to have social and political overtones at least as important as those of a more specifically religious character.

Within this shift towards adherence there was an undoubted paradox, for while the limits of practical undenominationalism were readily apparent, there was a sense in which the growth achieved through itinerancy displayed precisely that character. With its concentration upon the principal gospel themes and its lack of emphasis upon the obligation of church membership, village preaching tended to encourage the development of a rural chapel culture, conscious of its Nonconformity rather than specific denominational allegiance.

The evangelism of the 1790s and 1800s produced a growing demand for religious accommodation, and, influenced by the prevailing mood of optimism and progress, that desire increasingly turned towards the acquisition of premises that reflected success in visible terms by means of the size and quality of construction. Thus it is that most of the surviving records from this period display an increasing preoccupation with buildings and with the financial problems attendant upon their provision and maintenance. By the 1820s this material interest had combined with rising ministerial status to accentuate the contemporary concern for respectability and to hasten the change from individual spontaneity to a more formal assumption of responsibility for continuing expansion.

Whatever had been achieved by earlier effort and however impressive the continuing programme may have seemed, the practice of itinerancy by 1830 had lost much of its original relevance. At heart it remained a rural movement concerned with the religious condition of village society. In common with almost every other aspect of the wider Church it seemed unwilling or unable to address itself to the new focus of religious neglect located in the rapidly growing industrial centres and conurbations. But the later state of itinerancy does not provide an adequate basis for a wider evaluation of its importance. For that the historian must turn to other criteria and consider instead its function as one of the major components of that popular evangelicalism which formed such an active feature of English religion and society in the crucial period of unrest following the French Revolution. Even within the much narrower sphere of Protestant Dissent the implications of its adoption were far-reaching, for it is impossible to escape the conclusion that itinerant evangelism played a vital role throughout the entire spectrum of non-established Protestantism and not as traditionally supposed in the growth of Methodism alone.

Journal of T[homas] Wastfield, June 1797 – April 1798

June 18th [1797]

Went from Imber[1] about 6 o Clock; friend Ware & two others join'd in company with me in the way & about half past eight we reached Upheaven;[2] went round the place & gave notice of preachg. by the Baptists & immediately preached from Rev. 1.5.6 to about 100 people, who behaved very well in the general. I found the Lord present & hope good was done. I promised that day month to be there again at 8 o Clock in the morng., but if I should be there sooner would go round the place & give notice as on that day. Put up the horse at an Inn, expence 3d. At about half past 10 preachd at Entford[3] from Jhn 1.11.12 the people in general quiet & about 100 in number; 2d was given to some boys to run about & give notice of the preachg. The minister[4] sent two persons with an order for me to give off preachg. or they were to take me into custody. I said they had no authority to take me into custody & advised them to take heed of the consequences & said farther to them let the minister come himself. They went back to the minister who came & brought the constable & came up to me & insisted on my comg. down from the place on which I stood & to be guarded by those with him; I submitted, but kept on preachg in an irregular manner, while the minister was there I endeavoured to bring him to speak but in vain he said he would say nothg. to me. the persons to whom I was delivered did not confine me. I kept on preachg. & they let me go: The minister said if I came again he would carry me to the Justice, before he went off. The church service was just going in & so I stopt preachg. & went in to the Inn & had some beer with some bread I had in my pocket: We staid here till we thought the church were out in the next place & then went on to Haxon;[5] the church (was contrary to our thought) upon going in & there being a few people in the Street I began to talk to them of the things of God & as they increased to about 40 I expatiated on things which appeared needful for them to know for about ¼ of an hour when their church went in. I found much liberty in this exercise. Went on to Netherhaven[6] many people followed, preachd there to about 130 people. I found the Ld. present givg. me liberty & comfort, the people in general attentive & some appeared much impressed. One man came behind (me I preachd before two trees very near each other) & said he would bring the constable if I did not give off. I told him he had no authority & he went his way. Here appears a good promise of plantg. the Gospel if a house was set apart. I named no text. Here about 3 o Clock the service began.

Went on to Filiton,[7] called on frend Whitmarsh who kindly treated both me & my three friends about 30 people came up to his house, seemed desirous of hearg, I preached to them from Prov 8.35. I found myself dry, the words appeared only words I had but little comfort. O my God, do not leave me to myself, my words are nothing, O be ever present that I may feel thee & the people also.

Went on (my friends now returnd home) to Durrington, rode round & gave notice of preachg; attempted to shew them the doctrine of the new birth with its necessity but took no text; near the close of the service as I was singg. a hymn (the people desired me to sing) there appeared by the people something going forwd of an opposg. kind & presently an egg was flung wch struck no one; Confusion took place, the people in general were much offended with the person that did it, At first a general carelessness with talking was on the people but they got more serious as the service went on. I found peace & liberty to speak but not much sweet union. There were here near 100 people.

Went on to Bulford & near 30 of the Durrington people followed, from various motives as appeared by their conduct, some seemed to like to hear, & some to oppose particularly one man who opposed me almost thro' my discourse with mock preachg. & other abusive treatment. I preached to about 100 people but few could hear much the opposition was so noisy, some few eggs were flung, one struck me. A farmer came up to me & desired me to give off & go away I told him I would presently being unwillg to give off while I found some around me very attentive – He threatened me as he said he was a peace officer to force me – I told him he could not & so I kept on a little longer & left the place in much disorder about half past seven & reached home about 10. Glory to God for his tender care of me this day & for all his blessings.

The expences of the Horse at Uphaven 3d Entford 8 Netherhaven 3d Bulford Turnpike Gate 1d

in all	1 - 3	
Boys for givg notice	5	
My expences in Beer	3	
	1 - 11	

2nd July

Set out about six in the morng., preached at Isterton[8] to about 60 people between 8 & 9; went about the place & gave information of preachg; many people were not about but after I had breakfasted with friend Croock a congre[g]ation was gathered as above. All was peaceable. Text, Gal. 3.13.

Preached at Urchfont at the house set apart for worship by the independant brethren service began at half past ten (I believe) to about 50 people: many of these appeared acquainted with the power of religion; our meetg. was comfortable, Text, Rev. 1.5.6. Dined at friend Giddens's a carpenter, with Mr Garret who preaches at Urchfont generally. This place has not long been opened, it has a promisg. appearance; may the Ld. abundantly bless souls here. Immediately after dinner with four persons (who found it on their mind to go with me) set out for the places beyond Urchfont which lies in darkness: the first place we came into was Conock began by singg. a hymn, a few people gathered togr, (many could not be expected it being but a few houses, preached from Psm 8.4 "What is man" About 30 people were present, some of whom followed to the next place Charleton[9] where began by singing a hymn sch. drew about 80 people togr, preached from John 1.29 Behold the Lamb of God wh taketh away the sins of the world. The people were in general attentive. Went on to Mardon[10] but findg the people at Church went to Wilford;[11] called at some houses and informed them of preachg. Began by singg. a hymn wch. gathered many people togr.. I preached from Matt. 11.28 to about 100 & mainly attentive; some appeared to consider the truths delivered & expressed themselves desirous of hearing again when I could favour them. Returned to Marden, began by singg., about 90 people were assembled; preached from Ephes. 2. pt of 12th & 13 ver. "havg no hope & without God in the world, but now in Christ Jesus &c" After preachg I (as before in other places) thanked the people for their good behaviour &c – I had for answer the pleasg. reply "We ought to thank you, we love to hear &c" The people in general appeared to consider the word delivered, Glory to God for the same. Went from hence to Weddington[12] & began as before by singg.; preached from Matt 25.34th & 41st verses Come ye blessed & Go ye cursed &c. About the same number as at the last place were present but vastly different in appearance; levity appeared on the mind of many & those who were sober appeared not to be weighing the word in their minds. A person or two of respect however were an exception to these remarks. Went from hence to Isterton to friend Croaks who kindly refreshed me & got home about 11 o Clock havg. much reason to bless God for his causg. the different assemblies of the people during the day to be all free from opposition & blessg me with peace & comfort in the work. May the Lord abundantly bless the souls who have this day heard the Gospel from the lips of the most unworthy of His servants. Amen.

Expence

2 Turnpikes at Lavington	2d
1 afterwards	$\frac{1}{2}$
To a boy for holdg the horse during preachg	1
feedg the horse	6
	$9\frac{1}{2}$

As friend Whitmarsh of Ablington[13] was detained for me at Imber to supply in the evening[14] (he havg come on a friendly visit to unite with us in morng.) I gave him 1s/6d to defray his loss of time &c, he being a poor man & supports himself & family by his labour: he lives 12 or 13 miles from Imber.

friend Whitmarsh	1 - 6
Horse &c	$9\frac{1}{2}$
	2 - $3\frac{1}{2}$

16th July

Went from home a little before six in the morng., called on Mr Freeman of Rushsall[15] who desired me not to preach at Uphaven that morng. where I was going but go over & tell the people that I should preach at Rushsall (about a mile from Uphaven). Mr Freemans reasons were, he was informed by a person who heard the church minister appoint constables to apprehend me: I went over to Uphaven & talked to the people in the street for about half an hour, on the things of God but did not preach. I informed them I was going over immediately to Rushsall to preach where I did to about 3 or 4 score people. This place has a Baptist meeting house in it but the cause is very low indeed. Published preachg here again at 7 in the evening. At Mr Freeman's request went to Manningford, which place he said was very ignorant & preached in a common to about 80 people & from thence to Entford the place where the minister seized me a month before. Here my principle business was to get a house properly separated for worship. One Ann Carter[16] a widow a poor woman havg. a little house was disposed to devote it to the purpose of the worship of God. Having heard of her inclination before, carried paper which she signed & also five other persons. I read the scripture & enlarged as God gave me power; the people appeared desirous of hearing: about an hundred people were in & out of the house & all attentive. I returned from hence to Rushsall & preached in Mr Freeman's meeting house court to about 150 persons assembled from different parts, & then after refreshg myself at Mr Freemans returned home about 11 o'clock.

A comfortable day I experienced & hope the Ld. will raise the seed he enabled me to sow among the poor ignorant people who in general heard with attention

Expences		Texts	
Turnpike at Uphaven	1d	Rushsall in morng.	Rom 6:23
Feedg. horse at Uphaven &		Manningford	Jhn 3.36
horstler	6	Entford read pt of 23d psalm &	
Hay for the horse at Entford	2	enlarged	
A Glass of wine for myself	4	Rushsall in eveng	Heb 7.25
A feed of Corn for the horse		Cant recollect the exact time of	
at Rushsall	4	preachg but last a little after 7	
	1 - 5		

30th July

Set out a little before seven (it being wet early) & preached at Isterton to 40 or 50 people from Psm 8.4; then at Urchfont, at the house from Rev 20.6 for Mr Garrett on which account he preached at Imber at six in the evening. Dined with friend Giddens & went on for Cunk[17] where preached from Rom 1.16 to about 50 or 60 people; from thence to Churton[18] & preached from Mark 16.16 to 3 or 4 Score. Hitherto I had no interruption & the people in general seemed attentive. Went to Willsford & as we were singing (there being four of the Lavington &c. friends with me) Mr Hayward[19] the Constable of the hundred came up & insulted us with a person or two with him, insisted on our giving over or he would proceed to make us: he insisted on my not preachg in his hundred (swanborough). We gave off & the people were disappointed who came to hear peaceably. We told them if they would open a house we could licence it Free of all expence to them &c. – but could not find any one strong enough to bear such a cross. We next came to Marden where we had purposed to preach & there found a hundred people I suppose, but as this was in the constables hundred I did not preach but told them if they would open a house I would freely so do. Here we found a person of Patney who said we should have his house, we went to Patney & in the street saw a few people & began singing a hymn & then spoke to them of the things of God for a few minutes & went with this person to see his house; when at it the man had called to mind the consequences that were likely to ensue as his losg. his work &c he being a labourer & said he would consider about licensing his house as I asked him to sign his name for me to draw up an application to the bishop,[20] while we were there which was only a few minutes, a little company came up to his house some of whom were the farmers of the place; going away I ta[l]ked to them of the things of God & they did not seem offended but how the issue will be I dont know.

Went from this place to Weddington (had published to be there at 6 in the eveng.) & got there about half past six where was between 2 & 3 hundred people. As this was in swanborough hundred (& the constable before named seekg an opportunity against me) I told the people I should not preach but told them what we did preach about & so expatiated on the subjects we did preach on as the creation of man in the image of God, his fall & restoration by Christ – The people were all attentive. I told them they must open a house if I did come & preach there – There appears reason to conclude there will be a house opened in this place. Reached home a little before 11.

Expences

2 Turnpikes at Lavington	2d
Left the horse at Isterton & walked from place to place & found him very refreshg to ride home for I was much fatigued. The expence of the horse hire was	6d
Employed Henry Tinhams to be with my school in my absence	1 - 6
	2 - 2

Aug 13th

Preached at Rushall about half after ten to about 50 people from Ephes 2.8; at Entford in the licenced house from 1 Jhn 3.1 at half past one (purposed so but exceeded time a little) about 100 people within & without. spoke on the horse for about ¼ of an hour to 50 or 60 people at Haxon as was going down to Netherhaven: many of these & others from Entford &c went down to Netherhaven with me; One Thomas let me into his house where instructed the people by expatiating on such things as appeared to me to respect them; sung a hymn & promised to be there again the next sabbath, so left them; here were a great many people 100 or more within & without, some appeared to hear seriously & expressed themselves desirous of hearg. again. Returned to Rushall & preached in the meetg. court to the people as they could not conveniently all get into the meetg house. Text Rev. 20.6. Had promised to preach at 6 but exceeded a little. Got home about 10 & was during the day very comfortable. Glory to God for the same.

Expences

Myself	1d in beer at Entford
Horse	1 - 0
	1 - 1
Henry Tinhams wth. my boys	1 - 6
	2 - 7

Augst 20th

Being engaged by promise to be at Endford & Netherhaven to day & my wife being taken ill this morng & so improper for my leavg. the family, I sent a friend (H. Tinhams), to inform the people that I could not come: he went to prayer, sang & expounded the scripture &c; was well accepted, found it a very good day & returned home happy.[21]

The expence of the horse & himself   7½d

Augst. 26th[22]

Preach'd at Urchfont in the morng. from Phil 1.6 to a few people at the house set apart – Went on to Weddington & enquired respectg. a house; There seems a prospect of gettg. one but could not get persons to sign to day a Mrs Deane said we were welcome to a house of theirs in that place but the person livg. in it seem'd backward to sign for its being licenced; this business detained me some time here. Gave directions to some friends with one respectg. signg & they went to Hilcott & got two or three to sign. The owner of the house is a friend. Went from hence to Netherhaven, was detained some time in gettg persons to sign, but did one with the woman of the house & afterwds spoke to the people which were numerous but noisy. Named no text.

From this place went up to Endford & preached to a full house from Rom 8.1 Went from here to Rushall & preached to a good company for the place which is almost wholly deserted about 150 people were there I suppose; preached from 49 Psm 8 'The ridemn of soul is precious'. After being friendly accomodated by Mr Freeman returned home; the clock struck 11 as I was rubbing down the horse.

I havg desired Mr Freeman to get some oats for the horse paid him for the same & some gin ———— 1 - 6

I desired that a pint of cordial Gin might be gotten for me to take as I needed. I was both before & after sermon at Rushall in a perspiration; the places where I preached were full & very hot & my time between preachg very little indeed, so it was needful to take something of a hot kind.

Expences

Feedg horse at Netherhaven	5d
Puttg up horse & hay at Endford	3
a Glass peppermint water	2
Cunk Turnpike	$\frac{1}{2}$
Lavington turnpiks returng home it being dark travllg on the down	2
Oats as before observed some of which are yet for use	1 - 6
Henry Tinhams wth. my boys	1 - 6
	4 - 0$\frac{1}{2}$

Sepr 10th

Opened a house at Hilcott, a little company was there which seemed to hear wth. attention. Began about 11 o Clock. Before this service was a[t] Urchfont to get an application to the bishop, for a house at Wedhampton a place about a mile from Urchfont & considered to be in Urchfont parish. Got persons to sign it.

Preached at Netherhaven to many in the house lately licensed but very noisy in general, some few seemed to hear wh. attention.

Preached at Entford to many in the house, these people appear desirous of hearg. in general. Preached at Rushsall to a tolerable company in the eveng. the people appeared very attentive.

Expences

Horse at Netherhaven	6d
——— Entford	2
Myself at Entford	2
Turnpikes home at Lavington	2
Had corn at Rushall but was paid for before	
Henry wh. the boys	1 - 6
	2 - 6

Sep. 24

Preached in the morng. at Wedhampton & Hilcot. The people appear to hear attentively. Was at Endford & preached in the afternoon & at Netherhaven. The people behaved much better at Netherhaven than when there last. There appeared more to hear with attention – Yet many still of the noisy sort. All was well at Endford. I hope the Ld. will gather in souls in these places. In the eveng. preached at Rushall & Wedhampton. The people at Rushall appear to attend with some concern. I hope time will prove it so. At Wedhampton there were many more than in the morng. & very quiet. I was not exactly at the time appointed at all the places. The appointments were

Wedhampton	half past 8	in the morng	Rushall	5	Evening
Hilcot	half past 10	do.	Wedhampton	7	
Endford	half past 1½ afternoon		Was home about half past Eleven		
Netherhaven	3		o Clock. It was very dark & wet		

[The next leaf of the journal has been removed. The narrative resumes in the middle of a subsequent preaching excursion probably dated October 1st, 1797]

Mr Atkins, Shoemaker at Compton[23] near Endford appear'd with his father & his wife very friendly & ask'd me to his house, I called & was kindly treated. The Ld bless them, & dwell in them. Mr & Mrs Clifft of Hilcott were very friendly also. I dined there & last time also. The Ld gave me much of his presence today. Glory to his name.

Expences

Horse at Endford with 2d to		2 Turnpikes at Lavingn.	2d
Horstler	7d	Turnpike at Cunk	½
Netherhaven	6	Henry Tinhams wth. Boys	1 - 6
			3 - 11
pint Beer & Biscay	2½		
Feed Corn at Lavington comg		Monday Morng set shoes	
home being very wet &		for the horse	2. ——
horse hot	4	I ordered this. As I have	
horstler	1	used the shoes much I think	
Glass Wine	4	it right.	
To a boy in the day holdg.			
horse	2		

October 8

Preached in the morng at Wedhampton & Hilcott; in the afternoon at Endford & Netherhaven; the people here were many of them very attentive but many still unruly & noisy. I beg'd them much to be silent, used the kindest terms but it would not prevail with them; I went from preachg to talk to & intreat them but this would not do neither; then told them I must & would proceed against them legally for I was licenced & the house also & we would have order. This talking as I desired some of the friends to take notice of their names prevailed & we had silence afterwards tolerably well. They were not angry & I hope will be brought over to order without legal force. In the eveng I preached at Rushall & Wedhampton & got home a little before eleven. It was a cold eveng & took cold in my head which affects my hearing. Going out from a hot room into the cold over the down was I suppose the cause being by preachg worked into a perspiration, but I hope all will be well again soon. I found the Ld. good today.

Expences

Horse 2 feeds Standg & Horstlery	1s.
No Turnpike but Churton it being light & I	
went over the down	½
I ordered some Corn at Rushall for the	
horse & some Gin for me to take a little	
sometimes but did not pay for it now	
Henry Tinhams with the boys	1 - 6
	s.2 - 6½
Bought a Bridle for the Horse	5 - 6

The farmer's pleased him very well but as it broke with me & the horse sometime since threw me & it was by my hold (under the Ld) on the bridle that was the means of savg my life as my foot hung in the stirup I was fearful to ride with it.

Octob 22d

Preached at Netherhaven the morng. the noisey part was not there & had a comfortable opportunity for the first time. 50 people or upwards were there & very attentive.

Preached for the first time at Fifield[24] (a neighbourg. place) in the house lately lisensed: about 25 persons were there & attentive.

Preached at Endford at half past one & Rushall at a little after 4 & Wedhampton a little after 6 & returned home about 10.

Expences

	d.
Turnpikes	$2\frac{1}{2}$
Horse at Inn & Horsler	1 - 2
Paid for Oats to keep at Rushall	2 - 8
& for Gin	1 - 1
It was very cold wet & dark & thought	
it needful to have something at	
Lavington going home for I found	
myself in need & had a glass of	
brandy	4d
	$5 - 5\frac{1}{2}$
Henry Tinhams with the boys	1 - 6
	$6 .. 11\frac{1}{2}$

Nov 12th,

preached at Netherhaven in the morng about 9 o Clock at Fiddleton[25] a little before eleven & at Endford at half past one; was at Rushall in the afternoon but did not preach, I was not expected till next Sabbath by misapprehension of appointment. Was home about 8 o'Clock.

Expences

	s	d
Horse & Turnpikes	1 -	$5\frac{1}{2}$
Henry Tinhams with the Boys	1 -	6
	2 -	$11\frac{1}{2}$
paid for a Bushel of Oats to		
be kept at Netherhaven at		
the House where the		
preachg is	3	
	5 -	$11\frac{1}{2}$

Novr 26

Preached at Netherhaven at Fiddleton & Endford. Was home before seven. The weather was very wet & was wet but did not take cold.

175

Expences

Horse at Endford	3d
Turnpike at Cunk	$\frac{1}{2}$
Henry Tinhams with Boys	1 - 6
	1 - 9$\frac{1}{2}$

The man at Netherhaven at whose house the preachg is has need of relief from the Parish but they refuse helpg him except he refuses me his house. The poor man does not seem to know how to act; he likes for the preachg to be there & so does his wife but natures wants press them: how it will be I do not know. may the Ld open the hearts of the parish & give grace to these poor souls to enable them to bear suffering if called to it for his gospel. I wish friends were to support such persons who suffer loss for the Gospel in this respect: this would encourage the Gospel & be a means of spreadg. it.

10th Decr

One of the scholars being ill could not go myself to Endford &c – so sent H. Tinhams who engaged in prayer singing &c at the several places & found it good to be there. The expences attending him & the horse were 2s——

24 Decr

was at Netherhaven, Fifield & Entford

Expences   6d.

Janry 6, 1798

H. Tinhams carried up a Window to put in a poor mans House who proposed giving up his house for the Gospel & wanted a window to make it fit: This window, I having some old glass by me I put in a frame & sent it by H. Tinhams who stayed the Sabbath & found much of the Lords presence with the people: he was at Netherhaven Fifield & Endford: the people receive his Exhortation very well.

His Expences   1s - 6d

The poor man who opens his house at Netherhaven suffers much from the farmers because he opens his house for the gospel & on this account I accepted the other poor mans offer: but this house is very inconvenient & the other very commodious. Poor Tommas the man of the house at Netherhaven does not put me away, but says he will bear all but my feelings were much affected at hearing he earned only 2s..9d in the week at Stonepickg being turned out of his common work on the gospels account, & six or 7 persons in family & all wantg bread. I wish those who have ability would consider such cases & support such poor sufferers. Alas too many live in delicacy & spend much needlessly!!!

Jan 20th[26]
Preachd at Netherhaven, Fifield & Entford

Expences	6d	} 2 - 6
H. Tinhams being with the Boys	1 - 6	

Paid 2s..6d for repairg the windows at the house at Netherhaven wch. were broken by the opposers

Feby 4th
Being desired to go to Tisbury (Mr Morley the minister being out raising money by begging for the Lord's cause) sent H. Tinhams up to Netherhaven, Fifield & Entford.

Expences   9d

Feb 18th
Was at Tisbury & Henry Tinhams was at Endford & the other places.

Expences   1s

March 4th
Was at Netherhaven Fifield & Endford. The Cause appears to flourish, I trust many are seeking the Lord. Instead of the prophane songs which were sung sometime past, Watt's hymns now are adopted by many of the inhabitants of Endford. Most evenings assemblies are formed in different parts to learn to sing the hymns by those whose hearts I trust are touched by the Lord. Glory to his great name for the appearance of so much good done by the word as is to be seen here

Expences   1s..5d

March 18th
Sent H. Tinhams to Endford Netherhaven & Fifield – being called to go to Tisbury

Expences   1s..1d

April 1st
Being called to go to Corsham sent friend Tinhams to Endford Netherhaven & Fifield

Expences	6d	} 2 - 6
A set of shoes for the Horse	2 ____	

Expences during the whole of the former account:

June 18th	£0- 1-11		Brot. forwd.	£2..14.. 5
July 2d	0.. 2.. 3½		March 4	0.. 1.. 5
July 16	1.. 5		18	-.. 1.. 1
30th	2.. 2		April 1	-.. 2.. 6
Augst 13th	2.. 7		for a Boy who looks	
20th	7½		after the horse	-.. 6
26th	4.. 0½			2 19..11
Septr 10th	2.. 6		Paid house rent for	
24	5..11		preachg at Endford	
October 8	5.. 6		33 Weeks	£3..15.. -
October 22	6..11½			£6..14..11
Nov 12	5..11½		Mr Saffry paid the whole of	
26	1.. 9½		the above	
Decr 10	2.. -		April 3d, 1798	
24	-.. 6		T Wastfield	
1798 Jany 6	1.. 6		Brought Forward	£6-14-11
21	2.. 6		Registering Seven	
for repairg			Houses for Preaching	
Windows at			in different Villages	0-17- 6
Netherhaven	2.. 6			7-12- 5
Feb 4	- 9			
18	1 -			
	2-14.. 5			

[There follows an explanatory letter appended by John Saffery, pastor of Salisbury Baptist church, written to the sponsoring body, the Baptist Missionary Society.]

The Society (or at least Bror. Fuller)[27] will remember when we first proposed the Itinerancy of Mr Wastfield it was suggested his expences may amount to 10/6 pr week on acct. of Horse hire but by the foregoing acct. it will be seen the whole is much beneath that sum. – There was no Horse to be hired in the Village of Imber, nor nearer yn. Warminster (6 Miles) which threw a considerable difficulty in the way both as to Inconvenience & expence but we prevailed on a Farmer at Imber related to him to lend his Horse which he has continued to do & saved that expence.

His own expences are very trifeling, sometimes under 1/ when he has travelled at least 30 Miles & preached 6 or 7 times. The Parish of Endford used to allow the old Woman where the preaching is 2/ pr Week, but on her admiting him they would do it no longer, this was continued 15 Weeks, in which time Mr Wastfield applied to a Justice who is friendly to religion, who wrote to the overseers but in vain, & he cd. not compel them <u>because the House is her own.</u>

She then attended a Meeting of Justices & laid her complaint before them having nothing to subsist on, but they did nothing but ridicule, & refuse to make any order for an allowance – said the Parson must keep her if she took him in, but if she wd turn him out they wd order her 2/6 pr Week instead of 2/ This she was unwilling to do & since that Wastfield has given her 2/6 – I know the Bishops Register cd. demand but 6d for Registering the Houses, but long before I came here it has been the custom both by the Baptists & Independants to give 2/6 Applications from the whole Diocess came to us, & I suppose the best part of a 100 has been made within these two Years, & were we to refuse giving them their usual fee, it wd perhaps create considerable difficulties & place us (as constantly going to the office) in an awkward situation[28] – Henry Tinhams of whom mention is made so frequently is a Member of Bratton Church, liveing at Imber a very godly man. The reason of his sending him has been either thro' personal or relative affliction, or his having been called to supply Churches – I hope this will not be so frequent in future – Some places at first visited by him he has since declined. He has prevailed on a person of Pottern near Devizes who preaches occasionally, to Preach regularly at Wedhampton, as it was very inconvenient for him to continue it – At Hilcott after Registering a House, our good Independant Fds at Devizes took very unfriendly steps in prevailing with the man in whose House the Preaching is, to get rid of Wastfield, & take them in, & succeeded – W____ says (& he has a wonderful deal of Candour & liberality) it is because he is a Baptist. Perhaps it may be. However they are entered into another mans labors, I hear are building a small Meeting there & the prospect is pleasing – His labors at present are confined chiefly to Endford & it's Neighborhood (Netherhaven, Compton, Fifield &c) As to his success I can say nothing from any personal acquaintance with the places or people – They are 15 or 16 Miles from us, & I have had so many engagements nearer home that I have not yet been able to visit them, but hope to do it in 2 or 3 Weeks. But from all I can learn not only from him but others, appearances are very pleasing – The opposition fm ye Farmers &c is great, but a spirit of hearing prevails, & <u>many seem</u> concerned about their souls – I find Mr Freeman of Rushall (mentioned in the preceeding Journal) Baptized four of them a week or two since, & W____ asures me he has every reason to think they are real Believers – One of them has offered a piece of ground to build a Meeting & wished me to engage in it – But as I have not yet been with them, can say nothing as to the propriety of this – I have had so much to do with this at home & at Shrewton, & the times are so much agst it that I feel but little disposed to engage in such a matter at present – When it's considered that <u>none</u> of these places had the gospel before, the Society will not think the above £7–12–5 Ill bestowed – No man in the world I believe has his heart more set upon the

Saln. of men, & none will labor & live harder to promote it. His exertions has very much injured his health thro' the Winter, & tho' I persuaded him to relax a little & be more careful, there is no holding him in – He is now much better than he has been

I have told him I wd continue to pay his expences 'till the Society sd order me to desist – If possable intend to get a House at Endford without expence. Shall not have so much (at least in those places) to pay for Registering Houses; & he hopes to do without paying H. Tinhams 1/6 a day for looking after his Boys, at least for some time to come – But shall be glad to be guided by the Society.

Would submit the propriety of making him some small recompence He has nothing to depend for the Maintenance of himself, Wife, & I think six small Children but his School which is not large (about 14 Boys) I know he has not the most distant idea or wish the Society sd give him any thing (He even did not expect the £3–15–0 for the House rent but intended paying it himself, this I wd not suffer knowing he cd not afford it) I cannot say what it wd be proper to give him for the 12 Months but as he must wear his Clothes pretty much sd think 2 or 3 Guineas wd not be too much But as he expects Nothing, the Society* are quite at liberty to judge respecting it, whether proper to make him an allowance or not.

We have not been able to make up the Accts of the H & W Society[29] yet, hope to do it in two or three weeks, when I will remit to Mr King – Hope it will be nearly as much as last year exclusive of what I have paid Wastfield – Tho' we have called it the H & W Assisstt Society only 7 Churches in both Counties belong to it, & several of these are in the most miserable situation one or two we rece nothing from, & from some of the rest not more than one or two Guineas a Year – A little we recd from Portsea, but Bror Pearce[30] prevented us from haveing any from that quarter this year am glad he collected so much there –

I fear the removal of our dear Bror Steadman[31] will be a loss to the Society as well as the Neighborhood – Hope to be enabled to do what I can to keep alive Missionary exertions in this quarter, but fear I shall stand almost alone – Will thank the Society to direct to me if necessary to write to the H & W Sociy in future, as they have appointed me Secretary & Bror Bain of Downton, Treasurer –

J. Saffery Sarum
April 21. 1798

Shall be glad to have a parcel of Appendix's to No 4 sent soon as possable

*I think he well deserves more

Notes

1 Imber was an isolated downland settlement on the Salisbury Plain, 16 miles north-west of the city of Salisbury. The village was evacuated in 1943 for military purposes.
2 Upavon.
3 Enford.

4 In the period 1797–8 the Vicar of Enford was John Prince. His curate was William Gray.
5 Haxton.
6 Netheravon.
7 Probably Figheldean rather than Fittleton.
8 Easterton.
9 Charlton.
10 Marden.
11 Wilsford.
12 Wedhampton.
13 A small hamlet near Figheldean.
14 It appears from this remark that Thomas Wastfield may have acted as the lay leader of a small group of Dissenters at Imber in addition to his duties as a schoolmaster.
15 Rushall.
16 According to the Enford Baptismal and Burial Register an inhabitant named Ann Carter was buried on 7 February 1800.
17 Conock, a hamlet between Wedhampton and Chirton.
18 Chirton.
19 Possibly John Hayward who is mentioned with his wife Ann in Wilsford Baptismal Register.
20 Under the terms of the statute 1 William and Mary c.18, commonly termed the Toleration Act, the meeting-houses of Protestant Dissenters were required to be registered either with the diocesan authorities or at the local quarter sessions.
21 According to the Imber Marriage Register Henry Tinhams of Imber married Betty Mead of the same parish in March 1780 both marking a cross by way of signature, the ceremony being conducted by the curate, Lewis Joncs. In the same register an entry dated 26 December 1785 records the marriage of Thomas Wastfield and Hannah Scammell, both residents of Imber. Wastfield and Scammell, unlike the earlier couple, signed their names in firm, educated handwriting. Among the relatives of Wastfield's wife was one whose occupation is described in the register as that of 'yeoman'.
22 If this entry refers to a Sunday the date should be 27 August 1797.
23 An independent artisan living in an outlying hamlet: two of the factors which encouraged the spread of evangelical Dissent.
24 A hamlet situated midway between Enford and Netheravon.
25 Probably Fittleton.
26 If this entry refers to a Sunday the date should be 21 January 1798.
27 Andrew Fuller, pastor of the Baptist church at Kettering, Northamptonshire and secretary of the Baptist Missionary Society from its inception until his death in 1815.
28 These remarks provide independent confirmation of the surge in Dissenting activity which prompted Bishop John Douglas to voice his anxiety in August 1798 during his third triennial visitation of the Salisbury diocese.
29 The Hants and Wiltshire Society for Propagating the Gospel among the Heathen formed in Aid of the Society instituted for the same purpose at Kettering in Northamptonshire Oct 2, 1792 [Baptist Missionary Society].
30 Samuel Pearce, pastor of Cannon Street Baptist church, Birmingham and an active supporter of the Baptist Missionary Society.
31 William Steadman, pastor of the Baptist church at Broughton, Hampshire. Steadman moved to Plymouth Dock in June 1798 to become assistant minister to Isaiah Birt.

Calvinistic Dissenting organizations active in itinerant evangelism between 1780 and 1830

These are arranged as far as possible in chronological order. The dates listed denote the first recorded employment of itinerancy. The use of an asterisk indicates an earlier foundation for the society itself. The list, which for the most part excludes Dissenting academies and local church-based itineran-cies, should not be regarded as definitive. A number of factors make the compilation of a complete record impossible. In many cases the precise denominational composition of a body is unknown. Societies appeared, evolved and lapsed with little warning, their titles being quoted in ephemeral religious publications and in manuscript sources with scant regard for the precision desired by the historian. A number of groups were, moreover, merely local auxiliaries of national organizations.

Whitefield's Connexion
Rodborough Connexion
Countess of Huntingdon's Connexion
Baptist Western Association (1775)*
Northamptonshire Baptist Association (1775–79)*
Societas Evangelica (1776/revitalized 1796)
Kent Congregational Association (1792)
North Staffordshire and Shropshire Independent Association (1793)
Warwickshire Independent Association (1793)
Baptist Midland Association (1785)*: Society for the Promotion of Village
    Preaching (1794)
Particular Baptist Society for Propagating the Gospel amongst the Heathen
    (1795)*
County Union [Cambridgeshire] (1795)
Dorset Missionary and Itinerant Society (1795) [later known as the Dorset
    Congregational Association]
Ebenezer Itinerant Society, Chatham (not in existence before 1794)
Essex Baptist Association (1796)
Salop Independent Association (1796)
Somerset Independent Association (1796)
Village Itinerancy (1796)
Bedfordshire Union of Christians (1797)

Baptist Society in London, for the Encouragement and Support of Itinerant and Village Preaching (1797) [from 1821 known as the Baptist Home Missionary Society]
Congregational Society for Spreading the Gospel in England (1797)
Hampshire Association of Protestant Dissenting Ministers (1797)
Hants and Wiltshire Auxiliary Society for Propagating the Gospel among the Heathen (1797)
Kent and Sussex Association of Baptist Churches (1797)*
London Itinerant Society (1797)
Reading Evangelical Society for Village Preaching (1797)
Surrey Mission (1797)
Warwickshire Union of Christians (1797)
Wilts and East Somerset Independent Association (1797)
Essex Congregational Union (1798)
Evangelical Association for propagating the Gospel in the Villages of Cumberland, Durham, Northumberland and Westmoreland (1798)
Union of Ministers in the Eastern Division of Kent (1798)
Union of Independent and Baptist Ministers in the Western Division of Kent (1798)
Association of Congregational Ministers in Lancashire, Cheshire and Derbyshire (1798)/Lancashire Itinerant Society (1801)/Lancashire Congregational Union (1806)
Union Society of Greenwich (fl.1799)
Worcestershire and Herefordshire Union and Association (1799)
Cornwall Association of Congregational Churches (1802)
Association for Spreading the Gospel in Worcestershire and Staffordshire (fl.1805)
Cambridgeshire Society for Promoting Religious Knowlege (1806)
Cheshire Congregational Union (1806)
Evangelical Society (formed at Launceston 1806)
Hoxton Itinerant Society (fl.1806)
Shropshire and Cheshire Baptist Association (1806)
Devon Union (1808)
London Baptist Itinerant Preachers Society (1809)
Sussex Mission (fl.1809)
Hertfordshire Union (1810)
Gloucester Evangelistic Mission (fl.1810)
Northern Baptist Itinerant Society (1810)
Bristol Itinerant Society (1811)
Bucks and Herts Particular Baptist Association (1811)
Norfolk and Suffolk Association of Baptist Churches (fl.1811)
Itinerant Society for the West Riding of Yorkshire (1811)

Cornwall Baptist Association (1812)
Cumberland Association (fl.1812)
Zion Itinerant Society (dissolved in 1812)
London Association for Extending the Knowledge of the Gospel in the
    Metropolis (1813)
Oxfordshire and East Gloucestershire Baptist Association (fl.1813)
Holderness Itinerancy (fl.1814)
South Devon Itinerancy (1814)
Westmorland Congregational Union (fl.1815)
Carlisle Association for Three Counties (fl.1816)
East Devon Itinerancy (fl.1817)
Independent North Devon Association (1817)
Suffolk Association of Dissenting Ministers and Churches of the Indepen-
    dent Denomination (1817)
North Bucks Association of Independent Ministers and Churches (1818)
Home Missionary Society (1819)
Association of Independent Ministers for the Isle of Ely and the Southern
    parts of Lincolnshire (1820)
Durham and Northumberland Association of Congregational Ministers and
    Churches (1823)
Sussex Congregational Society (1823)
Bristol Baptist Itinerant Society (1824)
Independent Itinerant Society for East Sussex (1825)
East Essex Union (fl.1829)
North East Cambridge Christian Instruction Society (fl.1830)
Buckingham Christian Instruction Society (1830)
Newport Pagnell Christian Instruction Society (1830)
Olney Christian Instruction Society (fl.1830)

Baptismal statistics for the Midland, Northamptonshire and Western Baptist regional associations, 1770–1830

Year	Midland Association			Northamptonshire Association			Western Association		
	Associated churches	Baptisms	Baptisms per church	Associated churches	Baptisms	Baptisms per church	Associated churches	Baptisms	Baptisms per church
1770		35		12	89[a]			75	
1771		28					29	44	1.5
1772		38		14	48[a]		29	110	3.8
1773		43					32	150	4.7
1774		73					31	122	3.9
1775		90					33	97	2.9
1776		38		16	69[a]		30	121[a]	4.0
1777		35		17	56	3.3	29	58	2.0
1778		55		17	59	3.5	31	131	4.2
1779		38		17	75	4.4	36	85	2.4
1780	14	28	2.0	17	75	4.4	34	55	1.6
1781	16	54	3.4	16	59	3.7	34	61	1.8
1782		65		16	39	2.4	33	61	1.8
1783	18	55	3.1	16	24	1.5	33	101	3.1
1784		51		16	31	1.9	34	103	3.0
1785	17	69	4.1	16	25	1.6	34	114	3.4
1786	16	86	5.4	19	72	3.8	36	181	5.0
1787		59		22	79	3.6	38	186	4.9
1788		76		22	116	5.3	37	191	5.2
1789		98		22	95	4.3	39	165	4.2
1790	17	98	5.8	23	75	3.3	37	166	4.5
1791	14	75	5.4	23	101	4.4	37	176	4.8
1792	14	75	5.4	24	73	3.0	39	131	3.4
1793	18	87	4.8	25	88	3.5	39	100	2.6
1794	20	98	4.9	23	83	3.6	37	132	3.6
1795		61		24	128	5.3	41	88	2.1
1796		107		24[b]	139	5.8	42	161	3.8
1797		104		21[b]	122	5.8	41	190	4.6
1798	18	131	7.3	24	88	3.7	40	197	4.9
1799							41	158	3.9
1800				22	76	3.5	40	203	5.1
1801	22			22	101	4.6	45	225	5.0
1802		102		24	85	3.5	47	268	5.7

Year	Midland Association			Northamptonshire Association			Western Association		
	Associated churches	Baptisms	Baptisms per church	Associated churches	Baptisms	Baptisms per church	Associated churches	Baptisms	Baptisms per church
1803				24	36	1.5	48	267	5.6
1804		66		24	51	2.1	47	258	5.5
1805	24	112	4.7	24	116	4.8	47	296	6.3
1806		74		27	146	5.4	48	284	5.9
1807		119		27^c	119	4.4	49	316	6.4
1808	24	174	7.2	28	144	5.1	52	412	7.9
1809	22	89	4.0	29	101	3.5	54	331	6.1
1810	21	130	6.2	31	122	3.9	55	364	6.6
1811	21	148	7.0	31	183	5.9	55	304	5.5
1812	20	53	2.6	29^d	101	3.3	60	399	6.6
1813	23	114	5.0	31	159	5.5	63	471	7.5
1814	26	78	3.0	31	112	3.6	63	448	7.1
1815		129		31	185	6.0	68	448	6.6
1816	30	225	7.5	31	137	4.4	70	578	8.3
1817	27	170	6.3	33^e	165	5.0	74	507	6.9
1818		104		33^f	160	4.8	78	462	5.9
1819		211		34	153	4.5	77	397	5.2
1820	27	190	7.0	31^g	134	4.3	77	327	4.2
1821		149		33^h	125	3.8	78	369	4.7
1822		233					78	391	5.0
1823	29	187	6.4	33^i	115	3.5	78^i	325	4.2
1824	32	173	5.4	34	146	4.3	24^j	113^j	4.7^j
1825		131		36	108	3.0	26	75	2.9
1826		159		36	113	3.1	26	105	4.0
1827		264					27	91	3.4
1828		112					31	108	3.5
1829		171		36	235	6.5	34	124	3.6
1830		207		37^k	187	5.1	37	238	6.4

a including those received by letter of
dismission from other churches
b three churches not included
c one church not included
d two churches not included

e one church not included
f one church not included
g three churches not included
h one church not included

i one church not included
j new and smaller Western Association
created by division of existing body
k one church not included

Sources: Annual circular letters of the Midland, Northamptonshire and Western associations; J. Rippon (ed.), *Baptist Annual Register*; W. Stokes, *History of the Midland Association of Baptist Churches* (1855); Ms Account of the state of the churches belonging to the Baptist association in the West of England

Notes

1 The Established Church and England Separatism

1 H. Gee and W. J. Hardy (eds.), *Documents illustrative of English Church History compiled from original sources* (London, 1921), p. 587.
2 J. Lecler, *Toleration and the Reformation*, trans. T. L. Westow (2 vols., London, 1960), vol. 2, pp. 387–95. For a more positive assessment of the progress towards religious toleration under the later Tudor monarchy see W. K. Jordan, *The Development of Religious Toleration in England* (4 vols., London, 1932–40), vol. 1, pp. 159–62, 233–8.
3 J. Bossy, *The English Catholic Community 1570–1850* (London, 1975), pp. 121–5, 183.
4 Gee and Hardy, *Documents*, pp. 460–1, 463.
5 M. R. Watts, *The Dissenters From the Reformation to the French Revolution* (Oxford, 1978), pp. 15–16; P. Collinson, 'England and international Calvinism 1558–1640' in M. Prestwich (ed.) *International Calvinism 1541–1715* (Oxford, 1985), p. 210.
6 Gee and Hardy, *Documents*, pp. 468–71.
7 Gee and Hardy, *Documents*, pp. 492–5. In the case of convicted clerics 'benefit of clergy' had come to operate as a first offender's law, with the culprit escaping punishment where there was no previous conviction. T. F. T. Plucknett, *A Concise History of the Common Law*, 3rd edn (London, 1940), p. 18.
8 B. R. White, *The English Separatist Tradition from the Marian Martyrs to the Pilgrim Fathers* (London, 1971), pp. 86–90.
9 I. B. Horst, *The Radical Brethren Anabaptism and the English Reformation to 1558* (Nieuwkoop, 1972), pp. 49–58; D. Plumb, 'The social and economic spread of rural Lollardy: a reappraisal' in W. J. Sheils and D. Wood (eds.), *Studies in Church History*, 23 (1986), 111–29; Watts, *Dissenters*, pp. 7–14, 283–4.
10 The change was accomplished through a series of important statutes, namely: Act in Restraint of Appeals, 1533 (24 Hen. VIII, c. 12); Act in Absolute Restraint of Annates and concerning the Election of Bishops, 1534 (25 Hen. VIII, c. 20); Act forbidding Papal Dispensations and Payment of Peter's Pence, 1534 (25 Hen. VIII, c. 21); Act of Supremacy, 1534 (26 Hen. VIII, c. 1). A. G. Dickens and D. Carr (eds.), *The Reformation in England to the Accession of Elizabeth I* (London, 1967), pp. 55–65.
11 Watts, *Dissenters*, p. 14.
12 P. Collinson, *The Elizabethan Puritan Movement* (London, 1967), pp. 27–8, 101–6, 297–302; H. Davies, *The English Free Churches*, 2nd edn (London, 1963), pp. 29–31.
13 Watts, *Dissenters*, pp. 72–4; White, *English Separatist Tradition*, pp. 83–6.
14 Watts, *Dissenters*, pp. 285–9.
15 Watts, *Dissenters*, pp. 110–18, 132–4, 188–9; H. J. McLachlan, *Socinianism in Seventeenth-Century England* (London, 1951), pp. 187–95.
16 Jordan, *Development of Religious Toleration*, vol. 3, pp. 159–60, 451.
17 Watts, *Dissenters*, pp. 218–20, 260, 290; R. T. Jones, *Congregationalism in England 1662–1962* (London, 1962), pp. 105–7.

18 An Act for exempting Their Majesties Protestant Subjects, dissenting from the Church of England, from the Penalties of certain Laws (1 W. and M., c. 18), Sections VII–VIII, XVIII.

19 *A Sketch of the History and Proceedings of the Deputies Appointed to Protect the Civil Rights of the Protestant Dissenters. To which is annexed a Summary of the Laws affecting Protestant Dissenters with an Appendix of Statutes and Precedents of Legal Instruments* (London, 1814), pp. 27–9.

20 1 W. and M., c. 18, Section XVI.

21 The body which came to be known as the Protestant Dissenting Deputies was formed in 1732 at a gathering of lay Dissenters at Silver Street Meeting-house in London. The original purpose of the organization, to press for the repeal of the Test and Corporation Acts, was subsequently extended to the safeguarding of existing civil rights enjoyed by Dissenters. From 1736 each Baptist, Independent and Presbyterian congregation situated within ten miles of the metropolis was entitled to elect deputies annually from whom a standing committee was drawn. Although London-based, the Deputies showed a willingness to pursue provincial interests, and so became an important vehicle for the expression of Dissenting views on matters of civil and religious concern. See B. L. Manning, *The Protestant Dissenting Deputies*, ed. O. Greenwood (Cambridge, 1952).

22 Arian and Socinian ideas made considerable headway during the eighteenth century among Presbyterian and General Baptist ministers.

23 For example the high Calvinist views of John Gill and John Brine, two prominent London Particular Baptist ministers.

24 G. F. Nuttall, 'Northamptonshire and *The Modern Question*: a turning-point in eighteenth-century Dissent', *Journal of Theological Studies*, n.s.16 (1965), 101–23.

25 The Caroline divines were a group of prominent theologians and leaders within the Church of England whose writings were influential in restoring a traditional Catholic emphasis in the face of strong Presbyterian opposition. Their number included such figures as Richard Hooker (1554?–1600), Lancelot Andrewes (1555–1626), Jeremy Taylor (1613–67) and Herbert Thorndike (1598–1672).

26 R. R. Palmer, *Catholics and Unbelievers in Eighteenth Century France* (Princeton, 1939), pp. 3–7.

27 M.D.V.*** [Monsieur de Voltaire], *Lettres écrites de Londres sur les Anglois et autres sujets* (Basle, 1734), pp. 41–3.

28 J. H. Newman *et al.*, *Tracts for the Times* (5 vols., London, 1834–40), vol. 1, Tract 2, pp. 1–2; J. H. Newman, *Apologia Pro Vita Sua Being a history of his religious opinions*, ed. M. J. Svaglic (Oxford, 1967), pp. 24–5, 46, 50.

29 W. Warburton, *The Alliance between Church and State: or, The Necessity and Equity of an Established Religion and a Test Law, demonstrated from the essence and end of Civil Society, upon the fundamental principles of the Law of Nature and Nations* (London, 1736), p. 53.

30 N. Sykes, *Church and State in England in the XVIIIth Century* (Cambridge, 1934), p. 321; R. A. Soloway, *Prelates and People Ecclesiastical Social Thought in England 1783–1852* (London, 1969), p. 9. For a concise discussion of the theory and practice of Church-State relations in the early part of the eighteenth century see G. F. A. Best, *Temporal Pillars Queen Anne's Bounty, the Ecclesiastical Commissioners, and the Church of England* (Cambridge, 1964), pp. 35–46.

31 F. Atterbury, *A Letter to a Convocation-Man concerning the Rights, Powers, and Priviledges of that body* (1697); W. Wake, *The Authority of Christian princes over their ecclesiastical synods asserted; with particular respect to the Convocations of the clergy of the*

Realm and Church of England; occasioned by a late pamphlet intituled, A letter to a Convocation man (London, 1697).

32 Sykes, *Church and State*, pp. 285–7.
33 Sykes, *Church and State*, p. 310.
34 Sykes, *Church and State*, pp. 49–50.
35 R. K. Webb, *Modern England From the Eighteenth Century to the Present* (London, 1969), p. 50.
36 C. J. Abbey and J. H. Overton, *The English Church in the Eighteenth Century* (2 vols., London, 1878), vol. 2, p. 33.
37 Sykes, *Church and State*, p. 362.
38 Best, *Temporal Pillars*, pp. 46–7.
39 Sykes, *Church and State*, pp. 206–11.
40 Best, *Temporal Pillars*, pp. 29–31; Sykes, *Church and State*, pp. 226–7.
41 From the visitation records of Bishops Butler and Moss in the Oxford diocese it is possible to detect between 1778 and 1808 a lowering of standards with respect to clerical residence and to the performance of parochial duty. D. McClatchey, *Oxfordshire Clergy 1777–1869 A study of the Established Church and of the role of its Clergy in local society* (Oxford, 1960), pp. 31–2.
42 Norfolk CRO. VIS/35.
43 The returns examined concerned the parishes of: (Norfolk) Bunwell, Diss, Garboldisham, Kenninghall, Scole, South Lopham (Suffolk) Aldeburgh, Aldringham, Badingham, Benhall Street, Blythburgh, Bramfield, Chediston, Clare, Cransford, Cratfield, Great Bealings, Halesworth, Hintlesham, Horham, Hoxne, Kersey, Laxfield, Little Bealings, Mildenhall, Peasenhall, Rendham, Rumburgh, Saxmundham, Shelley, Southwold, Stoke Ash, Stradbroke, Syleham, Thrandeston, Walpole, Wenhaston, Westleton, Wetheringsett, Wickham Market, Wissett. Included in the figure for parishes having no curate is one case where parish affairs were in the hands of a sequestrator. In 1809 Arthur Young reported from Oxfordshire that the winter wage of an agricultural worker on the estate of the Rector of Lower Heyford amounted to 9s. per week. A. Young, *View of the Agriculture of Oxfordshire* (London, 1809), p. 321.
44 Norfolk CRO. VIS/35d. The modern spelling of Snetherton is Snetterton.
45 Dr McClatchey argues that the factors which caused non-residence also contributed to niggardly Sunday duty. McClatchey, *Oxfordshire Clergy*, p. 83.
46 Norfolk CRO. VIS/35a.
47 Norfolk CRO. VIS/35e. Blayney lived in London where he held an appointment as morning preacher at King Street Chapel, St James's, Westminster.
48 Cheshire CRO. EDV 7/1/191.
49 McClatchey, *Oxfordshire Clergy*, p. 21.
50 W. R. Ward, 'The tithe question in England in the early nineteenth century', *Journal of Ecclesiastical History*, 16 (1965), 72.
51 McClatchey, *Oxfordshire Clergy*, p. 109.
52 Cheshire CRO. EDV 7/1/191.
53 The Vicar of Leigh reported thirteen celebrations during the course of the year. By contrast Colne chapelry in the parish of Whalley reported at the 1804 visitation that communion was celebrated at Christmas, Good Friday, Easter and Michaelmas. Cheshire CRO. EDV 7/1/191, EDV 7/3/131.
54 In 1811 Edmund Gibson, Curate of the chapelry of Ashton in Makerfield, reported his duties as extending over an area of 20 square miles encompassing 24 villages with 855 houses and a total population of 5,000. Gibson, who was resident and who appears from his returns to have served his cure with exemplary diligence, reported a

mere 25 communicants in spite of the presence in the chapelry of 715 Roman Catholics and 137 Methodists and Dissenters of varying description. Cheshire CRO. EDV 7/4/6.

2 Itinerancy and Dissent

1 E. Halévy, *A History of the English People in 1815*, trans. E. I. Watkin and D. A. Barker (London, 1924), pp. 365–70.

2 D. J. Jeremy, 'A local crisis between Establishment and Nonconformity: the Salisbury village preaching controversy, 1798–1799', *Wiltshire Archaeological and Natural History Magazine*, 61 (1966), 63–84.

3 G. F. Nuttall, *The Significance of Trevecca College, 1768–91* (London, 1968).

4 R. J Carwardine, *Transatlantic Revivalism. Popular Evangelicalism in Britain and America, 1790–1865* (Westport, 1978).

5 Denominational journals also provide an important forum for Dissenting scholarship yet even in these publications itinerancy has not attracted much attention.

6 O. C. Robison, 'The Particular Baptists in England, 1760–1820', Oxford, D.Phil. thesis, 1963, pp. 95–106; P. E. Sangster, 'The life of the Rev. Rowland Hill (1744–1833) and his position in the Evangelical Revival', Oxford, D.Phil. thesis, 1965, esp. pp. 47–76.

7 T. W. Davis, 'Conflict and concord among Protestant Dissenters in London, 1787 to 1813', North Carolina, Ph.D. thesis, 1972; N. U. Murray, 'The influence of the French Revolution on the Church of England and its rivals, 1789–1802', Oxford, D.Phil. thesis, 1975.

8 R. H. Martin, 'Evangelical Dissenters and Wesleyan-style itinerant ministries at the end of the eighteenth century', *Methodist History*, 16 (1978), 169–84.

9 Two examples of Calvinistic Methodist congregations moving into independency are the Plymouth and Rodborough Tabernacles, which called their first ordained ministers in 1763 and 1778 respectively. See C. E. Welch, 'Andrew Kinsman's churches at Plymouth', *Transactions of the Devonshire Association*, 97 (1965), 228–9; C. E. Watson, *The Story of Rodborough Tabernacle* (Stroud, n.d., [ca. 1927]), p. 23. The first minister at Rodborough, Jehoiada Brewer, left the Countess of Huntingdon's Connexion to the considerable annoyance of his benefactress. Another prominent defector to independency was the former minister of the Countess's chapel at Wigan, William Roby.

10 N. S. Moon, 'Caleb Evans, founder of the Bristol Education Society', *Baptist Quarterly*, n.s. 24 (1971–2), 177–9; G. F. Nuttall, 'Questions and answers: an eighteenth-century correspondence', *Baptist Quarterly*, n.s. 27 (1977–8), 89.

11 R. Burls, *A Brief Review of the Plan and Operations of the Essex Congregational Union for Promoting the Knowledge of the Gospel in the County of Essex and its Vicinity. With an Appendix, containing Biographical Notices of the Principal Founders and Supporters of the Society* (Maldon, 1848), pp. 37–103.

12 Bossy, *English Catholic Community*, pp. 251–4.

13 H. Jephson, *The Platform Its Rise and Progress* (2 vols., London, 1892); E. M. Howse, *Saints in Politics The 'Clapham Sect' and the Growth of Freedom* (London, 1953), pp. 41–2, 163, 180–3; N. McCord, *The Anti-Corn Law League 1838–1846* (London, 1958), pp. 175–80, 187.

14 R. W. Dale, *History of English Congregationalism*, ed. A. W. W. Dale (London, 1907), p. 588.

15 F. Buffard, *Kent and Sussex Baptist Associations* (n.d. [ca. 1963]), p. 52.

16 W. Roby, *Anti-Swedenborgianism: or, a Letter to the Rev. J. Clowes, M.A., Rector of St John's Church, Manchester, and late Fellow of Trinity College, Cambridge; containing a Reply to his Strictures on those Passages in the Author's Lectures, which refer to the Honourable Emanuel Swedenborg, and his Disciples* (Manchester, 1819), p. 42.

17 Sketch for a projected autobiography, p. 21, MCC. William Roby Papers. Huntingtonianism was the particular brand of high Calvinist doctrine strongly flavoured with antinomianism that was propounded by the eccentric preacher William Huntington S.S. (1745–1813) and his followers.

18 'The doctrine of election', Yorkshire and Lancashire Baptist Association, circular letter 1810; 'The doctrine of election particularly with respect to its devotional and practical tendency', Baptist Midland Association, circular letter 1817.

19 Dale, *English Congregationalism*, pp. 588–90.

20 Jones, *Congregationalism*, p. 174.

21 A. C. Underwood, *A History of the English Baptists* (London, 1947), pp. 160–7. Underwood follows Joseph Ivimey, however, in pointing to the publication in 1781 by Robert Hall, senior, of *Help to Zion's Travellers* as marking the start of the theological change.

22 S. Clift, *An Incidental Letter, Addressed to the Lord Bishop of Sarum, August the 9th, 1798, the day of his Visitation held at Chippenham, Wilts. with some Observations and Reflections in Favour of Village Preaching* (Chippenham, n.d. [1798]), pp. 16–17.

23 R. Mant, *Puritanism Revived; or Methodism as old as the Great Rebellion. In a Series of Letters from a Curate to his Rector* (London, 1808), pp. 12, 32–7.

24 The London Independent Walter Wilson wrote, 'By giving way too much to that laxity of principle, and indiscriminate zeal which distinguish the Methodists, Dissenters have lost that peculiarity of character for which their forefathers were so eminent'. W. Wilson, *The History and Antiquities of Dissenting Churches and Meeting Houses, in London, Westminster, and Southwark; including the Lives of their Ministers, from the rise of Nonconformity to the present time* (4 vols., London, 1808–14), vol. 4, p. 550.

25 W. R. Ward, 'The Baptists and the transformation of the Church, 1780–1830', *Baptist Quarterly*, n.s. 25 (1973–4), 167–84; M. Warren, *The Missionary Movement from Britain in Modern History* (London, 1965), pp. 21–2. The Rev. John Gill DD. was pastor of Horsleydown Particular Baptist church, Southwark from 1720 to 1771.

26 E. P. Thompson, *The Making of the English Working Class* (London, 1963), p. 389. Other historians see little sign of working-class frustration during the 1790s and argue that the prosperity brought about by industrialization prevented any cause, apart from the war with France, from capturing men's hearts prior to 1800. See M. I. Thomis and P. Holt, *Threats of Revolution in Britain, 1789–1848* (London, 1977), p. 27.

27 Thompson, *English Working Class*, pp. 362–3. Unfortunately, while the author outlines the predominantly proletarian character of the Methodist following in the period after 1790, he does not indicate to what extent those who were attracted to the ranks of evangelical Dissent belonged to a significantly different social category.

28 E. J. Hobsbawm, *Primitive Rebels Studies in Archaic Forms of Social Movement in the 19th and 20th Centuries* (Manchester, 1959), pp. 129–30, 134–40.

29 See Chapter 7 below; D. Lovegrove, 'English evangelical Dissent and the European conflict 1789–1815' in W. J. Sheils (ed.), *Studies in Church History*, 20 (1983), 263–7. Professor Goodwin's suggestion that Dissenters turned from the rejection of their own plea for civic equality in 1790 to organize new types of radical society with political aims and working-class membership can be misleading, for he is speaking exclusively of the small but articulate group of Rational Dissenters associated with

Priestley, and makes no reference to the orthodox majority. A. Goodwin, *The Friends of Liberty: The English Democratic Movement in the age of the French Revolution* (London, 1979), pp. 98, 145.

30 Robison, 'Particular Baptists in England', caps 1–2; E. F. Clipsham, 'Andrew Fuller and Fullerism: a study in evangelical Calvinism', *Baptist Quarterly*, n.s. 20 (1963–4), 99–114, 146–54, 214–25, 268–76; Nuttall, 'Northamptonshire and *The Modern Question*', pp. 101–23. John Brine was pastor of the Baptist congregation at Curriers' Hall, Cripplegate from 1730 until his death in 1765, *Dictionary of National Biography*. Although there was a general rejection of predestined reprobation among the moderates, the essence of the theological change is to be found in their conviction that it was the duty of the unconverted to believe the gospel and the obligation of the converted to preach that gospel to those among the unconverted who would listen. Particular redemption with its emphasis upon the elect was still widely emphasized, but in practical terms it was reinterpreted by the widespread offer of the gospel and by the optimistic spirit in which the offer was made.

31 J. Ivimey, *A History of the English Baptists* (4 vols., London, 1811–30), vol. 3, pp. 270–5, 279–81, vol. 4, pp. 22–5.

32 Waterbeach Particular Baptist church book, 1827, pp. 27–8.

33 W. Roby, *A Defence of Calvinism; or, Strictures on a Recent Publication, entitled, 'St Paul against Calvin'* (London, 1810), pp. 8–9.

34 J. Gadsby (ed.), *A Memoir of the late Mr William Gadsby, upwards of thirty-eight years pastor of the Baptist Chapel, St George's-Road, Manchester, compiled from authentic sources* (Manchester, 1844), p. 50.

35 Blunham Baptist church, minutes February 1827, February 1828; *Biggleswade Baptist Church, 1771–1971* (1971), p. 77.

36 London Itinerant Society, minutes 16 January 1828, CL. MS I.i.37.

37 Burls, *Brief Review*, p. 17; Oxfordshire and East Gloucestershire Baptist Association, circular letter 1821, p. 23.

38 W. Kingsbury, *An Apology for Village Preachers; or an Account of the Proceedings and Motives of Protestant Dissenters, and Serious Christians of other Denominations, in their Attempts, to Suppress Infidelity and Vice, and to Spread Vital Religion in Country Places; especially where the Means of Pious Instruction, among the Poor, are Rare: with some Animadversions on an Anonymous 'Appeal to the People': and Replies to Objections* (Southampton, 1798), p. 37.

39 *Dictionary of National Biography*; W. Fancutt, *The Southern Baptist Association and its Churches, 1824–1974* (Andover, n.d. [1974]), p. 26.

40 Essex Baptist Association, circular letter 1841, p. 10. Ivimey gives the support of such itinerant preachers as one of the purposes of the general fund proposed at the first assembly. It was hoped that their preaching would encourage existing churches and break new ground. From the report of the 1691 assembly it appears that the fund had already been used in this manner. Ivimey, *English Baptists*, vol. 1, pp. 492, 512–13.

41 Joseph Oddy M.A. was ejected from a fellowship at Trinity College, Cambridge and from the living of Meldreth. Francis Holcroft M.A. was likewise ejected from a fellowship at Clare College, Cambridge and from the living of Bassingbourn. A. G. Matthews, *Calamy Revised Being a revision of Edmund Calamy's Account of the ministers and others ejected and silenced 1660–2* (Oxford, 1934), pp. 271, 371.

42 *Congregational Magazine*, 2 (1819), 183–4, 439.

43 W. Densham and J. Ogle, *The Story of the Congregational Churches of Dorset, from their foundation to the present time* (Bournemouth, 1899), p. 162.

44 The society was later known as the Dorset Congregational Association.

45 Nuttall, 'Questions and answers', pp. 83, 89. Francis was pastor of the Horsley congregation from 1759 to 1799.
46 A. G. Matthews, *The Congregational Churches of Staffordshire with Some Account of the Puritans, Presbyterians, Baptists and Quakers in the County during the Seventeenth Century* (London, 1924), p. 132.
47 Sangster, 'Rev. Rowland Hill', p. 138; G. F. Nuttall, 'Rowland Hill and the Rodborough Connexion, 1771–1833', *Transactions of the Congregational Historical Society*, 21 (1972), 71–3.
48 Robert Robinson, pastor of the Baptist congregation in Cambridge from 1759 to 1790, preached with varying degrees of regularity in fifteen neighbouring villages. Likewise William Roby acted as a tireless exponent of Independent itinerancy in Lancashire throughout his ministry in Manchester between 1795 and 1830. Both men began their preaching careers as Calvinistic Methodists.
49 Northern Education Society, report 1820, p. 4. The Bradford Academy admitted its first students in 1806.
50 J. Rippon (ed.), *The Baptist Annual Register* (4 vols., London, 1793–1802), vol. 2, pp. 461–3.
51 Samuel Mills to Joshua Wilson, 29 August 1845, DWL. New College MS 242/13.
52 Hereafter referred to as the Baptist Society.
53 Periodical Accounts Relative to a Society formed among the Particular Baptists, for Propagating the Gospel among the Heathen, 1792–1828, vol. 1, pp. 117, 153–6, 262. The objection concerning domestic infidelity was voiced for example in October 1797 by John Robison, Professor of Natural Philosophy at the University of Edinburgh, in a letter to Robert Haldane of Airthrey near Stirling in connection with his intention to go as a missionary to Bengal. R. Haldane, *Address to the Public concerning Political Opinions, and Plans lately adopted to promote Religion in Scotland*, 2nd edn (Edinburgh, 1800), p. 30.
54 The allocation of funds to Wastfield was made by the Hampshire and Wiltshire Auxiliary Society from the money it had collected for the parent body in Northamptonshire. See minute and account book of the Hants and Wiltshire Auxiliary Society for Propagating the Gospel among the Heathen, 1793–1818, 11 April 1798 to 21 April 1802, BMS. MSS; Journal of T. Wastfield, 18 June [1797] to 3 April 1798, BMS. MSS (see Appendix A). Even when official BMS support for home mission had ceased, this and other auxiliary missionary societies continued to finance both home and overseas mission. See *Baptist Magazine*, 7 (1815), 484 and 8 (1816), 41.
55 Jeremy, 'A local crisis', pp. 67–8; Societas Evangelica, minutes 18 September 1795 to 26 January 1821, DWL. New College MSS 122/1, 124/1.
56 The Eastern Association circular letter of 1780 illustrates the Baptist preoccupation with evidence of preparation by the Holy Spirit 'All needful qualifications for the work of the ministry, are from this divine agent. By his Almighty operations, he has made fishermen, tent-makers and other mechanics, lively, bold, spiritual, faithful, laborious and successful preachers of the gospel, and he can do the same still, and sometimes does. No qualifications are, or can be sufficient to capacitate for the ministry, no influences can render truly comfortable, or really useful in it, but such as come from him. And we would not have you forget, brethren, that you stand in need of the assistance and influence of the same spirit, as your ministers do.'
57 The available evidence is examined in chapter 3. In certain areas such as Essex Independents continued to show reluctance in the use of lay personnel. By contrast William Steadman the Baptist minister of Broughton in Hampshire had no hesitation

in commending the use of gifted laymen in village preaching. Rippon, *Register*, vol. 2, p. 463.

58 C. E. Welch (ed.), *Two Calvinistic Methodist Chapels, 1743–1811: the London Tabernacle and Spa Fields Chapel* (London, 1975), p. 94.

59 S. Bradley, W. Roby and I. Sharp, *A Discourse on the Nature of a Christian Church, by the Rev. S. Bradley; A Charge, by the Rev. W. Roby; A Sermon by the Rev. I. Sharp; with a Confession of Faith, etc., Delivered, December 7th, 1802, at the Independent Meeting-House, in Warrington, at the ordination of the Rev. Joseph Johnson* (Manchester, 1803), p. 32.

60 Sermon on 3 John 7–8, MCC. William Roby Papers.

61 William Roby to Sarah Roper, 14 July [17]88; Sketch for projected autobiography, pp. 9–12, MCC. William Roby Papers.

62 Sketch for projected autobiography, pp. 11–12.

63 Sketch for projected autobiography, p. 11; Yorkshire and Lancashire Baptist Association, circular letter 1818, pp. 5–7.

64 Best, *Temporal Pillars*, pp. 239–50.

65 Nuttall, 'Northamptonshire and *The Modern Question*', pp. 103–4.

66 W. R. Ward, *Religion and Society in England 1790–1850* (London, 1972), p. 50.

67 The subjects chosen for Particular Baptist association letters reflect this change of focus. Typical of the period before 1800 are the Northamptonshire Association letters on 'Divine Providence' (1779) and 'The authority and sanctification of the Lord's day' (1786). Post-1800 titles from the same association include such practical subjects as 'The assistance that people should render to their ministers in promoting the interest of Christ' (1806) and 'The nature, design and advantages of associations' (1812).

68 *Congregational Magazine*, 3 (1820), 172.

69 The practical tendencies of itinerant evangelism towards association and mutual acquaintance were noted by the Cheshire Congregational Union report for 1808, pp. 6–7.

70 J. Bennett, *Memoirs of the Life of the Rev. David Bogue, D.D.* (London, 1827), p. 38.

71 Richard Alliott to [?] editor of *Congregational Magazine*, 2 December 1841, DWL. New College MS L 52/2/11.

72 Agreement to form 'an Association of different Congregational Churches, in Lancashire and other neighbouring Counties', Bolton, 7 June 1786, Lancashire CRO. CUL 1.1.

73 Welch, *Two Calvinistic Methodist Chapels*, pp. 19–45.

74 L. Brown, *The Story of the Dorset Congregational Association* (Bridport, 1971), p. 7. Two years earlier a meeting of Independent ministers at Warwick had established a fund for the spread of the gospel at home and overseas, a move which led to the formation of an evangelistic association for the county of Warwickshire. *Evangelical Magazine*, 2 (1794), 509–10.

75 B. Nightingale, *The Story of the Lancashire Congregational Union, 1806–1906* (Manchester, 1906), pp. 16–18. The new body was formed in August 1798. In the following year Roby approached Job Wilson then at Northwich in Cheshire regarding the post of part-time itinerant. When Wilson declined the invitation George Greatbatch was appointed. Roby to Wilson, 6 November 1799, MCC. William Roby Papers.

76 Ivimey, *English Baptists*, vol. 4, p. 41; E. A. Payne, *The Baptist Union A Short History* (London, 1959), pp. 37–8; Underwood, *English Baptists*, p. 160.

77 The minute and accounts of the Northamptonshire association meetings were published annually with the circular letters to member churches. These are extant

from 1768 onwards. See especially minutes for 1779. The letter for 1812, p. 8, states that the Northamptonshire association fund, which listed the support of village preaching among its objects, commenced 'about ten years after this association was constituted'. The fund was established, therefore, around 1775; Records of the Baptist Western Association in the years 1733–1809, minutes of annual meetings and accounts, BBC. MSS G98.

78 Essex Baptist Association minute book, 1805–64, introductory notes, BU. MSS.

79 Shropshire and Cheshire Baptist Association, circular letter 1815.

80 Journal of T. Wastfield, 21 April 1798, BMS. MSS. Saffery's reference in this covering letter is to the Hampshire and Wiltshire Auxiliary of the BMS.

81 This body, officially designated The Evangelical Association for propagating the Gospel in the Villages of Cumberland, Durham, Northumberland and Westmoreland, is hereafter referred to as the Northern Evangelical Association.

82 Nightingale, *Lancashire Congregational Union*, p. 25.

83 Records of the Baptist Western Association in the years 1733–1809, minutes of annual meetings and accounts, 1776–1800, BBC. MSS G98.

84 Ward, *Religion and Society*, pp. 48–9; A. D. Gilbert, *Religion and Society in Industrial England: Church, Chapel and Social Change, 1740–1914* (London, 1976), pp. 58–9; Murray, 'The influence of the French Revolution', p. 202.

85 W. R. Ward, 'The French Revolution and the English churches. A case study in the impact of revolution upon the Church' in R. Peters (ed.), *Miscellanea Historiae Ecclesiasticae*, 4 (1970), 78.

86 S. Horsley, *The Charges of Samuel Horsley, LL.D., F.R.S., F.A.S., late Lord Bishop of St Asaph, Delivered at his Several Visitations of the Dioceses of St David's, Rochester, and St Asaph* (London, 1830), p. 104.

87 S. Greatheed, *General Union Recommended to Real Christians in a Sermon preached at Bedford, October 31, 1797. With an introductory account of an union of Christians of various denominations, which was then instituted to promote the knowledge of the Gospel; including a plan for universal union in the genuine Church of Christ* (London, 1798), pp. xvi–xviii. The postscript to this work is misleading, for Greatheed's remark that the union 'now comprehends six religious denominations' was made on 28 December 1797, only two months after its founding. Church of England, Moravian and Methodist participation was mentioned in the report of the union's second assembly [*Evangelical Magazine*, 6 (1798), 256], but whatever propaganda value this may have had, the true proportions of the inter-denominational co-operation were insignificant. In 1798 the leaders of the infant Methodist New Connexion pledged their support for the venture, but any practical assistance from that source has yet to be identified and was certainly very limited. For the New Connexion attitude see J. D. Crosland, 'The Bedford Association: an early ecumenical movement', *Proceedings of the Wesley Historical Society*, 28 (1951–2), 95.

88 Bedfordshire Union of Christians, original minutes, fol. 2r, Bedfordshire CRO. Z 206/1; Bedfordshire Union of Christians, report 1799, p. 12. Bedford's Moravian congregation owed its origin to a religious awakening in 1738 led by Benjamin Ingham and William Delamotte. A. J. Lewis, *Zinzendorf the Ecumenical Pioneer A Study in the Moravian Contribution to Christian Mission and Unity* (London, 1962), pp. 128–9.

89 *Baptist Magazine*, 1 (1809), 384.

90 Ward, 'The French Revolution', p. 80.

91 Societas Evangelica was formed originally in 1776 but was revitalized in 1796.

92 The latter were both formed in 1797, namely, the Congregational Society for

Spreading the Gospel in England (also referred to as the Congregational Society)
which survived only until 1809, and the Baptist Society which proved more enduring.
93 See Appendix B for a list of the principal bodies engaged in itinerancy.
94 Rippon, *Register*, vol. 3, p. 5.
95 C. Russell, *A Brief History of the Independent Church at Forest Green, Nailsworth*
(Nailsworth, 1847), p. 26.
96 Greatheed, *General Union Recommended*, p.v.
97 London Itinerant Society, minutes 18 October 1826, CL. MS I.i.37.
98 North Bucks Association of Independent Ministers and Churches, report 1823,
p. 13.
99 'Mr Wesley's People are our greatest Enemies who envy our Prosperity and go to the
greatest Lengths in blaspheming our Doctrine. They have repeatedly given themselves the Trouble of going over to the Neighbourhood where I preach in the Barn
and to warn the People against Hearing me, and to say their horrid Things of
Calvinism.' Roby to Sarah Roper, 4 July 1789, MCC. William Roby Papers.
100 Lord Teignmouth, who became the first president of the undenominational British
and Foreign Bible Society, was very sensitive concerning charges of Jacobinism.
C. J. Shore, *Memoir of the Life and Correspondence of John, Lord Teignmouth* (2 vols.,
London, 1843), vol. 1, pp. 62–3. Rowland Hill was ordained deacon in 1773 in
connection with the curacy of Kingston, near Taunton, but his ecclesiastical
preferment proceeded no further, and his permanent pastoral commitment lay
outside the Established Church in the form of Surrey Chapel built for him in St
George's Fields, Southwark in 1783. John Eyre was ordained priest in 1779 by
Bishop Thurlow, but after a succession of curacies under Cecil and Cadogan he was
appointed in 1785 as minister of Ram's Chapel at Homerton to the north of London,
a situation which gave him the freedom to pursue his wider evangelical interests until
his death in 1803. *Dictionary of National Biography*.
101 London Itinerant Society, minutes 16 March 1798, CL. MS I.i.35.
102 Village Itinerancy, minutes October 1816 to June 1817, DWL. New College MS
56/1.
103 M. Wells, *Memoir of Mrs Joanna Turner, as Exemplified in Her Life, Death, and
Spiritual Experience. With a Recommendatory Preface by the Rev. D. Bogue, D.D.*
(London, 1820), pp. 86–7, 206–7, 240.
104 Baptist Western Association, circular letter 1800, pp. 2–3. For a recent criticism of
this distinction between the undenominational spirit of the 1790s and the organizational limits placed upon practical co-operation in evangelism see D. M. Thompson, 'Denominationalism and Dissent, 1795–1835: a question of identity', *Friends of
Dr Williams's Library Lecture*, 39 (1985), 15.
105 T. Scott, *The Holy Bible containing the Old and New Testaments, according to the
Authorized Version; with Explanatory Notes, Practical Observations, and Copious Marginal References*, 6th edn (6 vols., London, 1823), vol. 2, commentary on 2 Chronicles
17.3–10.
106 Baptist Society, minutes 8 June 1798 to 22 July 1802, BMS. MSS.
107 Baptist Society, minutes 22 October 1801.
108 Ivimey, *English Baptists*, vol. 3, p. 279.
109 'Returns relating to Dissenters' places of worship, England and Wales', *Parliamentary Papers* (1852–3), vol. 78, pp. 83–170.
110 *Parliamentary Papers* (1852–3), vol. 78, p. 164.
111 Gilbert, *Religion and Society*, p. 35.
112 Gilbert, *Religion and Society*, pp. 53–5.

113 See Appendix B. It is important to note that neither local church-based itinerancies nor those associated with Dissenting academies are included in these figures.

114 The five societies are the Bedfordshire Union of Christians, the Baptist Society, the Northern Evangelical Association, Societas Evangelica and the Village Itinerancy. Societas Evangelica is eligible for inclusion by virtue of its reconstitution in 1796.

115 Allowing for omissions the true figure probably exceeded 250 locations. Because of the non-statistical nature of most society records all the figures probably erred on the conservative side. Three years earlier the Bedfordshire Union alone was reported to be employing 45 ministers and preachers together with 150 lay members in 100 towns, villages and hamlets [*Evangelical Magazine*, 6 (1798), 256]. The apparent conclusion to be drawn from this is that the general level of activity of the five societies was considerably greater than that reported.

116 Carwardine, *Transatlantic Revivalism*, pp. 60–3.

117 Mant, *Puritanism Revived*, pp. 9–17; V. Kiernan, 'Evangelicalism and the French Revolution', *Past and Present*, 1 (1952), 46.

118 According to the local press this formed the principal theme of John Douglas's third triennial visitation charge delivered in Salisbury cathedral. *Salisbury and Winchester Journal*, 20 August 1798.

119 *Sketch of the History and Proceedings of the Deputies*, pp. 115–19.

3 Preachers and sponsors

1 Horsley, *Charges*, p. 103.

2 R. Woodward, *The Causes and Pretences for Separation from the ancient Established Church considered and refuted* (London, 1802) quoted in J. Brown, *The History of the Bedfordshire Union of Christians. The Story of a Hundred Years*, ed. D. Prothero (London, 1946), pp. 43–6.

3 J. Brown, *History of the Bedfordshire Union of Christians*, p. 45.

4 R. I. and S. Wilberforce, *The Life of William Wilberforce* (5 vols., London, 1838), vol. 2, p. 361.

5 Wilson, *Dissenting Churches*, vol. 4, p. 550.

6 Ward, *Religion and Society*, pp. 49–51; Murray, 'The influence of the French Revolution', pp. 174–5.

7 Waterbeach Particular Baptist church book, 1827, gives the names of these 'Berrigers' as 'Messrs. Whitby, Price, Brown, Stittle, Sharp, Course, and Baxter'. It notes that although they were Calvinist in doctrine they had no particular awareness of the grounds of Dissent and made no attempt to form gathered churches among their hearers.

8 T. Whitehead, *History of the Dales Congregational Churches* (Bradford, 1930), pp. 227–8.

9 See Appendix A.

10 J. Brown, *History of the Bedfordshire Union of Christians*, p. 45; A. S. Langley, *Birmingham Baptists Past and Present* (London, 1939), pp. 33, 82; [W. M. Bowen], *An Appeal to the People on the Alleged Causes of the Dissenters' Separation from the Established Church: To which are Subjoined a few Cautionary Observations, in respect to their Present Political Views* (Salisbury, 1798), pp. 17–18.

11 Essex Baptist Association, minutes 19 October 1809, 29–30 May, 1810, BU. MSS. Garrington was a deacon of the church at Burnham and in 1811 was ordained as pastor.

12 See also Yorkshire and Lancashire Association, circular letter 1818 and Bucks and Herts Association, 1819.
13 Rippon, *Register*, vol. 3, pp. [1–2]; J. Malham, *A Broom for the Conventicle: or, the Arguments for Village Preaching Examined, and Fairly Discussed; more particularly obviating the unfounded assertions of Mr Kingsbury, of Southampton, and Mr Clift of Chippenham. With observations on the various replies to Mr H. W's Letter to the Bishop of Salisbury, And the other Publications on this Subject* (Salisbury, 1798), pp. 15, 25–6.
14 One example is the town of Nailsworth of which it was said in 1809 that within a seven mile radius 'not less than 70 gospel sermons are preached every Sabbath to more than 7,000 hearers'. *Baptist Magazine*, 1 (1809), 127.
15 Diary of Caleb Warhurst, 1755–9, MCC. William Roby Papers.
16 W. Steadman, *The Christian Minister's Duty and Reward. A sermon, addressed as a charge to Mr Richard Pengilly, when ordained pastor of the Baptist church at Newcastle upon Tyne, August 12, 1807* (Gateshead, 1807), pp. 38–9.
17 Lancashire Congregational Union, minutes 9–10 April 1816, Lancashire CRO. CUL 2.2. Such a plan of concerted itinerancy was tried briefly by the Independent ministers of the Manchester District but was relinquished under the pressure of pastoral commitments. Thereafter, apart from the work of those employed as itinerants, evangelistic activity remained a matter for local, unco-ordinated effort. R. Slate, *A Brief History of the Rise and Progress of the Lancashire Congregational Union; and of the Blackburn Independent Academy* (London, 1840), p. 99.
18 Franklin was a student at the Baptist Academy in Bristol.
19 Baptist Society minute book, p. 5, BMS. MSS.
20 Baptist Society, minutes 25 July 1799, 24 October 1799, 25 April 1805. The latter entry records Palmer as saying that through the society's help he had been assisted in preaching 'in 64 Towns Villages Farm houses and Cottages in Shropshire'.
21 Baptist Society, minutes 19 April 1804.
22 Congregational Society, minutes 12 July 1798, 23 April 1799, CL. MS I.i.41.
23 Societas Evangelica, minutes 28 February 1801, DWL. New College MS 122/1.
24 Baptist Society, minutes 26 April 1811, BMS. MSS.
25 Societas Evangelica, minutes 22 February 1799, 15 August 1811, DWL. New College MSS 122/1, 124/1. Dennant was still receiving financial support for local itinerancy in 1811 but Dunwich was not specifically mentioned.
26 Essex Congregational Union, minutes 22 April 1799, Essex CRO. D/NC 9/1.
27 Although evangelism as a Christian duty is an important and recurring theme in association records, the progression from principle to expediency is also clearly visible. The clearest manifestation of this change is found in the minutes of the Baptist Society. The argument from Christian duty took two forms: the example provided by the itinerant ministry of Jesus himself, and the Great Commission presented to the disciples in Matthew 28. 18–20.
28 Sketch for projected autobiography, p. 27, MCC. William Roby Papers.
29 Baptist Society, minutes 21 July 1808, BMS. MSS.
30 Baptist Society, minutes 19 October 1809.
31 Baptist Society, minutes 15 June, 22 July 1802. The minister was Mr Norman of Bampton who itinerated regularly over a wide area of North Devon and Somerset.
32 Slate, *Lancashire Congregational Union*, pp. 128–9. Rotherham and Idle Academies were Independent foundations: the institution at Bradford belonged to the Baptists.
33 An example would be Robert Woodward's description of the situation at Harrold.
34 Eyre to Cornelius Winter, 17 September 1796, DWL. New College MS 41/2. The agents in question were William Griffin and William Church.

35 The term 'itinerant' had a double usage. In a generic sense it was applied by opponents to travelling preachers of all kinds. As a technical abbreviation it was used within Dissent to refer to those who held appointments as full-time itinerant evangelists. Here the latter usage is intended.

36 These very points are made by the Northamptonshire Association circular letter 1821, p. 9: 'Notwithstanding the most zealous efforts of the pastor, and of those in a church who occasionally preach the word, there may be places too far distant for them to reach by their personal labours, or which may demand more frequent services than they can supply, consistently with their other engagements. In that case, it is the duty of christian churches to meet such opening for usefulness, by procuring and supporting, as far as their ability will allow, an Itinerant Preacher, who, free from more stated duties, may have leisure to go out into the highways and hedges, and invite sinners to the gospel feast.'

37 Essex Baptist Association minute book, 1805–64, introductory notes, BU. MSS.

38 Northern Evangelical Association, minutes 1798–1805, Durham CRO. B Ham/2. After 1820 Milnthorpe became the centre of a thriving Independent itinerancy, but no connection with the earlier initiative is apparent.

39 Hampshire Association of Protestant Dissenting Ministers [hereafter referred to as the Hampshire Congregational Association], minutes 25 April 1804.

40 Whitchurch (Hants) Independent church, minutes 16 November 1813.

41 Societas Evangelica, minutes 25 January 1799 to 30 January 1807, DWL. New College MSS 122/1, 124/1. As late as 1828 William Norris, senior, received some financial assistance with occasional itinerancy, by which time he was Independent pastor at Boroughbridge in North Yorkshire. Minutes 5 February 1828, 124/1.

42 Lancashire Congregational Union, minutes 1806–1813, Lancashire CRO. CUL 2. 1–2.

43 *Congregational Magazine*, 5 (1822), 635–6. The letter dated 1812 was addressed to Mr S. This was probably the itinerant named Silvester who was stationed at Sandbach for many years. See Cheshire Congregational Union, reports 1808–22.

44 Letters to John Eyre concerning the Village Itinerancy, 5 October 1797 to 19 December 1800, DWL. New College MSS 41/14–81.

45 North Bucks Independent Association, reports 1820–6. The village of Marsh Gibbon was covered by an agent of the Home Missionary Society working in consultation with the local association.

46 Most Particular Baptist area associations employed no full-time agent. The only exceptions were those responsible for Essex and Shropshire.

47 Essex Baptist Association, minutes 27–28 May 1818, 16–17 May 1826, BU. MSS.

48 Rippon, *Register*, vol. 2, pp. 462–3.

49 Densham to Eyre, 29 July 1800, DWL. New College MS 41/68.

50 Burls, *Brief Review*, pp. 25–6.

51 Cheshire Congregational Union, report 1808, pp. 4, 6 and financial statement attached; C. E. Surman, 'Students at the Yorkshire Independent academies during the eighteenth and nineteenth centuries' (3 vols.), vol. 1, MCC; C. E. Surman, 'Roby's academy, Manchester, 1803–08', *Transactions of the Congregational Historical Society*, 13 (1937–9), 51–2.

52 Surman, 'Roby's academy', pp. 46–52.

53 Itinerants at Burslem and Ormskirk respectively. Surman, 'Students at the Yorkshire Independent academies', vols. 1–2.

54 A. T. Sears, 'Christians in Kent: a brief account of Congregational churches from the 17th to 19th centuries', pp. 4–5, unpublished notes; Matthews, *Congregational*

Churches of Staffordshire, p. 172; Address to the ministers of the Lancashire association regarding the formation of an itinerant seminary (1797), MCC. William Roby Papers; Northern Evangelical Itinerant Academy, plan (ca. 1818), CL. MS II.c.48.

55 Slate, *Lancashire Congregational Union*, p. 21.

56 In 1814 the Baptist Society in London, for the Encouragement and Support of Itinerant and Village Preaching was reorganized on a public basis, being renamed the Baptist Home Missionary Society seven years later. In 1819 the Home Missionary Society emerged from the ashes of the Congregational Society for Spreading the Gospel in England. Like its overseas counterpart, the London Missionary Society, the new body was at first theoretically undenominational, but in practice most of its support came from Congregational churches.

57 *Baptist Magazine*, 7 (1815), 436.

58 C. Brown, *The Story of Baptist Home Missions* (London, 1897), pp. 30, 32; *Congregational Magazine*, 3 (1820), 332; A. Mearns, *England for Christ: a record of the Congregational Church Aid and Home Missionary Society* (London, 1886), pp. 60–1.

59 North Bucks Independent Association, report 1826, p. 33.

60 Mearns, *England for Christ*, p. 50.

61 Cheshire Congregational Union, report 1814, p. 11.

62 North Bucks Independent Association, reports 1820–5. The better paid itinerant received between £50 and £80 p.a., a level of remuneration comparable with that of the average pastorate.

63 Lancashire Congregational Union, minutes 10 September 1810, Lancashire CRO. CUL 2.2.

64 Baptist Society, minutes 22 November 1804, 12 July 1808, BMS. MSS.

65 C. Brown, *Baptist Home Missions*, p. 31. The second secretary was J. Edwards.

66 Mearns, *England for Christ*, pp. 59–60.

67 In 1822 the 21 Particular Baptist churches in Hampshire were reported as having 'Considerably more than twenty brethren ... employed in village preaching, in addition to the itinerating excursions of the pastors, most of whom [were] thus laudably engaged.' *Baptist Magazine*, 14 (1822), 202–3.

68 Haddenham Particular Baptist church book 1809–50. See especially minutes concerning James Wood (January–February 1816), Francis Collindridge and John Bates (December 1816, January–February 1820), a church member named Wall (21 October 1822), and the general subject of members speaking at villages (16 December 1816), Buckinghamshire CRO. NB 9/1.

69 S. P. Carey, *William Carey D.D., Fellow of Linnaean Society*, 6th edn (London, 1925), pp. 47–8.

70 North Bucks Independent Association, report 1824, p. 23: ordination of Mr Hood as Home Missionary Society itinerant for the Banbury area; Cheshire Congregational Union, report 1809 [p. 1]: ordination of William Silvester as county itinerant based at Sandbach. Exceptionally the minutes of the Lancashire Congregational Union make no mention of itinerants being ordained, apart from William Alexander who had already held a pastorate at Prescot. For Baptist practice see Essex Association minute book, 1805–64, introductory notes, BU. MSS.

71 Essex Baptist Association, minutes 29 May 1821.

72 Gilbert, *Religion and Society*, pp. 62–7, especially tables 3.1–2; J. Brown, *History of the Bedfordshire Union of Christians*, p. 45.

73 Bowen, *Appeal*, p. 17.

74 D. Douglas, *History of the Baptist Churches in the North of England from 1648–1845*

(London, 1846), p. 229. The Hamsterley library formed in 1790 is presently housed within the premises of Durham City Baptist church.

75 [T. G. Crippen], 'The London Itinerant Society', *Transactions of the Congregational Historical Society*, 7 (1916–18), 350, 355; London Itinerant Society, minutes 19 January 1798. CL. MS I.i.35.

76 R. Hall, 'Fragment on Village Preaching', in *The Works of Robert Hall, A.M.*, ed. O. Gregory (6 vols., London, 1832), vol. 3, p. 359.

77 J. Clark, *Memoirs of the Late Reverend John Clark, Written by Himself*, ed. W. Jay (Bath, 1810), pp. 8–9.

78 J. Brown, *History of the Bedfordshire Union of Christians*, pp. 46–7.

79 In the first decade of the nineteenth century two of the largest and most progressive farmers in the Bicester area were parish clergymen: the Rectors of Lower Heyford and Wendlebury. McClatchey, *Oxfordshire Clergy*, p. 116.

80 Andover Congregational church, minutes 5 December 1817.

81 Bethel Independent Chapel, Sheerness, minutes 16 June 1826, Kent CRO. N/C 254 B/1 A1.

82 At the assembly of Particular Baptist elders and messengers held at Bristol in 1693 it had been recommended that intending preachers should submit to examination by their churches for the sake of internal harmony and external reputation. Ivimey, *English Baptists*, vol. 1, pp. 527–8.

83 J. Edwards, *Stubborn Facts; or, a plain statement of the proceedings of a Particular Baptist Church with respect to two of their members, who were found guilty of praying, reading, and expounding the Scriptures, in the villages, under the patronage of the London Itinerant Society, without a regular call to the work of the ministry, in a series of letters to a friend* (London, 1808), pp. [iii]–13.

84 T. Chalmers, *Lectures on the Establishment and Extension of National Churches*, 2nd edn (Glasgow, 1838), pp. 48–54.

85 The building in London which in 1790 became Sion Chapel was acquired at a rent of £130 p.a. and was fitted out as a place of worship at a total cost to the Countess of Huntingdon of £2,600. Earlier, in 1775, she had spent nearly £800 on a similar conversion in order to provide a second chapel for Bristol. *The Life and Times of Selina Countess of Huntingdon* (2 vols., London, 1844), vol. 2, pp. 322–3, 393. During the same period Hope Chapel was erected by Lady Glenorchy at Hotwells on the outskirts of Bristol at an estimated cost of £2,200. T. S. Jones, *The Life of the Right Honourable Willielma, Viscountess Glenorchy, containing extracts from her diary and correspondence* (Edinburgh, 1822), p. 509.

86 John Lloyd to Countess of Huntingdon, April 1783, John Williams to Countess of Huntingdon, 21 February 1788, WC. Cheshunt MSS F1/11/514, F1/15/706.

87 *Life and Times of Selina Countess of Huntingdon*, vol. 2, p. 432.

88 T. S. Jones, *Life of the Viscountess Glenorchy*, p. 517.

89 *Congregational Magazine*, 2 (1819), 501.

90 Among the members of Eyre's congregation were Edward Hanson and Mary Mather, both of whom were co-founders and generous benefactors of the Village Itinerancy. Hanson also provided the financial stimulus which led to the establishment in 1800 of the academy at Idle.

91 Letters to John Eyre concerning the Village Itinerancy, 27 August 1796 to 19 December 1800, DWL. New College MSS 41/1–81.

92 Nightingale, *Lancashire Congregational Union*, pp. 120–4.

93 Wells, *Memoir of Mrs Joanna Turner*, pp. 132–95.

94 Northern Evangelical Association, minutes 12 August 1801, Durham CRO. B/Ham

2; Douglas, *Baptist Churches in the North of England*, pp. 218–19, 241; D. J. Rowe, *Lead Manufacturing in Britain a History* (London, 1983), pp. 21–2, 31–3; Slate, *Lancashire Congregational Union*, p. 22.

95 Bennett, *Life of David Bogue*, p. 119; Hampshire Congregational Association, minutes 4 May 1796. According to Joshua Wilson the anonymous benefactor was Welch. J. Wilson, *A Memoir of the Life and Character of Thomas Wilson, Esq., Treasurer of Highbury College* (London, 1846), p. 149.

96 F. W. Bull, 'The Newport Pagnell Academy', *Transactions of the Congregational Historical Society*, 4 (1909–10), 307; Rippon, *Register*, vol. 1, pp. 129–30.

97 Wilson acted as treasurer for Societas Evangelica from 1794 until at least 1828, the latest date recorded in the society's minutes. Between 1813 and 1822, apart from making donations to building projects in various parts of the country, he advanced the money needed to erect three large chapels in the metropolis designed to serve areas with rapidly expanding populations. The combined cost of the Paddington, Claremont and Craven Chapels came to more than £25,000 of which a large proportion was eventually written off by the lender.

98 Wilson, *Memoir of Thomas Wilson*, pp. 176–9. The academy at Hoxton for which Wilson acted as treasurer should be distinguished from an earlier institution bearing the same name which was dissolved in 1785 by the Coward trustees because of its heterodox tendencies. The later seminary started in 1779 as the English Evangelic Academy. In 1791 it migrated from Mile End to the old academy house at Hoxton, and moved yet again to purpose-built premises at Highbury in 1826.

4 The academic leaven

1 The existence of a general connection seems all the more likely in the light of a statement on local itinerancy published in the 1813–15 report of Idle Academy. The statement concluded: 'The Academy at Idle must therefore be considered as the life blood of our [West Riding] Itinerant Society.'

2 W. Jay, *Memoirs of the Life and Character of the late Rev. Cornelius Winter*, 2nd edn (London, 1812), pp. 254–6. It is possible that a connection existed between the preaching parties mentioned by Wilberforce and the evangelistic activities of the Bath Sunday School Union. See Ward, *Religion and Society*, pp. 15–16.

3 Clift, *Incidental Letter*; Kingsbury, *Apology*; Hall, 'Fragment on Village Preaching', *Works*, vol. 3; For reference to the pamphlet by 'Clero Mastix' see D. Bogue and J. Bennett, *History of Dissenters, from the Revolution in 1688, to the year 1808* (4 vols., London, 1808–12), vol. 4, pp. 216–17.

4 Resistance to formal ministerial training was not a new phenomenon. The earliest annual assemblies of Particular Baptist churches held at the end of the seventeenth century spent considerable time debating the question of the spiritual gifts required for the ministry and their relationship to human learning. Ivimey, *English Baptists*, vol. 1, p. 528.

5 Bristol Education Society, reports vol. 2, 1791–1806. The normal objection to ministerial education was based upon a concern for the sovereignty of God, as might be expected of Calvinists, and not upon the possible threat to gospel preaching as suggested by Robison, 'Particular Baptists in England', p. xvii.

6 Baptist Western Association, circular letter 1804, pp. 14–15.

7 Baptist Western Association, circular letter 1823, p. 4. A similar prejudice pervaded the churches of Yorkshire and Lancashire and was only overcome by the efforts of John Fawcett and William Steadman. S. M. Stone, unpublished dissertation entitled

'A survey of Baptist expansion in England from 1795 to 1850 with special reference to the emergence of permanent structures of organisation', pp. 35–9, BBC. MSS G98.

8 Hoxton Academy, report 1804, pp. 10–11. The 1825 report of Rotherham Academy adopted a less defensive tone and attempted to trace an historical connection between careful attention to ministerial training and the incidence of religious revival.

9 H. McLachlan, *English Education under the Test Acts. Being the History of the Nonconformist Academies, 1662–1820* (Manchester, 1931), p. 16 quoting W. A. Shaw; M. D. Stephens and G. W. Roderick, 'Education and the Dissenting academies', *History Today*, 27 (1977), 49, 54; J. W. A. Smith, *The Birth of Modern Education. The Contribution of the Dissenting Academies, 1660–1800* (London, 1954), pp. 265–8.

10 McLachlan, *English Education*, pp. 163, 169.

11 Halévy, *History of the English People in 1815*, pp. 366–7.

12 Nuttall, *Trevecca College*, p. 5.

13 W. G. Robinson, *William Roby (1766–1830) and the Revival of Independency in the North* (London, 1954), p. 32.

14 Sketch for projected autobiography, p. 6, MCC. William Roby Papers. 'J.J.' was John Johnson, minister of the Countess of Huntingdon's chapel, Wigan, 1784–9.

15 *Life and Times of Selina Countess of Huntingdon*, vol. 2, pp. 348–9.

16 Williams to Countess of Huntingdon, 21 February 1788, WC. Cheshunt MS F1/15/706.

17 *Life and Times of Selina Countess of Huntingdon*, vol. 2, pp. 317–18; Countess of Huntingdon to Thomas Wills, 13 September 1781, CL. MS II.c.7. Tension between Hill and the Countess of Huntingdon over the subject of Trevecca had appeared ten years earlier when as a young Cambridge graduate he had shown an understandable reluctance to accept her invitation to enter the college as a student. Rowland Hill to the Countess of Huntingdon, undated but probably ca.1771. Cheshunt MSS F1/24/1197, 1199.

18 Nuttall, *Trevecca College*, p. 20.

19 R. H. Martin, *Evangelicals United: Ecumenical Stirrings in Pre-Victorian Britain, 1795–1830*, Studies in Evangelicalism, No. 4 (Metuchen, N.J., 1983), esp. p. 19. The Baptists' tendency to dissociate themselves from the pan-evangelical movement noted by Martin was, as this study suggests, more than matched by a paedobaptist reluctance to work with those of an antipaedobaptist persuasion.

20 List of supplies provided by Mr. R[oby] for different congregations in the neighbourhood of Manchester, 1807–8–9, MCC. William Roby Papers; Idle Academy, reports 1802–30; Hampshire Congregational Association, minutes 5 April 1797; Northern Education Society, reports 1804–25.

21 Northern Education Society, report 1804–5, p. 7.

22 Nightingale, *Lancashire Congregational Union*, pp. 34, 37, 42–3. Similar comments are to be found in county association records concerning villages in many parts of the country. See for example the description of exploratory visits to Charlton, Northants in 1825–6. North Bucks Independent Association, report 1826, pp. 29–30.

23 Among those who trained at Newport Pagnell between 1782 and 1830 were seven who on leaving the academy became pastors of Baptist congregations. Bull, 'Newport Pagnell Academy', pp. 316–19. H. C. Leonard (ed.), *A History of the Churches forming the Hertfordshire and Bedfordshire Baptist Association* (Hemel Hempstead, 1875), p. 17, mentions an eighth man, Joseph James (d. 1791), a miller from Keysoe, who was ordained as pastor of the newly formed congregation at Leighton Buzzard in 1775. James, who engaged in weekday village preaching and who partly supported himself by keeping a day school, walked regularly to Newport Pagnell to receive instruction in

the classics from William Bull. A small number of Newport students also found their way into the ministry of the Established Church. For the limits to undenominational tolerance elsewhere see: Hoxton Academy, minutes 9 June 1797, DWL. New College MS 126/1; Village Itinerancy, minutes 3 February 1817, New College MS 56/1; Apostolic Society, minutes 14 December 1791, WC. Cheshunt MS C1/1. The Apostolic Society was the body responsible for the support and management of the colleges at Trevecca and Cheshunt.

24 Apostolic Society, minutes 4 April 1804, Cheshunt MS C1/3.

25 Slate, *Lancashire Congregational Union*, pp. 15–21; Surman, 'Roby's academy', pp. 46–52.

26 Bogue died in 1825 and the academy closed in 1829. Hampshire Congregational Association, minutes 22 April 1829.

27 Leaf Square Academy and School, minutes 22 December 1813, MCC. Lancashire Independent College Papers; C. E. Surman, 'Leaf Square Academy, Pendleton, 1811–1813', *Transactions of the Congregational Historical Society*, 13 (1937–9), 112.

28 Idle Academy, report 1808–10, p. 3.

29 North Bucks Independent Association, report 1824, pp. 15–16, 26–7.

30 Highbury College, minutes 14 December 1827, 10 October 1828, New College MS 129/1; Airedale Independent College, Idle Academy, report 1830, p. 5.

31 English Evangelic Academy, minutes pp. 2, 9, New College MS 126/1.

32 G. F. Nuttall, *New College, London and Its Library* (London, 1977), p. 11.

33 Village Itinerancy, minutes 20 September 1813, New College MS 56/1.

34 During 1820 applications were received by the trustees of Cheshunt College from James Tackle of Gloucester, Joseph Woods of Bristol and Leonard Wake of Norwich, all of whom had been active for some time in local village preaching. Apostolic Society, minutes 2 March, 8 November 1820, Cheshunt MS C1/4.

35 Apostolic Society, minutes 6 August 1806, Cheshunt MS C1/3.

36 Village Itinerancy, minutes 20 November 1822, New College MS 59/1.

37 Jay, *Life of Cornelius Winter*, pp. 253–61.

38 J. Bull, *Memorials of the Rev. William Bull, of Newport Pagnel* (London, 1864), p. 121. John Newton, the moving spirit behind the academy at Newport Pagnell, intended the course to be severely biblical with a smattering of logic, history and polite literature. The classical languages would be taught for the sake of biblical interpretation but he envisaged the complete omission of science, philosophy and natural religion. McLachlan, *English Education*, pp. 241–4.

39 Apostolic Society, minutes 1 September 1802, Cheshunt MS C1/3.

40 Village Itinerancy, minutes 29 July 1806, New College MS 55/1. At the committee meeting held on 4 September 1811 eight men were accepted as probationer students. Of this group one left in May 1813, but the names of five others still appeared on the list of preaching arrangements for the following summer vacation. During the third academic year (1813–14) five of the original group entered the ministry either in an itinerant or settled capacity, and of the eight entrants only one remained at the academy for more than three years. Village Itinerancy, minutes 4 September 1811 to April 1815, New College MSS 56/1, 57.

41 Hoxton Academy, minutes 9 June 1797, New College MS 126/1.

42 Bristol Education Society, reports vol. 2, 1791–1806, pp. x–xi; Cheshunt College, report 1795, pp. 2–3.

43 The course details mentioned in this passage are derived from the records of the evangelical academies at Hackney, Hoxton, Bradford, Bristol and Cheshunt. The following references apply unless otherwise stated: Village Itinerancy, minutes 29 July

1806, New College MS 55/1; Hoxton Academy, minutes 14 July 1809, New College MS 125/1; Northern Education Society, report 1823, pp. 21–2; Bristol Education Society, report 1815, pp. 16–17; Cheshunt College, report 1828, pp. 10–11.

44 The proposals for William Roby's academy at Manchester included the following provision for practice in sermon preparation: '4th Quarter. Sermonizing. Producing the Plan of a Sermon every Day from some given Text; and alternately delivering a short Sermon every Day for the Purpose of habituating them to public Speaking, and for exposing their Improprieties to Correction'. Address to the ministers of the Lancashire association regarding the formation of an itinerant seminary (1797), MCC. William Roby Papers.

45 Apostolic Society, minutes October 1791 to May 1792, Cheshunt MS C5/2.

46 Jay, *Life of Cornelius Winter*, pp. 6, 13, 128.

47 *Congregational Magazine*, 2 (1819), 7.

48 Hoxton Academy, minutes 9 January 1808, 14 July 1809, New College MS 125/1.

49 For formal resolutions see Hoxton Academy, minutes 14 December 1810 and Bristol Education Society, report 1804, p. 9.

50 Hoxton Academy, minutes 8 October 1813, New College MS 125/1.

51 J. Leifchild, *Memoir of the late Rev. Joseph Hughes, A.M.* (London, 1835), p. 39.

52 Bogue and Bennett, *History of Dissenters*, vol. 4, pp. 299–300. However, they added (pp. 305–7) that most authorities acknowledged the Dissenting academies to be more than equal to the universities in biblical studies and theology, and it appears, therefore, that their comments were directed particularly at deficiencies in the sphere of classical studies. This view is reinforced by the examiners' comment at Cheshunt College in 1831 that 'although some areas of knowledge had perhaps been neglected, particular attention had been paid to those most immediately connected with Theology'. Apostolic Society, minutes 27–28 April 1831, Cheshunt MS C1/4.

53 Hoxton Academy, minutes 14 April 1815, New College MS 125/1; Idle Academy, report 1821.

54 Hoxton Academy, minutes 15 January 1813, New College MS 125/1; Blackburn Independent Academy, minutes 28 December 1820, MCC. Lancashire Independent College Papers.

55 D. W. Lovegrove, 'Particular Baptist itinerant preachers during the late 18th and early 19th centuries', *Baptist Quarterly*, n.s. 28 (1979–80), 130–1.

56 Though by the 1790s it had become primarily a means of encouraging settled minsters to itinerate in conjunction with their pastoral responsibilities, Societas Evangelica had been formed in 1776 for the purpose of providing lay preachers for the suburban villages of the metropolis and defraying their expenses. Three years later the English Evangelic Academy (later Hoxton) had been opened in London to provide those employed by the itinerant society with rudimentary theological instruction. Samuel Mills to Joshua [Wilson], 29 August 1845, New College MS 242/13. The relationship between Hackney Academy and the Village Itinerancy developed in a similar fashion.

57 Honley is situated three miles south of Huddersfield. At various times regular student supplies were sent from Idle to places as far distant as Chester-le-Street, Monkwearmouth, Northallerton and Malton. For Sunday 24 April 1825 with only 15 students available Vint received requests for supplies from 22 congregations, namely: Eccleshill, Allerton, Bradford, Elland, Blubberhouses, Morley, Wetherby, Wortley, Otley, Marsden, Selby, Holmfirth, Heckmondwike, Flockton, Boroughbridge, Sedbergh, St Helens, Driffield, Cleckheaton, Heckmondwike (New Chapel), Brighouse and Bedale.

58 Idle Academy, report 1810–12, p. 6. Similar causes were commenced and maintained at other places including Blubberhouses, Pateley Bridge, Ripon and Harrogate. Report 1818, pp. 6–10.

59 Cheshunt College, student preaching lists, 1820–8, Cheshunt MS C9/11/1.

60 Whitehead, *Dales Congregational Churches*, pp. 332–3; Idle Academy, reports 1813–15, p. 4, 1821, p. 5.

61 Whitehead, *Dales Congregational Churches*, p. 63.

62 Village Itinerancy, minutes 31 May 1813, New College MS 56/1.

63 Rippon, *Register*, vol. 3, pp. 56–9.

64 J. Brown, *History of the Bedfordshire Union of Christians*, p. 54.

65 Village Itinerancy, weekly occurrences book, p. 10. New College MS 57. The prison ships in use at the time included *Retribution* and *Justitia*, both anchored off Woolwich between Gallions Reach and Barking Reach. W. B. Johnson, *The English Prison Hulks*, 2nd edn (London, 1970), pp. 4, 32, 36. The records of Societas Evangelica note the allocation of funds to support itinerant preachers engaged in visiting the convicts at Woolwich. Minutes 30 January 1807, 26 October 1810, New College MS 124/1.

66 *Congregational Magazine*, 1 (1818), 166, 222, 331–2; Cheshunt College, student preaching lists, 25 June 1820, Cheshunt MS C9/11/1. For a full account of the creation of the Port of London floating chapel see R. Kverndal, 'Seamen's missions: their origin and early growth A contribution to the history of the Church maritime', Oslo, D.Theol. thesis, 1984, pp. 150–65.

67 Bennett, *Life of David Bogue*, pp. 135–6.

68 English Evangelic Academy, minute book, p. 4, New College MS 126/1.

69 Hoxton Academy, minutes 9 June 1797, 14 July 1809, New College MSS 126/1, 125/1.

70 Idle Academy, minute book 1804–31 [p. 5], MCC. Yorkshire United Independent College Papers.

71 Idle Academy, reports 1808–10, p. 4, 1810–12, pp. [3]–4.

72 Jay, *Life of Cornelius Winter*, pp. 254–6.

73 Idle Academy, minutes 30 December 1816, 20 October 1817, Yorkshire United Independent College Papers.

74 Hoxton Academy, report 1814, pp. 8–10.

75 Typical of these was John Dennant, Independent minister at Halesworth, Suffolk, who had been a student at Hoxton from 1791–3. From Halesworth he itinerated to the villages of Rumburgh, Wissett, Chediston, Cratfield, Laxfield, Wenhaston, Bramfield, Blythburgh, Westleton and Dunwich. Societas Evangelica, report 1799, p. 2.

76 From Hoxton this group included John Mitchell (Quebec), Robert Morrison (China), John Philip (Cape Colony), and Aaron Buzacott.

77 B. Cracknell, *The Utility of Academical Institutions to the Church of Christ* (London, n.d. [1806]) pp. 17–18.

78 English Evangelic Academy, minutes 11 June 1779, 15 October 1782, New College MS 126/1.

79 Hoxton Academy, minutes 14 October 1803 to 8 June 1804, New College MS 125/1.

80 Highbury College, minutes 6 November 1829, New College MS 129/1.

81 See Rotherham Independent Academy, report 1817, p. [3]; Airedale Independent College, report 1826, p. 8.

5 Organization and infrastructure

1 Burls, *Brief Review*, pp. 97–8.
2 Baptist Society, minutes 12 February 1805, BMS. MSS.
3 Copies of this letter are preserved among the society's correspondence: see DWL. New College MSS 42/45–6.
4 [T. G. Crippen], 'The Surrey Mission', *Transactions of the Congregational Historical Society*, 6 (1913–15), 305.
5 C. Hull to Countess of Huntingdon, 16 September 1771, S. Phillips to Countess of Huntingdon, 23 December 1783, WC. Cheshunt MSS F1/3/135, F1/12/588.
6 Baptist Society, minutes 24 October 1799.
7 The itinerancy centred upon Deddington, Oxfordshire in 1821 followed this pattern. North Bucks Independent Association, report 1821, p. 18.
8 This was the experience for example at Dry Drayton in Cambridgeshire. Baptist Society, minutes 19 October 1809.
9 North Bucks Independent Association, report 1830.
10 Baptist Society, minutes 14 March 1809.
11 Lancashire Congregational Union, minutes 20 April 1814 to 8 April 1824, Lancashire CRO. CUL 2.2.
12 Baptist Society, minutes 24 April 1800.
13 Baptist Society, minutes 22 October 1801.
14 B. Nightingale, *Lancashire Nonconformity; or, sketches, historical and descriptive of the Congregational and Old Presbyterian Churches in the County* (6 vols., Manchester, 1890–3), vol. 2, p. 208; Whitehead, *Dales Congregational Churches*, pp. 332–4.
15 See Idle Academy, report 1810–12, pp. 4–5 which cites the examples of Eastwood, Brighouse and Skipton; London Itinerant Society, minutes vol. 1, p. 11, CL. MS I.i.35 mention a similar case at Streatham.
16 Thomas Wilson, Autobiographical notes and correspondence, pp. 6–7, 17, 36, CL. MS. II.d.5.
17 Ward, *Religion and Society*, pp. 15–16; Gilbert, *Religion and Society*, pp. 56–7.
18 Cheshire Congregational Union, report 1816, pp. 13–14.
19 P. Laslett, *The World We Have Lost*, 2nd edn (London, 1971), pp. 108–11.
20 Village Itinerancy, minutes 29 July 1806, New College MS 55/1. For a more general examination of this development see T. W. Laqueur, *Religion and Respectability Sunday Schools and Working Class Culture 1780–1850* (New Haven, 1976), pp. 148–51.
21 North Bucks Independent Association, reports 1821, p. 20, 1823, p. 21; Cheshire Congregational Union, report 1816, p. 7.
22 Burls, *Brief Review*, p. 19.
23 Baptist Society, minutes 19 July 1798, 8 July 1800, 24 September 1805.
24 Bedfordshire Union of Christians, minutes north-western district September 1804, Bedfordshire CRO. Z 206/1; *The Publications of the Religious Tract Society. To which is prefixed, an account of the origin and progress of the society, with extracts of correspondence, foreign and domestic* (4 vols., London, 1812–14).
25 *Proceedings of the first twenty years of the Religious Tract Society: being a compendium of its reports, and extracts from the appendices* (London, 1820), p. 143.
26 Densham to Eyre, 5 September 1800, New College MS 41/72.
27 London Itinerant Society, minutes 27 March 1811, CL. MS I.i.36.
28 North Bucks Independent Association, report 1827, p. 30.

29 Lancashire Congregational Union, minutes 7 April 1825, Lancashire CRO. CUL 2.2.
30 'That the melancholy extent of the ignorance still existing in numerous counties of Great Britain, the inadequacy of societies already formed to effect its removal, added to the entreaties for assistance from county associations, and of many villages for the blessings of an evangelical ministry, present a strong claim on our Christian sympathies; that it is therefore highly necessary that a society be formed, which shall aid county associations in their grand objects of sending forth itinerants, establishing Sunday schools, and in other ways endeavouring to promote the spread of Divine truth throughout the country; and that it be called the HOME MISSIONARY SOCIETY.' Mearns, *England for Christ*, pp. 31–2.
31 L. Brown, *Dorset Congregational Association*, p. 23.
32 Mearns, *England for Christ*, p. 36.
33 Greatheed, *General Union Recommended*, pp. 50–1.
34 Northern Evangelical Association, minutes 1801 and 1803, Durham CRO. B Ham/2.
35 A brief examination of the society's account book for 1797–1809, CL, reveals the extent of this failure. For 1800–1 total income was £208.1s.3d. of which £179.15s.6d. represented the previous year's balance. In 1801–2 £142.19s.2d. was received. From May 1802 onwards no income was recorded apart from small dividend payments on stock held by the society and two 1gn. subscriptions in 1803.
36 Societas Evangelica, minutes 30 January 1807 to 5 February 1828, New College MS 124/1.
37 See especially the entry referring to Graham of Darlington and the society's refusal to make a grant towards the cost of a horse purchased for itinerating. Societas Evangelica, minutes 30 May 1806, New College MS 124/1.
38 Village Itinerancy, minutes 19 March, 23 April 1828, New College MS 60/1.
39 Village Itinerancy, minutes 22 October, 17 November 1830, New College MS 60/1.
40 The minutes for 25 July 1799 and 24 April 1800 mention two sums of £20 voted to John Palmer of Shrewsbury for the year 1799–1800. See also minutes 24 April 1798.
41 North Bucks Independent Association, report 1822, p. 28.
42 Congregational Society, minutes 1 May 1798, 23 April 1799, 30 April 1800, CL. MS I.i.41.
43 Cheshire Congregational Union, report 1816, p. 13; North Bucks Independent Association, report 1827, pp. 32, 34.
44 Village Itinerancy, minutes 16 December 1814, 22 October 1830 concerning Haslemere and Hoarwithy, Herefordshire, New College MSS 56/1, 60/1; Societas Evangelica, minutes 26 May 1797 concerning Salisbury, New College MS 122/1; Baptist Society, minutes 26 April 1811 concerning East Bergholt.
45 Gilbert, *Religion and Society*, pp. 62–7.
46 Journal of T. Wastfield, 10 December [1797] to 1 April 1798, BMS. MSS (See Appendix A).
47 News of terminations did nothing to stimulate giving and were usually passed over in silence. Little evidence is available on the matter, yet it is clear from occasional, incidental comments that some itinerant preachers regarded their work as a failure. In 1825, after spending several years preaching at Steeple Claydon, a member of the Winslow Independent church named Hedgecock relinquished the task feeling that little progress had been made. North Bucks Independent Association, report 1826 pp. 25–6.
48 Roby to Sarah Roper, 9 May [17]89, MCC. William Roby Papers; Journal of T.

Wastfield, 2 July [1797]; Densham to Eyre, 7 August 1800, New College MS 41/69; Bucks and Herts Particular Baptist Association, report 1819, pp. 3–4.

49 Burls, *Brief Review*, pp. 21–22.
50 Essex Baptist Association, minutes July 1805, BU. MSS.
51 Societas Evangelica, minutes 18 September 1795, New College MS 122/1. Ministers supported by the society were on other occasions reminded of a 1796 resolution not to defray the expenses of any preaching station for longer than three years. See also Baptist Society, minutes 28 March 1800, 15 April 1802.
52 Societas Evangelica, minutes 18 September 1795 to 28 February 1801, New College MS 122/1.
53 Essex Baptist Association, minutes 1809, 23 September 1816, 29 May 1821.
54 Slate, *Lancashire Congregational Union*, p. 45.
55 *Baptist Magazine*, 2 (1810), 592.
56 Densham to Eyre, 5 September 1800, New College MS 41/72.
57 Lancashire Congregational Union, minutes 9 April 1807, 14 September 1808, Lancashire CRO. CUL 2.1; Slate, *Lancashire Congregational Union*, pp. 23–4.
58 Village Itinerancy, minutes 21 April 1830, New College MS 60/1.
59 Cheshire Congregational Union, report 1814, pp. 11–12.
60 Cheshire Congregational Union, reports 1816, p. 19, 1820, p. 2, 1822, p. 10.
61 Cheshire Congregational Union, report 1829, pp. 4–8, 10. The locations suggested in Wirral were Parkgate, Neston, Sutton, Tranmere, Birkenhead, Woodside and Seacombe.

6 Support and opposition

1 Baptist Society, minutes 22 July 1802, BMS. MSS.
2 Baptist Society, minutes 24 July 1800, 22 October 1801.
3 Densham to Eyre, 7 August, 2 October, 20 October 1800, DWL. New College MSS 41/69, 74, 77. The transformation of attitudes may have been exaggerated by Densham since the Village Itinerancy minutes for 2 May 1803 record that in Rogate 'at the death of Mr Densham, the bells were rung for joy'. New College MS 55/1.
4 Densham to Eyre, 25 June 1798, New College MS 41/27.
5 Baptist Society, minutes 21 October 1802.
6 North Bucks Independent Association, report 1824, p. 20.
7 North Bucks Independent Association, report 1828, pp. 24–5. Thomas Radcliffe was the itinerant involved.
8 See for example the criticism voiced by Walter Wilson.
9 Kingsbury, *Apology*, pp. 35–40. Kingsbury was minister of the Independent church at Above Bar, Southampton from 1764–1809. His *Apology* appeared as a component of the Salisbury village preaching controversy of 1798. In his refutation of the charge that evangelism was leading to the neglect of existing congregations he mentioned plans in progress in various parts of the country for the appointment of supernumerary ministers as full-time itinerants.
10 Robinson, *William Roby*, p. 42.
11 In 1806 Aspland and Eaton took part in the establishment of a Unitarian Fund for Promoting Unitarianism by Means of Popular Preaching. *Monthly Repository*, 20 (1825), 337–40, 479–83; Aspland had become minister to the Unitarian congregation worshipping at Gravel Pit Chapel, Hackney in 1805. *Dictionary of National Biography*; Eaton, for a short while the pastor of a General Baptist congregation at Billericay, had by 1806 established himself in London as a bookseller. *Monthly Repository*, n.s. 3

(1829), 357; R. Wright, *A Review of the Missionary Life and Labors of Richard Wright. Written by himself* (London, 1824); S. Mews, 'Reason and emotion in working-class religion, 1794–1824' in D. Baker (ed.), *Studies in Church History*, 9 (1972), 365–82.

12 E. D. P. Evans, 'The history of the Presbyterian Chapel, Bank Street, Bury, Lancashire, 1719–1919', unpublished dissertation, Manchester Unitarian College, 1919, pp. 399, 423.

13 Cheshire Congregational Union, report 1814, p. 8.

14 Village Itinerancy correspondence, New College MSS 41/25–7, 45, 58.

15 Nightingale, *Lancashire Congregational Union*, pp. 35–6.

16 It was criticism of this kind voiced by the young Jesuit priest Joseph Curr which prompted William Roby to produce his three part tract entitled *Protestantism: or an Address particularly to the Labouring Classes, in defence of the Protestant Principle, 'That the Scriptures, not Tradition, are the Rule of Faith'* (London, 1821–2).

17 Slate, *Lancashire Congregational Union*, p. 54.

18 *Tract Magazine; or, Christian Miscellany*, 2 (1825), 107–8.

19 I. Bridgman, *A Candid Appeal to the Religious Public, in a Letter, Addressed to the Inhabitants of the Forest of Dean, Gloucestershire, occasioned by the Dismissal of the Rev. Isaac Bridgman, A.B. of St Edmund's Hall, Oxford, from the Curacy of Trinity Church, in the said Forest. With a Preface, by the Rev. Rowland Hill, A.M.* (Ross, 1823) [p. 15]; Village Itinerancy, minutes 18 December 1822, 25 February 1824, New College MS 59/1. In 1822 the Bishop of Gloucester was Henry Ryder, brother of the first Earl of Harrowby, and the first avowed Evangelical to sit on the episcopal bench. Ryder occupied the see of Gloucester from 1815 until 1824 when he was translated to Lichfield and Coventry. G. C. B. Davies, *The First Evangelical Bishop. Some aspects of the life of Henry Ryder* (London, 1958), pp. 4, 7–8.

20 For the attitude of Wilberforce and his followers see I. C. Bradley, 'The politics of godliness; Evangelicals in Parliament, 1784–1832', Oxford, D.Phil. thesis, 1974, pp. 172–4. Wilberforce also showed his sympathy for evangelical Dissent by practical support, becoming, for example, in 1815, one of the subscribers to the fund for the new Baptist academy building in Bristol. Bristol Education Society, report 1815, p. 62.

21 This suggestion is made by Murray, 'The influence of the French Revolution', p. 273 on the basis of a report in the *Evangelical Magazine* for 1798.

22 Clift, *Incidental Letter*, p. 20.

23 V. E. Neuburg, *Chapbooks. A guide to reference material on English, Scottish and American chapbook literature of the eighteenth and nineteenth centuries*, 2nd edn (London, 1972), pp. 1–15.

24 *Proceedings of the first twenty years of the Religious Tract Society*, p. iv. George Burder was minister of an Independent church at Coventry from 1783 to 1803. *Dictionary of National Biography*.

25 *Publications of the Religious Tract Society*, vol. 1, pp. 279–304, vol. 2, pp. 282–94. Hannah More's personal output of popular religious literature designed to counter the Jacobinical tendencies of contemporary chap-books was published between 1794 and 1798 under the title *Cheap Repository Tracts*.

26 *Proceedings of the first twenty years of the Religious Tract Society*, pp. 74–5; see also *Baptist Magazine*, 5 (1813), 470.

27 *Proceedings of the first twenty years of the Religious Tract Society*, p. 79.

28 *Tract Magazine*, 1 (1824), 57.

29 *Tract Magazine*, 1 (1824), 46, 2 (1825), [1]–2.

30 *Tract Magazine*, 2 (1825), 59.

31 A. Everitt, *The Pattern of Rural Dissent: the Nineteenth Century*, English Local History

Occasional Papers, 2nd Series, ed. A. Everitt, No. 4 (Leicester, 1972), pp. 20–2; For consideration of this relationship in a strongly Methodist area see J. Obelkevich, *Religion and Rural Society: South Lindsey 1825–1875* (London, 1976), pp. 8–14. The changing patterns of land ownership and settlement which help to explain the growing religious diversity of early nineteenth-century rural society are examined by Mills and Gleave in studies of contrasting parishes in Lincolnshire and the Yorkshire Wolds. D. R. Mills (ed.), *English Rural Communities: the impact of a specialised economy* (London, 1973).

32 Laslett, *The World We Have Lost*, p. 64.
33 Baptist Society, minutes 22 November 1804.
34 Village Itinerancy, minutes 16 May 1827 to 19 March 1828, New College MS 60/1.
35 Journal of T. Wastfield, 30 July [1797], BMS. MSS (see Appendix A).
36 Journal of T. Wastfield, 6 January 1798. In 1800 the committee of the Dissenting Deputies decided to take no action in a similar situation at Long Buckby, Northamptonshire where the parish clergyman and others had ejected a pauper from one of the almshouses for having registered his home for preaching. Protestant Dissenting Deputies, minutes 29 November 1799 to 31 January 1800, GL. MS 3083.
37 Baptist Society, minutes 21 January, 1808.
38 This body, hereafter referred to as the Protestant Society, was formed in May 1811.
39 *Baptist Magazine*, 10 (1818), 157–8.
40 Essex Baptist Association, minutes February–March, 1807, BU. MSS.
41 *Protestant Dissenter's Magazine*, 2 (1795), 252–6. Hinton, who was a prominent advocate of itinerant evangelism, was also known for his liberal political opinions, and hence the cry of 'Jacobin Rascal' raised against him by the mob. The riot at Woodstock did not involve open air preaching but rather a meeting held in a private house which had been properly registered.
42 The number of cases of disturbance of worship recorded by the Deputies was always small, never exceeding nine in any five year period. Nevertheless the pattern suggested by the organization's undoubtedly conservative figures resembles the general growth profile of Dissenting itinerancy. The picture is complicated in the early 1790s by popular hostility directed against the political views of Joseph Priestley and his supporters.

1740–4	2 cases	1785–9	6 cases
1745–9	No cases reported	1790–4	7 cases
1750–4	1 case	1795–9	9 cases
1755–9	No cases reported	1800–4	6 cases
1760–4	1 case	1805–9	5 cases
1765–9	No cases reported	1810–14	7 cases
1770–4	3 cases	1815–19	5 cases
1775–9	2 cases	1820–4	2 cases
1780–4	3 cases	1825–9	3 cases

Sketch of the History and Proceedings of the Deputies, pp. 159–64; Dissenting Deputies, minutes 1732–1830, GL. MS 3083.
43 Densham to Eyre, 2 October 1800, New College MS 41/74.
44 Dissenting Deputies, minutes 21 January 1791.
45 *Publications of the Religious Tract Society*, vol. 1, pp. 181–9.
46 Dissenting Deputies, minutes 29 November to 27 December 1805.
47 Dissenting Deputies, minutes 6 November, 18 December 1795. No mention of this case appears in the Suffolk quarter sessions records. The Suffolk assize court records are incomplete. Those that do exist yield no further information.

48 Densham and Ogle, *Congregational Churches of Dorset*, pp. 13–14, 290–2; R. Hine, *History of Beaminster* (Taunton, 1914), pp. 97–8.

49 Dorset quarter sessions order book 1798–1806, p. 70. Dorset CRO. Under the Toleration Act there was the alternative of registering premises with the diocesan authorities. Quarter sessions functioned only at fixed intervals and it was often more convenient to make an ecclesiastical registration. In the case of Stoke Abbott doubt is raised by the October entry in the secular records. For further details of eighteenth-century practice see E. Welch, 'The registration of meeting houses', *Journal of the Society of Archivists*, 3 (1966), 116–18.

50 Dorset quarter sessions order book 1798–1806, p. 165.

51 Dissenting Deputies, minutes 25 January 1799.

52 Western circuit, estreat book 1740–1800, PRO. ASSI 24.17; process book 1785–1807, PRO. ASSI 24.43.

53 T. J. Hosken, *History of Congregationalism and Memorials of the Churches of our order in Suffolk* (Ipswich, 1920), p. 308; V. B. Redstone, *The Annals of Wickham Market and other papers* (Woodbridge, 1896), p. 48; Suffolk quarter sessions order book 1809–15, pp. 76, 78, Suffolk CRO. 105/2/54.

54 Court of King's Bench, indictments (modern-out counties) 1811, PRO. KB 11.68.1.

55 *Evangelical Magazine*, 19 (1811), 370–1; Protestant Society, minutes 12 August 1811, DWL. MS 38.193; Redstone, *Annals of Wickham Market*, p. 48 suggests that the money was donated to the Bible Society for the purchase of bibles for the poorer inhabitants of the town.

56 Protestant Society, minutes 24 September 1811, 12 May 1812, DWL. MS 38.193; *Evangelical Magazine*, 20 (1812), 243.

57 J. S. Pearsall, *Historical Memorials of a Christian Fellowship*, 2nd edn (n.d.), pp. 28–31; Hampshire quarter sessions order book, Midsummer 1814–Easter 1817, p. 107b, Hampshire CRO. QO/30; Court of King's Bench, indictments (modern-out counties) 1815, PRO. KB 11.72.19–20; King's Bench, orders and writs 1811–15, KB 16.25; King's Bench, rule (or order) book, 1813 Hil.–1817 Hil., pp. 609, 618, 621, KB 21.50.

58 Burrough's presence is demonstrated by the entries in the baptismal register for the parish of Abbotts Ann. In 1814 and 1815 25 out of 28 entries were signed by Burrough as the clergyman performing the rite. Abbotts Ann, register of baptisms 1813–1862, Hampshire CRO. 24M 68A/PR4.

59 Abbotts Ann, parish registers: baptisms and burials, 1740–1812/1813–62; marriages 1740–53/1754–1812/1813–58, Hampshire CRO. 24M68A/PR1–4.

7 Criticism and legality

1 Essex Baptist Association minute book, 1805–64, introductory notes, BU. MSS.

2 Clift, *Incidental Letter*, p. 19.

3 Densham to Eyre, 5 June 1799, New College MS 41/46.

4 Bowen, Malham and Bowles represented the Established Church in the Salisbury village preaching controversy of 1798. William Mogg Bowen (b. ca. 1767) was the ambitious but by no means impoverished Curate of Newton Tony, eight miles N.E. of Salisbury. John Malham, by 1798 already aged 51, was Curate of West Grimstead, four miles S.E. of the city. He also acted as chaplain to the county gaol at Fisherton Anger. William Lisle Bowles (b. 1762) was Rector of Dumbleton, Gloucestershire and a notable composer of sonnets. Jeremy, 'A local crisis', pp. 71–3.

5 Malham, *A Broom for the Conventicle*, pp. 32–3, 53.

6 Malham, *A Broom for the Conventicle*, p. 15; W. Mawer, *The Examiner Examined, or an Apology for the Methodists; Being an Answer to Mr Neesham's Examination; Together with some Further Remarks on the Reverend Mr Hett's Letters to Lord A, B, C &c.*, (Lincoln, 1810), p. 13.

7 Baptist Society, minutes 19 April 1798, BMS. MSS.

8 Malham, *A Broom for the Conventicle*, pp. 24, 30.

9 W. S. Goddard, *A Sermon, Preached in the Cathedral Church of Chichester, August 8, 1811, at the Triennial Visitation of the Right Reverend Father in God, John, Lord Bishop of Chichester*, 2nd edn (Winchester, 1812), pp. 34–5.

10 *Salisbury and Winchester Journal*, 20 August 1798, p. 4; Jeremy, 'A local crisis', pp. 63–5.

11 F. Wollaston, *A Country Parson's Address to his Flock, to Caution them against being Misled by the Wolf in Sheep's Cloathing, or Receiving Jacobin Teachers of Sedition, who intrude themselves under the Specious Pretense of Instructing Youth and Preaching Christianity* (London, 1799), pp. 30–1. An anonymous reply to Wollaston insisted on the purely religious and benevolent character of the maligned itinerant society. *A Letter to a Country Parson, or, a Reply to the Rev. F. Wollaston's Address to his Flock, to Caution them against being Misled by the Wolf in Sheep's Clothing, or Receiving Jacobin Teachers of Sedition, . . . By a Lover of his Country, and a Friend to Truth* (London, n.d.).

12 Horsley, *Charges*, pp. 103–4.

13 J. Ehrman, *The Younger Pitt The Reluctant Transition* (London, 1983), pp. 450–8; C. Emsley, *British Society and the French Wars 1793–1815* (London, 1979), pp. 41–9; E. A. L. Moir, 'Local government in Gloucestershire, 1775–1800: a study of the Justices of the Peace and their work', Cambridge, Ph.D. thesis, 1955, pp. 259–61.

14 The figures for the registration of meeting-houses recorded by the London diocesan authorities showed an increase between 1797 and 1799 which at its peak was approximately 150 per cent above the normal level. Annual figures for registrations between 1791 and 1801 were as follows:

1791 – 22	1794 – 21	1797 – 30	1800 – 22
1792 – 20	1795 – 19	1798 – 48	1801 – 10
1793 – 15	1796 – 19	1799 – 29	

Diocese of London, register of Dissenters' meeting-houses, 1791–1830, GL. MS 9580. Dr Cookson's suggestion that the response of Dissent to loyalist persecution in the 1790s was that of a vigorous and sometimes defiant assertion of the minority sub-culture, though based on cultural and political action, may also provide a useful insight into the growth of itinerant preaching. J. E. Cookson, *The Friends of Peace Anti-war liberalism in England, 1793–1815* (Cambridge, 1982), pp. 13–14.

15 Horsley, *Charges*, pp. 113–14; Kingsbury, *Apology*, p. 40.

16 *Salisbury and Winchester Journal*, 20 August 1798, p. 3; Malham, *A Broom for the Conventicle*, pp. 49n, 57–60. In September 1798 the committee of the Baptist Society was at pains to repudiate a report published in *The Times* which had connected the society with a convicted bigamist named Curtis. The report had accused the society of paying a £20 fine on the offender's behalf. Minutes 20 September 1798.

17 Malham, *A Broom for the Conventicle*, p. 54. 'So many are the horses wanted for the purpose of mounting these self-created and self-sufficient preachers, that the regular Ministers are frequently disappointed, if they do not keep horses of their own (which, in these times, very few of the Country Curates can afford); and it is no unusual thing to see the latter trudging through mire and dirt, whilst these Village Preachers sally forth and canter along the roads, compelling all before them to make way. Who, indeed, are half so important as themselves! Confined in the week to the shop-board

or the lap-stone, or whatever may be their respective occupations, we behold them on the Sunday morning dressed out cap-a-pee, in pantaloons, with shining boots, and glittering spurs, issuing from their retirements to dispense THE WORD, in the villages to which they have been respectively appointed for the day.'

18 *Salisbury and Winchester Journal*, 20 August 1798, p. 4; Horsley, *Charges*, pp. 57–60, 107–14, 122.
19 Bowen, *Appeal* [p. 1].
20 Jeremy, 'A local crisis', pp. 72, 79.
21 Hall, 'Fragment on Village Preaching', *Works*, vol. 3, p. 360.
22 R. Hill, *An Apology for Sunday Schools. The substance of a sermon, preached at Surry Chapel, February 22, 1801, for the benefit of the Southwark Sunday Schools: With incidental remarks on the late Charge of the Right Rev. the Lord Bishop of Rochester* (London, n.d. [ca. 1801]), p. ix.
23 J. Hinton, *A Vindication of the Dissenters in Oxford, addressed to the Inhabitants; in reply to Dr Tatham's Sermon, lately published, after having been preached in Oxford many Sundays successively*, 3rd edn (London, n.d.), pp. 13, 15, 17–18.
24 Kingsbury, *Apology*, p. 47.
25 Bradley, Roby and Sharp, *Discourse*, pp. 34–5.
26 Baptist Society, minutes, p. 4. In spite of these protestations of non-involvement in politics and the absence of any evidence to the contrary, a recent study of the period repeats the idea that village preaching by evangelical Dissenters involved explicit social and political disaffection. J. C. D. Clark, *English Society 1688–1832 Ideology, social structure and political practice during the ancien regime* (Cambridge, 1985), p. 378.
27 Hill, *Apology*, pp. 34–5, 39n.
28 Hill, *Apology*, pp. 40, 41n.
29 Hill, *Apology*, pp. xi, 30–3, 42n.
30 Hill, *Apology*, p. 39n.
31 H. W[ansey], *A Letter to the Bishop of Salisbury on his late Charge to the Clergy of his Diocese* (Salisbury, 1798), p. 19.
32 Baptist Society, minutes pp. 3–4.
33 Essex Baptist Association, circular letter 1818, p. 2.
34 North Bucks Independent Association, report 1827, p. 37.
35 Bogue and Bennett, *History of Dissenters*, vol. 4, pp. 216–17.
36 Wansey, *Letter to the Bishop of Salisbury*, p. 4.
37 Everitt, *Pattern of Rural Dissent*, pp. 13–46; Gilbert, *Religion and Society*, cap. 5.
38 Clift, *Incidental Letter*, p. 4.
39 Kingsbury, *Apology*, pp. 14–17.
40 Clift, *Incidental Letter*, pp. 7, 21–2.
41 Horsley, *Charges*, pp. 119–21.
42 Baptist Western Association, circular letter 1804, p. 14. The 1800 circular letter expressed the prevailing attitude succinctly: 'Political ideas we do not mean to obtrude; the less Christians trouble themselves about temporal governments the better. My kingdom, said our Lord, is not of this world, else would my servants fight. May it suffice you to know by whom kings reign, and princes decree justice.' The other organization passed loyal resolutions on no less than ten occasions between May 1800 and March 1820. General Body of Protestant Dissenting Ministers, minutes, DWL. MS 38.107. Only over the Sidmouth Bill of 1811 were evangelical organizations unanimously prepared to lay aside their political reserve.
43 Densham to Eyre, 2 October 1800, New College MS 41/74.
44 Malham, *A Broom for the Conventicle*, pp. 36–7. The use of initials to refer to the

preacher, 'the Rev. J. A. of Sarum', provided only a thin disguise for John Adams who was pastor of one of the two Independent congregations in the city.

45 North Bucks Independent Association, reports 1823–6.
46 Societas Evangelica, minutes 29 August 1800, New College MS 122/1.
47 London Itinerant Society, minutes 20 July, 17 August 1798, CL. MS I.i.35.
48 or preacher.
49 Ward, 'The French Revolution', pp. 81–2.
50 An Act To prevent preaching by Persons not duly qualified by Law, Jamaica, 17 December 1802 (reprinted London, 1803).
51 Correspondence and printed papers relating to an act passed by the Jamaica Assembly, 17 December 1802, BMS. MSS; Dissenting Deputies, minutes 1802–4, GL. MS 3083.
52 The text of the bill is preserved in *Cobbett's Parliamentary Debates* [*Hansard*], 19 (1811), 1133–40.
53 *Sketch of the History and Proceedings of the Deputies*, pp. 108–14. The minutes of the Deputies also mention the meeting but give less detail concerning the exchange of views which took place.
54 The anonymous article entitled 'Protestant Society for the Protection of Religious Liberty', *Transactions of the Congregational Historical Society*, 6 (1913–15) wrongly attributes the process of petitioning to the Dissenting Deputies acting in concert with the Wesleyan committee. The minutes of the Protestant Society, 17 May 1811, DWL. MS 38.193 and the resolutions passed by the same body on 24 May 1811, DWL. MS. 38.199 make it clear that the real responsibility for success lay in a combination of Methodist exertions and its own efforts. The minutes of the Deputies for 13–15 May 1811 show that the older Dissenting body contented itself with passing and publicizing a list of resolutions deploring Sidmouth's intentions and submitting one formal petition to the House of Lords signed by those present at a general meeting in the King's Head Tavern. While the scale of petitioning undoubtedly influenced the parliamentary outcome the precise number of petitions submitted is uncertain. Estimates range from 'about five hundred' in *Cobbett's Parliamentary Debates*, 20 (1811), 237 to 'above seven hundred' in the *Sketch of the History and Proceedings of the Deputies*, p. 130. The Protestant Society resolutions of 24 May 1811 give a total of 366 Dissenting petitions while the *Evangelical Magazine*, 19 (1811), 248, in what is probably a conservative figure, suggests 256 as the Methodist contribution.
55 General Body of Protestant Dissenting Ministers, minutes 16 May 1811, DWL. MS. 38.107. As might be expected the Protestant Society with its more evangelical complexion included among its list of grievances against the bill Sidmouth's preoccupation with the notion of self-assumed authority and the effect, therefore, that the proposed legislation would have upon itinerant preachers and all whose concern was to spread religious instruction throughout society. *Evangelical Magazine*, 19 (1811), 240.
56 G. F. A. Best, 'Church and State in English politics, 1800–1833', Cambridge, Ph.D. thesis, 1955, p. 190.
57 *Sketch of the History and Proceedings of the Deputies*, p. 106n.
58 *Sketch of the History and Proceedings of the Deputies*, p. 116. Sidmouth included Norfolk in his list, but the evidence available suggests that the magistrates in Suffolk were equally if not more determined to enforce a strict interpretation of the law.
59 Dissenting Deputies, minutes 28 November 1806, 26 June, 28 August 1807; Suffolk quarter sessions order book, pp. 54, 109, 123–4, Suffolk CRO. 105/2/54.
60 See G. Kitson Clark, *Churchmen and the Condition of England, 1832–1885* (London,

1973), pp. 34–8 for a brief assessment of the growing importance of clerical magistrates in this period. McClatchey, *Oxfordshire Clergy*, cap. 12, also examines this function.

61 Protestant Society, minutes 29 October, 3 December 1811; Court of King's Bench, rule (or order) book, 1807–12, pp. 745, 848, PRO. KB 21.49.

62 Protestant Society, minutes 3 December 1811, 30 January 1812; John Wilks acted as solicitor for Hoxton Academy.

63 Thomas Pellatt and John Wilks to Spencer Perceval, 5 May 1812, Liverpool Papers, vol. 58, BL. Add. Mss 38, 247, fol. 201r; Court of King's Bench, rule (or order) book, 1807–12, p. 848. For the text of Ellenborough's speech see *Evangelical Magazine*, 20 (1812), 241–2.

64 Pellatt and Wilks to Perceval, 31 January 1812, BL. Add. Mss 38, 247, fol. 53v.

65 Perceval sent letters to this effect to the Protestant Society, the Dissenting Deputies and the Committee for Guarding the Privileges of the Methodists on 10 April 1812. For his letter to the Protestant Society see BL. Add. Mss 38, 247, fol. 163.

66 The removal from the statute-book of the Five Mile Act (17 Cha. II, c.2) and the Conventicle Act (22 Cha. II, c.1).

8 Developments and trends

1 Gilbert, *Religion and Society*, pp. 149–57.

2 In the London diocese the average number of meeting-house registrations during the period 1791–1810 was 24 p.a. The 1798 total of 48 registrations was, therefore, 100 per cent above the average. Subsequent peaks were recorded in 1808 and 1811 with 37 and 43 registrations respectively. Diocese of London, register of Dissenters' meeting-houses, 1791–1830, GL. MS 9580. In 1814 the *Sketch of the History and Proceedings of the Deputies*, pp. 108n–9n reprinted the statistical findings of the enquiry into preachers' licences and meeting-house registrations initiated by Lord Sidmouth in 1809. It noted in the preamble that no returns were received from the counties of Worcester and Caernarvon or from the diocese of St David's, and that many of the returns commenced long after 1760. The figures for preachers were as follows:

'Number of persons who have taken the oaths and subscribed the declarations prescribed by 1st W. and M. c.18, and 19th G.3. c.44. at the Quarter Sessions, in periods of seven years, and in each year of the last period.

From	1760 to 1766	80	In 1802	105
	1767 to 1773	38	1803	188
	1774 to 1780	179	1804	113
	1781 to 1787	379	1805	114
	1788 to 1794	610	1806	171
	1795 to 1801	1318	1807	162
	1802 to 1808	1068*	1808	215
		3672		1068*'

3 Matthews, *Congregational Churches of Staffordshire*, p. 214.

4 Certain records also survive for associations in the northern and eastern counties, but these are less complete and in some cases refer to bodies which were in existence for only a few years.

5 See Appendix C for baptismal statistics for the three associations.

6 Rippon, *Register*, vol. 3, p. 37.

7 See above, p. 48.

8 North Bucks Independent Association, reports 1823, 1829.

9 Baptist Society, minutes 24 April 1806, BMS. MSS.
10 Cheshire Congregational Union, report 1811, p. 4.
11 North Bucks Independent Association, report 1821, p. 13. The minister referred to was Thomas Skeene of Wendover.
12 *Congregational Magazine*, 2 (1819), 59, 4 (1821), 499.
13 Village Itinerancy, minutes 21 October 1818. DWL. New College MS 58/1; *Congregational Magazine*, 1 (1818), 553; North Bucks Independent Association, report 1821, p. 12; *Congregational Magazine*, 5 (1822), 165.
14 *Evangelical Magazine*, 5 (1797), 340–1.
15 Hill, *Apology*, pp. 32n–3n.
16 Professor Jones draws attention to the distinction between members and hearers as it existed in the fourth decade of the nineteenth century. *Congregationalism*, p. 222. However, the change in emphasis from membership to adherence occurred 30–40 years earlier, parallel to the introduction of itinerant, and only loosely denominational, evangelism. The idea that Dissent brought to nineteenth-century Nonconformity a well-established tradition of growth and expansion runs counter to the suggestion of a general decline in its fortunes made by Pamela Horn, *The Rural World 1780–1850 Social change in the English countryside* (London, 1980), p. 159. The impression of decline stems from the all too common failure to distinguish between the fortunes of the well-known Rational minority and the much less prominent orthodox majority.
17 Both societies also initiated short-lived evangelistic experiments in areas where Dissent was weak: Societas Evangelica in North Yorkshire, County Durham and Lincolnshire and the Baptist Society in Cornwall.
18 Village Itinerancy, record of formation, New College MS 44.
19 Village Itinerancy, report 1811, New College MS 47. Subsequent expansion by the society was also confined to the southern counties.
20 Acton, Barnes, Bromley, Dulwich, Ealing, Enfield Highway, Garratt, Lewisham, Merton, Mortlake, Ponders End, Scotland Green, Southend (near Lewisham), Streatham, Sydenham, West Norwood and Wimbledon. London Itinerant Society, minutes 1797–1800, CL. MS I.i.35.
21 North Bucks Independent Association, reports 1823, pp. 18–21, 1826, p. 17.
22 Densham to Eyre, 2 October 1800, New College MS 41/74. A similar instance of failure resulting from popular hostility but involving Wesleyan preachers occurred at Barford in Oxfordshire around 1800. North Bucks Independent Association, report 1821, p. 17.
23 North Bucks Independent Association, report 1825, pp. 26–7. Similar seasonal difficulty was experienced at Shillington, Bedfordshire during the winter of 1798–9. Bedfordshire Union of Christians, report 1799, p. 8.
24 Bedfordshire Union of Christians, minutes north-western district 26 November 1799, Bedfordshire CRO. Z 206/1.
25 Bedfordshire Union of Christians, accounts 1812–27, Bedfordshire CRO. Z 206/15.
26 Ivy's programme of village preaching received financial support in 1817 from the Independent churches in Northumberland and from the funds of the Village Itinerancy. A former student at Hackney Academy, Ivy was Independent minister at Brampton between 1817 and 1822. Village Itinerancy, minutes 16 June, 17 December 1817, New College MS 56/1.
27 Lancashire Congregational Union, minutes Preston district 1818–30, Lancashire CRO. CUPf16. At Alston William Norris was able with support from Societas

Evangelica to establish a regular network of preaching stations in the surrounding mining communities. Societas Evangelica, minutes 27 January 1804, 25 January 1805, New College MS 124/1.

28 The latest extant minutes of the Northern Evangelical Association, formed in 1798, date from 1805.

29 Baptist Society, minutes 19 July, 1 October 1799.

30 Slate, *Lancashire Congregational Union*, pp. 72–3. The church referred to was at Ulverston.

31 Congregational Society, draft report 1799 inserted loose in minute book, CL. MS. I.l.41.

32 Baptist Society, minutes 14 November 1809, 9 January 1810. Between 1822 and 1825, spurred into action by a proposal from the Rev. G. C. Smith of Penzance for a new specialist body, the London Itinerant Society turned its attention to the poorer sections of the capital. Difficulties were encountered in finding suitable preaching stations and the various attempts to begin evangelistic meetings were short-lived. No further mention of the metropolis was made after 1825. London Itinerant Society, minutes 2 October 1822 to 15 June 1825, CL. MS I.i.37.

33 Yorkshire and Lancashire Baptist Association, circular letter 1807, p. 15.

34 E. R. Wickham, *Church and People in an Industrial City* (London, 1957), pp. 84–5.

35 J. Bennett, *The Claims of London on the Zeal of Christians. A sermon, in behalf of the London Association, for Extending the Knowledge of the Gospel in the Metropolis, preached at the Meeting-House in New Broad-Street, Moorfields, London* (Rotherham, 1815), p. 37.

36 In Liverpool attempts had been made to preach among the seafaring community and to visit the city's warren of cellar dwellings but this had been the work of individual ministers. I. Sellers, 'Liverpool Nonconformity (1786–1914)', Keele, Ph.D. thesis, 1969, pp. 11, 114.

37 *Baptist Magazine*, 14 (1822), 315–16. Similar tent missions appeared in suburban areas of London including Kentish Town and Kingsland under the auspices of the Home Missionary Society, and in Liverpool. Mearns, *England for Christ*, pp. 54–6; Sellers, 'Liverpool Nonconformity', p. 94.

38 Densham to Eyre, 7 May 1798, New College MS 41/22.

39 R. W. Dale (ed.), *The Life and Letters of John Angell James* (London, 1861), pp. 311–12.

40 Village Itinerancy, minutes 6 November 1811, New College MS 57.

41 Village Itinerancy, correspondence 19 February 1828, New College MS 42/59. A similar process of withdrawal can be seen in Cornwall. R. Ball, *Congregationalism in Cornwall* (London, 1955), pp. 30–2.

42 Bedfordshire Union of Christians, report 1802, p. 5; accounts 1812–27, Bedfordshire CRO. Z 206/15. The term premises includes such items of expenditure as rent, cleaning, furnishing and lighting.

43 Village Itinerancy, minutes 23 April 1807, 21 April 1819, 15 October 1828, New College MSS 57, 58/1, 60/1. Variations in size and location pose difficult problems for the strict comparison of building costs.

44 Wilson, *Memoir of Thomas Wilson*, pp. 309–9.

45 North Bucks Independent Association, report 1824, p. 15.

46 Village Itinerancy, minutes 24 September 1817, New College MS 56/1.

47 J. Sheppard to Matthew Wilks, 3 July 1821, New College MS 42/18.

48 London Itinerant Society, minutes 20 January 1815, CL. MS I.i.36. The debt related to the chapels at West Norwood and Wimbledon.

49 *Congregational Magazine*, 6 (1823), 390–1.

50 Bedfordshire Union of Christians, accounts 1827–44, entry for 1 February 1830, Bedfordshire CRO. Z 206/16.

51 Village Itinerancy, minutes 24 September 1817, 15 March 1820, 2 May 1803, 16 December 1829, New College MSS 56/1, 58/1, 55/1, 60/1. In 1803 the society received two bequests amounting to £11,000. Its subsequent capital of £20,000 yielded an income of £805 p.a. In a further legacy in 1829 it received stock worth £6,000.

52 Slate, *Lancashire Congregational Union*, p. 31.

53 For example Bilston in Staffordshire. See Baptist Midland Association, circular letter 1816, p. 2. In 1820 the same body, noting the serious impact of the recession on its member churches, called for a day of humiliation and prayer to seek divine mercy. Circular letter 1820, p. 8.

54 Gilbert, *Religion and Society*, p. 92. Dr Gilbert argues that Methodism faced similar difficulties.

55 Cheshire Congregational Union, report 1816, p. 13; North Bucks Independent Association, report 1829, pp. 7–10. The North Bucks report compared the attendance at the annual meeting (the largest ever) and the collection (the second largest) with 'the depressed condition of trade'.

56 Village Itinerancy, minutes 15 December 1824, 19 January, 16 March 1825, New College MS 59/1; Ball, *Congregationalism in Cornwall*, pp. 32–3. The collapse brought financial distress to a number of places in Cornwall, but especially to the port of Mevagissey.

57 North Bucks Independent Association, report 1830, pp. 18–19.

58 The circular letters of the Bucks and Herts Particular Baptist Association illustrate the disparity in mission finance very clearly: 1822 (home mission £4/overseas mission £97), 1823 (£4/£61), 1827 (£11/£62), 1828 (£16/£77). Giving for Irish evangelism is included in the overseas figures. In similar fashion the half-yearly meeting of the Northamptonshire Independent Association in 1822 agreed to allocate £80 to the London Missionary Society but only £26 to its domestic counterpart, the Home Missionary Society. *Congregational Magazine*, 5 (1822), 558.

59 The Baptist Home Missionary Society with 26 itinerants experienced a deficit of £131 in the financial year 1827–8. Its Independent counterpart, the Home Missionary Society, went through a more serious crisis the following year which its historian attributed to the widespread commercial depression then prevailing. *Baptist Magazine*, 20 (1828), 279, 321; Mearns, *England for Christ*, pp. 59–60.

60 Congregational Society, minutes 8–30 January 1798, CL. MS I.i.41.

61 North Bucks Independent Association, report 1830, p. 17.

62 Hoxton Academy, minutes 13 January 1809, New College MS 125/1.

63 Hoxton Academy, report 1824, p. xvii.

Bibliography

1. Manuscripts

Because of the importance to this study of local records and archives, and of manuscript material derived from autonomous congregations and societies, the sources are listed *in extenso* with an abbreviated note indicating their present location. Where no archive reference is given, the document is either held privately or by the institution to which it refers.

Abbotts Ann, parish registers, Hampshire CRO.

Richard Alliott, letter concerning early Congregational associations in Nottinghamshire, Derbyshire and Leicestershire, New College MSS., DWL.

Andover Congregational church, minutes.

Apostolic Society/Cheshunt College, minutes and student preaching lists, WC.

Assize court records: home, south eastern and western circuits, PRO.

Baptist Society in London, for the Encouragement and Support of Itinerant and Village Preaching, minutes, BMS.

Bedfordshire Union of Christians, minutes and accounts, Bedfordshire CRO.

Blackburn Independent Academy, minutes, MCC.

Blunham Baptist church, minutes, Bedfordshire CRO.

Bucks and Herts Particular Baptist Association, minutes, Buckinghamshire CRO.

Diocese of Chester, episcopal visitation returns, Cheshire CRO.

Congregational Society for Spreading the Gospel in England, minutes and accounts, CL.

William Davis, letters to Thomas Wilson regarding the establishment of a society in East Sussex for village preaching, New College MSS., DWL.

Dorset quarter sessions records, Dorset CRO.

Eastern Association of Baptist Churches, minutes, RPC.

Enford, parish registers, Wiltshire CRO.

English Evangelic Academy/Hoxton Academy/Highbury College, minutes and correspondence, New College MSS., DWL.

Essex Baptist Association, minutes, BU.

Essex Congregational Union, minutes, Essex CRO.

Evangelical Association for propagating the Gospel in the Villages of Cumberland, Durham, Northumberland and Westmoreland, minutes, Durham CRO.

General Body of Protestant Dissenting Ministers of the Three Denominations, minutes, DWL.

Haddenham (Bucks) Particular Baptist church book, Buckinghamshire CRO.

Hampshire Association of Protestant Dissenting Ministers/Hampshire Congregational Association, minutes and accounts.

Hampshire quarter sessions records, Hampshire CRO.

Hants and Wiltshire Auxiliary Society for Propagating the Gospel among the Heathen, minutes and accounts, BMS.

Hertfordshire quarter sessions records, Hertfordshire CRO.

Hertfordshire Union of Baptist Churches, minute book, containing report on the founding of the earlier Hertfordshire Union of Independent and Baptist Churches, Hertfordshire CRO.
Countess of Huntingdon, connexional papers, WC.
Countess of Huntingdon, letters to Thomas Wills, CL.
Idle Academy, minutes, MCC.
Imber, parish registers, Wiltshire CRO.
Correspondence and printed papers relating to an act passed by the Jamaica Assembly 17 December 1802, BMS.
Kent Evangelical Charity, syllabus of declaration of trust, New College MSS., DWL.
Court of King's Bench records, PRO.
Lancashire Congregational Union, minutes, Lancashire CRO.
Lancashire quarter sessions, register of Dissenters' meeting-houses, Lancashire CRO.
Leaf Square Academy and School, Pendleton, minutes, MCC.
Liverpool Papers, BL.
Diocese of London, register of Dissenters' meeting-houses, GL.
London Itinerant Society, minutes, CL.
London Particular Baptist Education Society, minutes, RPC.
Diocese of Norwich, episcopal visitation returns, Norfolk CRO.
Particular Baptist Society for Propagating the Gospel amongst the Heathen, minutes and accounts, BMS.
Petitions of Protestant Dissenters at Kettering and College Lane, Northampton, against the Protestant Dissenting Ministers bill of May 1811, BU.
Protestant Dissenting Deputies, minutes, GL.
Protestant Society for the Protection of Religious Liberty, records, DWL.
William Roby Papers, MCC.
Diocese of Salisbury, episcopal visitation returns, Wiltshire CRO.
Bethel Independent Chapel, Sheerness, minutes, Kent CRO.
Societas Evangelica, minutes and letter from Samuel Mills to Joshua Wilson giving an outline history of the society, New College MSS., DWL.
Suffolk Association of Dissenting Ministers and Churches of the Independent Denomination, minutes, Suffolk CRO.
Suffolk quarter sessions records, Suffolk CRO.
Village Itinerancy/Hackney Academy, minutes and correspondence, New College MSS., DWL.
Diary of Caleb Warhurst, MCC.
Journal of T. Wastfield, BMS.
Waterbeach Particular Baptist church book.
Baptist Western Association, minutes and accounts, BBC.
Whitchurch (Hants) Independent church, minutes.
Wilsford, parish registers, Wiltshire CRO.
Thomas Wilson, Autobiographical notes and correspondence, CL.

2. Association records (printed)

The annual reports circulated by societies and associations form an important source of information on itinerancy. Having been issued to supporters in the form of flimsy pamphlets most copies have not survived. Where collections do exist they are often incomplete. The presence of more than one abbreviation against a title indicates that the combined holdings of more than one library are necessary for the optimum reconstruction of the series.

Bedfordshire Association of Baptist Churches, circular letter, RPC.

Bedfordshire Union of Christians, annual reports, BU; Bedfordshire CRO.

Berks and West London Association of Particular Baptist Churches, circular letter and minutes, BU.

Bristol Association of Baptist Churches, circular letters and minutes, BU.

Bristol Education Society, annual reports, BBC.

Bucks and Herts Particular Baptist Association, circular letters and minutes, BU.

North Bucks Association of Independent Ministers and Churches, annual reports.

Cheshire Congregational Union, annual reports.

Cheshunt College, Fifteen Articles and annual reports, WC.

Independent North Devon Association and Home Missionary Society, annual report, DWL.

Eastern Association of Baptist Churches, circular letters and minutes, BU; RPC.

Essex Baptist Association, circular letters and minutes, BU; RPC.

Hampshire Association of Protestant Dissenting Ministers, circular letters.

Hoxton Academy, annual reports, DWL.

Idle Academy, annual reports, MCC.

Kent and Sussex Association of Baptist Churches, circular letters and minutes, BU; RPC.

Agreement to form 'an Association of different Congregational Churches, in Lancashire and other neighbouring Counties', Bolton 1786, Lancashire CRO.

London Particular Baptist Association, circular letter, RPC.

Baptist Midland Association, circular letters and minutes, BU; BBC; RPC.

Missionary Society, annual reports, CL.

Norfolk and Suffolk Association of Baptist Churches, circular letters and minutes, BU; RPC.

Northamptonshire Baptist Association, circular letters and minutes, BU; BBC; RPC.

Northern Association of Particular Baptist Churches, circular letters and minutes, BU.

Northern Education Society, annual reports, MCC.

Northern Evangelical Itinerant Academy, plan (ca. 1818), CL.

Oxfordshire and East Gloucestershire Baptist Association, circular letters and minutes, BU; RPC.

Particular Baptist Society for Propagating the Gospel amongst the Heathen [Baptist Missionary Society], annual reports, BMS.

Religious Tract Society, annual reports, BMS.

Rotherham Independent Academy, annual reports, circular letters, financial statements and subscription lists, MCC.

Shropshire and Cheshire Baptist Association, circular letters and minutes, BU; RPC.

Societas Evangelica, annual reports, DWL.

Suffolk and Norfolk New Association of Particular Baptist Churches, circular letter and minutes, RPC.

Baptist Western Association, circular letters and minutes, BU.

Yorkshire and Lancashire Association of Particular Baptist Churches, circular letters and minutes, BU; RPC.

3. Contemporary publications

Andrews, J. and Dury, A., *A Survey Map of Wiltshire*, 1773.

Anon., *A Letter to a Country Parson, or, a Reply to the Rev. F. Wollaston's Address to his Flock, to Caution them against being Misled by the Wolf in Sheep's Clothing, or*

Receiving Jacobin Teachers of Sedition, ... By a Lover of his Country, and a Friend to Truth, London, n.d.

Simple Facts, Illustrative of the Beneficial Results of Village Preaching, London, 1814.

Anti-Jacobin Review and Magazine; or, Monthly Political and Literary Censor.

Baptist Magazine.

Bennett, J., *The Claims of London on the Zeal of Christians. A sermon, in behalf of the London Association, for Extending the Knowledge of the Gospel in the Metropolis, preached at the Meeting-House in New Broad-Street, Moorfields, London*, Rotherham, 1815.

Memoirs of the Life of the Rev. David Bogue, D.D., London, 1827.

Benson, J., *A Defence of the Methodists, in Five Letters, Addressed to the Rev. Dr Tatham, containing Sundry Remarks on a late Discourse, preached by that Gentleman at four of the Churches in Oxford, and entitled 'A Sermon suitable to the Times'*, 2nd edn, London, 1793.

A Farther Defence of the Methodists, in Letters, Addressed to the Rev. W. Russel, Curate of Pershore, in Answer to his Hints to the Methodists and Dissenters, London, 1793.

Bogue, D., *The Great Importance of having Right Sentiments in Religion: a sermon, preached at an association of ministers, at Ringwood, Hants ... the 29th of July, 1788*, London, 1788.

The Diffusion of Divine Truth. A sermon preached before the Religious Tract Society, on Lord's Day, May 18, 1800, London, 1800.

The Removal of an Eminently Wise and Good Man lamented and improved. [Joseph Hardcastle], London, 1819.

Bogue, D. and Bennett, J., *History of Dissenters, from the Revolution in 1688, to the year 1808*, 4 vols., London, 1808–12.

Booth, A., *Glad Tidings to Perishing Sinners; or, the Genuine Gospel a complete warrant for the ungodly to believe in Jesus*, London, 1796.

[Bowen, W. M.], *An Appeal to the People on the Alleged Causes of the Dissenters' Separation from the Established Church: To which are Subjoined a few Cautionary Observations, in respect to their Present Political Views*, Salisbury, 1798.

Strictures, on a letter to the Bishop of Salisbury, on his late Charge to the Clergy of his Diocese: by H.W. of Salisbury, a Dissenter; Author of 'A Tour to the United States of America', Salisbury, 1798.

Brian Monckhouse [Bowen, W. M.], *A Letter to W. Kingsbury, of Southampton, M.A. in Answer to his Apology for Village Preachers; and his Animadversions on a part of An Appeal to the People*, Salisbury, 1798.

G.W. [Bowles, W. L.], *A Rowland for an Oliver, Addressed to Mr Wansey, on his Letter to the Bishop of Salisbury*, Salisbury, 1798.

[Bowles, W. L.], *The Dissenter Done Over; or The Woeful Lamentation of Mr H.W. a Wiltshire Clothier; setting forth How the Clergy of this Realm, all dressed in fiery Scarlet, have attacked with Mastiffs, Guns, and Pistols, the poor Lamb-like and inoffensive Dissenters. Describing also The dreadful Vicar of Scarborough, with a Turban on his Head, and the Koran in his Hand, crying out, 'Fee, faw, fum'. The whole Faithfully translated from the inimitable Production of the same Mr H.W.; and set to the Tune of 'The Taylor Done Over'*, Salisbury, 1798.

P.P. [Bowles, W. L.], *A True Account of the Deplorable Malady of H...y W....y, a Wiltshire Clothier: shewing How he mistook a Barber for a Clergyman in a red Coat; and a Lancet, with which it was attempted to bleed him, for a Scymitar. Being an Epistle From his Cook-maid, Doll Dish-clout, to Mrs Bacon, the Tallow-chandler's Wife*, Salisbury, 1798.

[Bowles, W. L.], *Fair Play is a Jewel: or, The Language and Conduct of the Discussers Discussed; in which the Case is fairly stated respecting the Bishop of Salisbury's late Charge, and Mr Wansey's Letter: the Illiberal Charges brought against the Clergy are repelled; and the Pretensions of Some, among Dissenters, to Exclusive Wisdom and Charity, are examined: Occasioned by a Pamphlet, entitled 'Rights of Discussion'*, Salisbury, 1799.

Bradley, S., Roby, W. and Sharp, I., *A Discourse on the Nature of a Christian Church, by the Rev. S. Bradley; A Charge, by the Rev. W. Roby; A Sermon by the Rev. I. Sharp; with a Confession of Faith, etc., Delivered, December 7th, 1802, at the Independent Meeting-House, in Warrington, at the ordination of the Rev. Joseph Johnson*, Manchester, 1803.

Bridgman, I., *A Candid Appeal to the Religious Public, in a Letter, Addressed to the Inhabitants of the Forest of Dean, Gloucestershire, occasioned by the Dismissal of the Rev. Isaac Bridgman, A.B. of St Edmund's Hall, Oxford, from the Curacy of Trinity Church, in the said Forest. With a Preface, by the Rev. Rowland Hill, A.M.*, Ross, 1823.

Bullar, J., *Memoirs of the late Rev. William Kingsbury, M.A.*, London, 1819.

Burder, G., *The Good Old Way: or, the Religion of our forefathers, as expressed in the Articles, Liturgy, and Homilies of the Church of England ...*, 7th edn, Coventry, 1792.

Village Sermons; or ... plain and short discourses on the principal doctrines of the Gospel, 7 vols., London, 1798–1816.

Burke, E., *Reflections on the Revolution in France, and on the Proceedings in Certain Societies in London relative to that event*, London, 1790.

Carey, W., *An Enquiry into the Obligations of Christians to use Means for the Conversion of the Heathens*, Leicester, 1792.

Clift, S., *An Incidental Letter, Addressed to the Lord Bishop of Sarum, August the 9th, 1798, the day of his Visitation held at Chippenham, Wilts. with some Observations and Reflections in Favour of Village Preaching*, Chippenham, n.d. [1798].

Cobbett's Parliamentary Debates.

Cottage Sermons: Twelve Short and Plain Discourses, Adapted for General Circulation, and also for Reading in Families, vols. 2 and 3, n.d.

Cracknell, B., *The Utility of Academical Institutions to the Church of Christ. A sermon, preached at Hoxton Chapel, June 26, 1806, before the supporters of the Hoxton College, at their Anniversary*, London, n.d. [1806].

Edwards, J., *Stubborn Facts; or, a plain statement of the proceedings of a Particular Baptist Church with respect to two of their members, who were found guilty of praying, reading, and expounding the Scriptures, in the villages, under the patronage of the London Itinerant Society, without a regular call to the work of the ministry, in a series of letters to a friend*, London, 1808.

Evangelical Magazine.

Exall, J., *Sketches of the Kent and Sussex Baptist Associations from 1779 to 1829*, London, 1829.

[Fisher, J.], *Rights of Discussion; or A Vindication of Dissenters, of Every Denomination: With a Review of the Controversy, occasioned by a late Pastoral Charge of the Bishop of Salisbury. To which is added, Hints for Pastoral Charges*, London, 1799.

Foley, R., *A Defence of the Church of England, in a Series of Discourses, preach'd at Old Swinford, in Worcestershire; on Ephesians 5, 27*, Stourbridge, 1795.

Fuller, A., *The Gospel of Christ worthy of all acceptation ...*, Northampton, 1785.

Gentleman's Magazine; and Historical Chronicle.

Goddard, W. S., *A Sermon, Preached in the Cathedral Church of Chichester, August 8, 1811, at the Triennial Visitation of the Right Reverend Father in God, John, Lord Bishop of Chichester*, 2nd edn, Winchester, 1812.

Greatheed, S., *General Union Recommended to Real Christians in a Sermon preached at Bedford, October 31, 1797. With an introductory account of an union of Christians of various denominations, which was then instituted to promote the knowledge of the Gospel; including a plan for universal union in the genuine Church of Christ*, London, 1798.

Griffin, J., *'The Encouraging Aspect of the Times: or, the Christian's Duty to Study the Prophecies of Revelation, in connection with the Events of Providence.' A sermon preached in Orange-Street Chapel, Portsea, February 26, 1806*, Portsea, 1806.

Haldane, R., *Address to the Public concerning Political Opinions, and Plans lately adopted to promote Religion in Scotland*, 2nd edn, Edinburgh, 1800.

Hall, Robert (Senr), *Help to Zion's Travellers; being an attempt to remove various stumbling-blocks out of the way, relating to doctrinal, experimental, and practical religion*, Bristol, 1781.

Hall, Robert (Junr), *The Works of Robert Hall, A.M. With a brief memoir of his life by Dr Gregory; and observations on his character as a preacher, by John Foster*, ed. O. Gregory, 6 vols., London, 1832 edn.

Hett, W., *Christian Morality; or, a Hint to Gospel Preachers: A sermon, delivered in the Cathedral Church of Lincoln, October 13, 1816*, London, 1817.

Hill, R., *An Apology for Sunday Schools. The substance of a sermon, preached at Surry Chapel, February 22, 1801, for the benefit of the Southwark Sunday Schools: With incidental remarks on the late Charge of the Right Rev. the Lord Bishop of Rochester*, London, n.d. [ca. 1801].

Hinton, J., *A Vindication of the Dissenters in Oxford, addressed to the Inhabitants; in reply to Dr Tatham's Sermon, lately published, after having been preached in Oxford many Sundays successively*, 3rd edn, London, n.d.

Hinton, J. H., *A Biographical Portraiture of the late Rev. James Hinton, M.A., Pastor of a Congregational Church in the City of Oxford*. Oxford, 1824.

Home Missionary Magazine: or, Record of the Transactions of The Home Missionary Society.

Horsley, S., *The Charges of Samuel Horsley, LL.D., F.R.S., F.A.S., late Lord Bishop of St Asaph, Delivered at his Several Visitations of the Dioceses of St David's, Rochester, and St Asaph*, London, 1830.

Ivimey, J., *A History of the English Baptists*, 4 vols., London, 1811–1830.

Jay, W. (ed.), *Memoirs of the Late Reverend John Clark, Written by Himself; And at His Request, Published, with Remarks, by William Jay*, Bath, 1810.

Jay, W., *Memoirs of the Life and Character of the late Rev. Cornelius Winter*, 2nd edn, London, 1812.

Jones, T. S., *The Life of the Right Honourable Willielma, Viscountess Glenorchy, containing extracts from her diary and correspondence*, Edinburgh, 1822.

Kingsbury, W., *An Apology for Village Preachers; or an Account of the Proceedings and Motives of Protestant Dissenters, and Serious Christians of other Denominations, in their Attempts, to Suppress Infidelity and Vice, and to Spread Vital Religion in Country Places; especially where the Means of Pious Instruction, among the Poor, are Rare: with some Animadversions on an Anonymous 'Appeal to the People': and Replies to Objections*, Southampton, 1798.

Liddon, J., *Thoughts on Intolerance, Occasioned by the New Interpretation of the Toleration Act as it respects the Protestant Dissenters*, London, 1812.

London Christian Instructor; or, Congregational Magazine.

[Malham, J.], *Remarks on a Letter to the Bishop of Salisbury, on his late Charge to the Clergy of his Diocese: by H.W. of Salisbury, a Dissenter. With some Cursory Hints in Defence of the Inferior Clergy*, Salisbury, 1798.

Malham, J., *A Broom for the Conventicle: or, the Arguments for Village Preaching Examined, and Fairly Discussed; more particularly obviating the unfounded assertions of Mr Kingsbury, of Southampton, and Mr Clift of Chippenham. With observations on the various replies to Mr H.W's Letter to the Bishop of Salisbury, And the other Publications on this Subject*, Salisbury, 1798.

Mant, R., *Puritanism Revived; or Methodism as old as the Great Rebellion. In a Series of Letters from a Curate to his Rector.* London, 1808.

Mawer, W., *The Examiner Examined, or an Apology for the Methodists; Being an Answer to Mr Neesham's Examination; Together with some Further Remarks on the Reverend Mr Hett's Letters to Lord A, B, C &c,* Lincoln, 1810.

Monthly Repository of Theology and General Literature.

More, H. *et. al., Cheap Repository Tracts,* 3 vols., London, 1798.

Orthodox Churchman's Magazine; or, A Treasury of Divine and Useful Knowledge.

Price, R., *A Discourse on the Love of our Country,* London, 1790.

Protestant Dissenter's Magazine.

The Publications of the Religious Tract Society. To which is prefixed, an account of the origin and progress of the society, with extracts of correspondence, foreign and domestic, 4 vols., London, 1812–14.

Quarterly Register of the Baptist Home Missionary Society.

Report from the Clergy of a district in the Diocese of Lincoln, convened for the purpose of considering the state of religion in ... the said district, as well as the best mode of promoting the belief and practice of it, London, 1800.

Resolutions of the Methodist Ministers of the Manchester District, assembled at Liverpool, May 23, 1811, on the subject of a Bill introduced into Parliament by the Right Hon. Lord Viscount Sidmouth: to which is annexed, an Abstract of the Debate in the House of Lords, on Tuesday, May 21st, 1811, when the said Bill was rejected, Liverpool, n.d.

Rippon, J. (ed.), *The Baptist Annual Register,* 4 vols., London, 1793–1802.

Roby, W., *A Short Treatise on the Absolute Necessity of the Satisfaction of Christ; or, the Dangerous Tendency of Socinianism considered,* Wigan, 1791.

A Defence of Calvinism; or, Strictures on a Recent Publication, entitled, 'St Paul against Calvin', London, 1810.

The Glory of the Latter Days: A Discourse delivered on Wednesday Evening, Jan. 12th, 1814 in the Independent Chapel, Mosley-Street, Manchester, at one of the associated Monthly Lectures, 2nd edn, London, 1814.

Academical Institutions: or the Importance of Preparatory Instruction for the Christian Ministry, illustrated in a Sermon, Preached at the Anniversary of the Blackburn Independent Academy; held on the 23d, and 24th of July, 1819, Manchester, 1819.

Anti-Swedenborgianism: or, a Letter to the Rev. J. Clowes, M.A., Rector of St John's Church, Manchester, and late Fellow of Trinity College, Cambridge; containing a Reply to his Strictures on those Passages in the Author's Lectures, which refer to the Honourable Emanuel Swedenborg, and his Disciples, Manchester, 1819.

Protestantism: or an Address particularly to the Labouring Classes, in defence of the Protestant Principle, 'That the Scriptures, not Tradition, are the Rule of Faith', 3 parts, London, 1821–22.

Salisbury and Winchester Journal and General Advertiser of Wilts, Hants, Dorset, and Somerset.

Scott, T., *The Holy Bible containing the Old and New Testaments, according to the Authorized Version; with Explanatory Notes, Practical Observations, and Copious Marginal References,* 6th edn, 6 vols., London, 1823.

Shrubsole, W., *Christian Memoirs ...; including A Memoir of the Life of the Rev. William Shrubsole,* London, 1807.

Simpson, D., *A Plea for Religion and the Sacred Writings, Addressed to the Disciples of Thomas Paine, and Wavering Christians of Every Persuasion,* 3rd edn, London, 1804.

A Sketch of the History and Proceedings of the Deputies Appointed to Protect the Civil Rights of the Protestant Dissenters. To which is annexed a Summary of the Laws affecting Protestant

Dissenters with an Appendix of Statutes and Precedents of Legal Instruments, London, 1814.

Steadman, W., *The Christian Minister's Duty and Reward. A sermon, addressed as a charge to Mr Richard Pengilly, when ordained pastor of the Baptist church at Newcastle upon Tyne, August 12, 1807*, Gateshead, 1807.

Tatham, E., *A Sermon suitable to the times*, London, 1792.

Tract Magazine; or, Christian Miscellany.

Transactions of the Missionary Society.

Village Discourses. Six sermons designed for the use of village congregations, families and Sunday schools, London, 1813.

H.W. [Wansey, H.], *A Letter to the Bishop of Salisbury on his late Charge to the Clergy of his Diocese*, Salisbury, 1798.

Wells, M., *Memoir of Mrs Joanna Turner, as Exemplified in Her Life, Death, and Spiritual Experience. With a Recommendatory Preface by the Rev. D. Bogue, D.D.*, London, 1820.

Whitfield, C., *The Obligations to Mental Improvement Stated, and the Use of Books Recommended, Especially to Youth. A sermon preached to the congregation of Protestant Dissenters, in Hamsterley, Durham, January 22, 1792*, Newcastle, 1792.

Wilson, W., *The History and Antiquities of Dissenting Churches and Meeting Houses, in London, Westminster, and Southwark; including the Lives of their Ministers, from the rise of Nonconformity to the present time*, 4 vols., London, 1808–14.

Wollaston, F., *A Country Parson's Address to his Flock, to Caution them against being Misled by the Wolf in Sheep's Cloathing, or Receiving Jacobin Teachers of Sedition, who intrude themselves under the Specious Pretense of Instructing Youth and Preaching Christianity*, London, 1799.

Woodward, R., *The Causes and Pretences for Separation from the ancient Established Church considered and refuted*, London, 1802.

Wright, R., *A Review of the Missionary Life and Labors of Richard Wright. Written by himself*, London, 1824.

Young, A., *View of the Agriculture of Oxfordshire*, London, 1809.

4. Other sources

Abbey, C. J. and Overton, J. H., *The English Church in the Eighteenth Century*, 2 vols., London, 1878.

Anon., *Biggleswade Baptist Church, 1771–1971*.

The Life and Times of Selina Countess of Huntingdon, 2 vols., London, 1844.

Memoir of the late Mr. William Hogg, of Painswick, Cheltenham, 1862.

'Protestant Society for the Protection of Religious Liberty', *Transactions of the Congregational Historical Society*, 6 (1913–15), 364–76.

'The defeat of Lord Sidmouth's bill, 1811', *Transactions of the Congregational Historical Society*, 7 (1916–18), 344–7.

Antrobus, A., *History of the Wilts and East Somerset Congregational Union*, London, 1947.

Atterbury, F., *A Letter to a Convocation-Man concerning the Rights, Powers, and Priviledges of that body*, 1697.

Ball, R., *Congregationalism in Cornwall*, London, 1955.

Best, G. F. A., 'Church and State in English politics, 1800–1833', Cambridge, Ph.D. thesis, 1955.

Temporal Pillars Queen Anne's Bounty, the Ecclesiastical Commissioners, and the Church of England, Cambridge, 1964.

Binfield, C., *So Down to Prayers Studies in English Nonconformity 1780–1920*, London, 1977.

Bolam, C. G., Goring, J., Short, H. L., and Thomas, R., *The English Presbyterians from Elizabethan Puritanism to Modern Unitarianism*, London, 1968.

Bossy, J., *The English Catholic Community 1570–1850*, London, 1975.

Bradley, I. C., 'The politics of godliness: Evangelicals in Parliament, 1784–1832', Oxford, D.Phil. thesis, 1974.

Bretherton, F. F., *The Countess of Huntingdon*, London, 1940.

Brown, C., *The Story of Baptist Home Missions*, London, 1897.

Brown, J., *The History of the Bedfordshire Union of Christians. The Story of a Hundred Years*, ed. D. Prothero, London, 1946.

Brown, L., *The Story of the Dorset Congregational Association*, Bridport, 1971.

Browne, J., *History of Congregationalism, and Memorials of the Churches in Norfolk and Suffolk*, London, 1877.

Buffard, F., *Kent and Sussex Baptist Associations*, n.d. [ca.1963].

Bull, F. W., 'The Newport Pagnell Academy', *Transactions of the Congregational Historical Society*, 4 (1909–10), 305–22.

Bull, J., *Memorials of the Rev. William Bull, of Newport Pagnel*, London, 1864.

Burder, H. F., *Memoir of the Rev. George Burder*, London, 1833.

Burls, R., *A Brief Review of the Plan and Operations of the Essex Congregational Union for Promoting the Knowledge of the Gospel in the County of Essex and its Vicinity. With an Appendix, containing Biographical Notices of the Principal Founders and Supporters of the Society*, Maldon, 1848.

Carey, S. P., *William Carey, D.D., Fellow of Linnaean Society*, 6th edn, London, 1925.

Carwardine, R. J., *Transatlantic Revivalism. Popular Evangelicalism in Britain and America, 1790–1865*, Westport, 1978.

Chalmers, T., *Lectures on the Establishment and Extension of National Churches*, 2nd edn, Glasgow, 1838.

Champion, L. G., 'The preaching baronet', *Baptist Quarterly*, n.s. 10 (1940–1), 429–33.

Champion, L. G., Moon, N. S. and Mowvley, H., *The Bristol Education Society, 1770–1970*, Bristol, n.d. [1970].

Clark, G. Kitson, *Churchmen and the Condition of England, 1832–1885*, London, 1973.

Clark, J. C. D., *English Society 1688–1832. Ideology, social structure and political practice during the ancien regime*, Cambridge, 1985.

Cleal, E. E. and Crippen, T. G., *The Story of Congregationalism in Surrey*, London, 1908.

Clipsham, E. F., 'Andrew Fuller and Fullerism: a study in evangelical Calvinism', *Baptist Quarterly*, n.s. 20 (1963–4), 99–114, 146–54, 214–25, 268–76.

Cockin, J., *Memoirs of the Rev. Joseph Cockin*, 2nd edn, London, 1841.

Collinson, P., *The Elizabethan Puritan Movement*, London, 1967.

Cookson, J. E., *The Friends of Peace. Anti-war liberalism in England, 1793–1815*, Cambridge, 1982.

[Crippen, T. G.], 'The Surrey Mission', *Transactions of the Congregational Historical Society*, 6 (1913–15), 297–314.

'The London Itinerant Society', *Transactions of the Congregational Historical Society*, 7 (1916–18), 310–23, 350–62.

Crosland, J. D., 'The Bedford Association: an early ecumenical movement', *Proceedings of the Wesley Historical Society*, 28 (1951–2), 95.

Currie, R., Gilbert, A. and Horsley, L., *Churches and Churchgoers. Patterns of Church Growth in the British Isles since 1700*, Oxford, 1977.

Curry, W., *A Letter, containing some account of the life and character of the late Rev. William Vint, with extracts from his correspondence*, London, 1834.

Dale, R. W. (ed.), *The Life and Letters of John Angell James*, London, 1861.

Dale, R. W., *History of English Congregationalism*, ed. A. W. W. Dale, London, 1907.

Davies, G. C. B., *The First Evangelical Bishop. Some aspects of the life of Henry Ryder*, London, 1958.

Davies, H., *The English Free Churches*, 2nd edn, London, 1963.

Davies, R., George, A. R. and Rupp, G. (eds.), *A History of the Methodist Church in Great Britain*, 3 vols., London, 1965–83.

Davis, R. W., *Dissent in Politics, 1780–1830: the political life of William Smith, M.P.*, London, 1971.

Davis, T. W., 'Conflict and concord among Protestant Dissenters in London, 1787 to 1813', North Carolina, Ph.D. thesis, 1972.

Densham, W. and Ogle, J., *The Story of the Congregational Churches of Dorset, from their foundation to the present time*, Bournemouth, 1899.

Dickens, A. G. and Carr, D. (eds.), *The Reformation in England to the Accession of Elizabeth I*, London, 1967.

Dictionary of National Biography.

Douglas, D., *History of the Baptist Churches in the North of England from 1648–1845*, London, 1846.

Drewery, M., *William Carey. Shoemaker and Missionary*, London, 1978.

Ehrman, J., *The Younger Pitt. The Reluctant Transition*, London, 1983.

Emsley, C., *British Society and the French Wars 1793–1815*, London, 1979.

Evans, E. D. P., 'The history of the Presbyterian Chapel, Bank Street, Bury, Lancashire, 1719–1919', Manchester Unitarian College, unpublished dissertation, 1919.

Evans, E. J., 'Some reasons for the growth of English rural anti-clericalism c.1750–c.1830', *Past and Present*, 66 (1975), 84–109.

Everitt, A., *The Pattern of Rural Dissent: the Nineteenth Century*, English Local History Occasional Papers, 2nd Series, ed. A. Everitt, No. 4, Leicester, 1972.

Fancutt, W., *The Southern Baptist Association and its Churches, 1824–1974*, Andover, n.d. [1974].

Gadsby, J. (ed.), *A Memoir of the late Mr William Gadsby, upwards of thirty-eight years pastor of the Baptist Chapel, St George's-Road, Manchester, compiled from authentic sources*, Manchester 1844.

Gay, J. D., *The Geography of Religion in England*, London, 1971.

Gee, H. and Hardy, W. J. (eds.), *Documents illustrative of English Church History compiled from original sources*, London, 1921.

Gilbert, A. D., *Religion and Society in Industrial England: Church, Chapel and Social Change, 1740–1914*, London, 1976.

Gill, J., *A Body of Doctrinal Divinity; or, a System of Evangelical Truths, Deduced from the Sacred Scriptures*, 2 vols., London, 1769.

Goodwin, A., *The Friends of Liberty: The English Democratic Movement in the age of the French Revolution*, London, 1979.

Gray, D., *Spencer Perceval. The Evangelical Prime Minister 1762–1812*, Manchester, 1963.

Griffin, J., *Memoirs and Remains of the Rev. John Griffin of Portsea*, London, 1840.

Halévy, E., *A History of the English People in 1815*, trans. E. I. Watkin and D. A. Barker, London, 1924.

Hamlin, A. G., 'The Bristol Baptist Itinerant Society', *Baptist Quarterly*, n.s. 21 (1965–6), 321–4.

Hempton, D., *Methodism and Politics in British Society 1750–1850*, London, 1984.

Henriques, U., *Religious Toleration in England 1787–1833*, London, 1961.

[M. Hewitt], 'Sutcliff: the meeting and the man', Bristol Baptist College, unpublished dissertation, n.d.

BIBLIOGRAPHY

Higgs, L. F., 'The calling and ordination of ministers in the eighteenth century', *Baptist Quarterly*, n.s. 16 (1955–6), 277–9.

Hine, R., *History of Beaminster*, Taunton, 1914.

Hobsbawm, E. J., 'Methodism and the threat of revolution in Britain', *History Today*, 7 (1957), 115–24.

Primitive Rebels Studies in Archaic Forms of Social Movement in the 19th and 20th Centuries, Manchester, 1959.

Horn, P., *The Rural World 1780–1850 Social change in the English countryside*, London, 1980.

Horst, I. B., *The Radical Brethren Anabaptism and the English Reformation to 1558*, Nieuwkoop, 1972.

Hosken, T. J., *History of Congregationalism and Memorials of the Churches of our order in Suffolk*, Ipswich, 1920.

Howse, E. M., *Saints in Politics The 'Clapham Sect' and the Growth of Freedom*, London, 1953.

Itzkin, E. S., 'The Halévy thesis – a working hypothesis? English revivalism: antidote for revolution and radicalism 1789–1815', *Church History*, 44 (1975), 47–56.

Jay, C., *Recollections of William Jay, of Bath: with occasional glances at some of his contemporaries and friends*, London, 1859.

Jebb, H. H., *A Great Bishop of one hundred years ago: being a sketch of the life of Samuel Horsley*, London, 1909.

Jephson, H., *The Platform Its Rise and Progress*, 2 vols., London, 1892.

Jeremy, D. J., 'A local crisis between Establishment and Nonconformity: the Salisbury village preaching controversy, 1798–1799', *Wiltshire Archaeological and Natural History Magazine*, 61 (1966), 63–84.

Johnson, W. B., *The English Prison Hulks*, 2nd edn, London, 1970.

Jones, R. T., *Congregationalism in England 1662–1962*, London, 1962.

Jones, W., *Memoirs of the life, ministry and writings of the Rev. Rowland Hill*, London, 1834.

Jordan, W. K., *The Development of Religious Toleration in England*, 4 vols., London, 1932–40.

Kiernan, V., 'Evangelicalism and the French Revolution', *Past and Present*, 1 (1952), 44–56.

Kverndal, R., 'Seamen's missions: their origin and early growth A contribution to the history of the Church maritime', Oslo, D.Theol. thesis, 1984.

Langley, A. S., *Birmingham Baptists Past and Present*, London, 1939.

Laqueur, T. W., *Religion and Respectability Sunday Schools and Working Class Culture 1780–1850*, New Haven, 1976.

Laslett, P., *The World We Have Lost*, 2nd edn, London, 1971.

Lecler, J., *Toleration and the Reformation*, trans. T. L. Westow, 2 vols., London, 1960.

Leifchild, J., *Memoir of the late Rev. Joseph Hughes, A.M.*, London, 1835.

Leonard, H. C. (ed.), *A History of the Churches forming the Hertfordshire and Bedfordshire Baptist Association*, Hemel Hempstead, 1875.

Lewis, A. J., *Zinzendorf the Ecumenical Pioneer A Study in the Moravian Contribution to Christian Mission and Unity*, London, 1962.

Lincoln, A., *Some Political and Social Ideas of English Dissent 1763–1800*, Cambridge, 1938.

Lovegrove, D. W., 'Particular Baptist itinerant preachers during the late 18th and early 19th centuries', *Baptist Quarterly*, n.s. 28 (1979–80), 127–41.

'English evangelical Dissent and the European conflict 1789–1815' in W. J. Sheils (ed.), *Studies in Church History*, 20 (1983), 263–76.

'Idealism and association in early nineteenth century Dissent' in W. J. Sheils and D. Wood (eds.), *Studies in Church History*, 23 (1986), 303–17.

McClatchey, D., *Oxfordshire Clergy, 1777–1869: A study of the Established Church and of the role of its Clergy in local society*, Oxford, 1960.

McCord, N., *The Anti-Corn Law League 1838–1846*, London, 1958.

McLachlan, H., *English Education under the Test Acts. Being the History of the Nonconformist Academies, 1662–1820*, Manchester, 1931.

McLachlan, H. J., *Socinianism in Seventeenth-Century England*, London, 1951.

Manley, K. R., 'The making of an evangelical Baptist leader. John Rippon's early years, 1751–1773', *Baptist Quarterly*, n.s. 26 (1975–6), 254–74.

Manning, B. L., *The Protestant Dissenting Deputies*, ed. O. Greenwood, Cambridge, 1952.

Martin, R. H., 'Evangelical Dissenters and Wesleyan-style itinerant ministries at the end of the eighteenth century', *Methodist History*, 16 (1978), 169–84.

Evangelicals United: Ecumenical Stirrings in Pre-Victorian Britain, 1795–1830, Studies in Evangelicalism No. 4, Metuchen, N.J., 1983.

Mathias, P., *The First Industrial Nation. An Economic History of Britain 1700–1914*, London, 1969.

Matthews, A. G., *The Congregational Churches of Staffordshire with Some Account of the Puritans, Presbyterians, Baptists and Quakers in the County during the Seventeenth Century*, London, 1924.

Calamy Revised Being a revision of Edmund Calamy's Account of the ministers and others ejected and silenced, 1660–2, Oxford, 1934.

Mayor, S. H., *Cheshire Congregationalism, a brief history*, n.d. [ca.1957].

Mearns, A., *England for Christ: a record of the Congregational Church Aid and Home Missionary Society*, London, 1886.

Mews, S., 'Reason and emotion in working-class religion, 1794–1824' in D. Baker (ed.), *Studies in Church History*, 9 (1972), 365–82.

Mills, D. R. (ed.), *English Rural Communities: the impact of a specialised economy*, London, 1973.

Moir, E. A. L., 'Local government in Gloucestershire, 1775–1800: a study of the Justices of the Peace and their work', Cambridge, Ph.D. thesis, 1955.

Moon, N. S., 'Caleb Evans, founder of the Bristol Education Society', *Baptist Quarterly*, n.s. 24 (1971–2), 175–90.

Murray, N. U., 'The influence of the French Revolution on the Church of England and its rivals, 1789–1802', Oxford, D.Phil. thesis, 1975.

Neuburg, V. E., *Chapbooks. A guide to reference material on English, Scottish and American chapbook literature of the eighteenth and nineteenth centuries*, 2nd edn, London, 1972.

Newman, J. H. *et al.*, *Tracts for the Times*, 5 vols., London, 1834–40.

Newman, J. H., *Apologia Pro Vita Sua Being a history of his religious opinions*, ed. M. J. Svaglic, Oxford, 1967.

Nightingale, B., *Lancashire Nonconformity; or, sketches, historical and descriptive of the Congregational and Old Presbyterian Churches in the County*, 6 vols., Manchester, 1890–3.

The Story of the Lancashire Congregational Union, 1806–1906, Manchester, 1906.

Norman, E. R., *Church and Society in England 1770–1970 A Historical Study*, London, 1976.

Nuttall, G. F., 'Northamptonshire and *The Modern Question*: a turning-point in eighteenth-century Dissent', *Journal of Theological Studies*, n.s. 16 (1965), 101–23.

The Significance of Trevecca College, 1768–91, London, 1968.

'Assembly and association in Dissent, 1689–1831' in G. J. Cuming and D. Baker (eds.), *Studies in Church History*, 7 (1971), 289–309.

'Rowland Hill and the Rodborough Connexion, 1771–1833', *Transactions of the Congregational Historical Society*, 21 (1972), 69–73.

New College, London and Its Library, London, 1977.

'Questions and answers: an eighteenth-century correspondence', *Baptist Quarterly*, n.s. 27 (1977–8), 83–90.

Obelkevich, J., *Religion and Rural Society: South Lindsey 1825–1875*, London, 1976.

Orchard, S. C., 'English Evangelical eschatology 1790–1850', Cambridge, Ph.D. thesis, 1969.

Overton, J. H., *The Evangelical Revival in the Eighteenth Century*, London, 1900.

Owen, W. T., *Edward Williams, D.D. 1750–1813. His Life, Thought and Influence*, Cardiff, 1963.

Palmer, R. R., *Catholics and Unbelievers in Eighteenth Century France*, Princeton, 1939.

Parker, I., *Dissenting Academies in England: their rise and progress and their place among the educational systems of the country*, Cambridge, 1914.

'Returns relating to Dissenters' places of worship, England and Wales', *Parliamentary Papers*, 78 (1852–3).

Payne, E. A., *The Baptist Union – A Short History*, London, 1959.

'Abraham Booth, 1734–1806', *Baptist Quarterly*, n.s. 26 (1975–6), 28–42.

Pearsall, J. S., *Historical Memorials of a Christian Fellowship*, 2nd edn, n.d. [Andover Congregational Church].

Pellew, G., *The Life and Correspondence of the Right Honble Henry Addington, First Viscount Sidmouth*, 3 vols., London, 1847.

Plucknett, T. F. T., *A Concise History of the Common Law*, 3rd edn, London, 1940.

Plumb, D., 'The social and economic spread of rural Lollardy: a reappraisal' in W. J. Sheils and D. Wood (eds.), *Studies in Church History*, 23 (1986), 111–29.

Powicke, F. J., *A History of the Cheshire County Union of Congregational Churches, prepared to commemorate its centenary, 1806–1906*, Manchester, 1907.

Prestwich, M. (ed.), *International Calvinism 1541–1715*, Oxford, 1985.

Rack, H. D., 'Domestic visitation: a chapter in early nineteenth century evangelism', *Journal of Ecclesiastical History*, 24 (1973), 357–76.

Ransome, M. (ed.), *Wiltshire Returns to the Bishop's Visitation Queries 1783*, Devizes, 1972.

Redford, G. and James, J. A. (eds.), *The Autobiography of William Jay*, London, 1854.

Redstone, V. B., *The Annals of Wickham Market and other papers. A contribution towards a history of Wickham Market*, Woodbridge, 1896.

Reeves, M. E., 'Protestant Nonconformity' in R. B. Pugh and E. Crittall (eds.), *Victoria County History of Wiltshire*, vol. 3, London, 1956.

Robinson, W. G., *William Roby (1766–1830) and the Revival of Independency in the North*, London, 1954.

Robison, O. C., 'The Particular Baptists in England, 1760–1820', Oxford, D.Phil. thesis, 1963.

Rowe, D. J., *Lead Manufacturing in Britain a History*, London, 1983.

Royle, E., *Radical Politics 1790–1900 Religion and Unbelief*, London, 1971.

Russell, C., *A Brief History of the Independent Church at Forest Green, Nailsworth*, Nailsworth, 1847.

Salt, H. R., *Gleanings from Forgotten Fields: Being the Story of the Berks Baptist Association, 1652–1907*, Reading, 1907.

Sangster, P., *Pity my Simplicity. The Evangelical Revival and the Religious Education of Children 1738–1800*, London, 1963.

'The life of the Rev. Rowland Hill (1744–1833) and his position in the Evangelical Revival', Oxford, D.Phil. thesis, 1965.

Sears, A. T., *James Prankard; Minister of the Bethel Independent Chapel Sheerness from 19th February 1811 to 11th January 1838 with extracts from his Church Book*, 1962.

'Christians in Kent: a brief account of Congregational churches from the 17th to 19th centuries', unpublished notes.

Sellers, I., 'Liverpool Nonconformity (1786–1914)', Keele, Ph.D. thesis, 1969.

Nineteenth Century Nonconformity, London, 1977.

Semmel, B., *The Methodist Revolution*, London, 1974.

Shore, C. J., *Memoir of the Life and Correspondence of John, Lord Teignmouth*, 2 vols., London, 1843.

Sibree, J. and Caston, M., *Independency in Warwickshire; a brief history of the Independent or Congregational Churches in that County; containing biographical notices of their pastors*, Coventry, 1853.

Sidney, E., *The Life of the Rev. Rowland Hill*, London, 1834.

Slate, R., *A Brief History of the Rise and Progress of the Lancashire Congregational Union; and of the Blackburn Independent Academy*, London, 1840.

Smith, J. W. A., *The Birth of Modern Education. The Contribution of the Dissenting Academies, 1660–1800*, London, 1954.

Soloway, R. A., *Prelates and People Ecclesiastical Social Thought in England 1783–1852*, London, 1969.

Steadman, T., *Memoir of the Rev. William Steadman, D.D.*, London, 1838.

Stell, C. F., 'The Eastern Association of Baptist Churches, 1775–1782', *Baptist Quarterly*, n.s. 27 (1977–8), 14–26.

Stephens, M. D. and Roderick, G. W., 'Education and the Dissenting academies', *History Today*, 27 (1977), 47–54.

Stone, S. M., 'A survey of Baptist expansion in England from 1795 to 1850 with special reference to the emergence of permanent structures of organisation', Bristol Baptist College, unpublished dissertation, n.d.

Surman, C. E., 'Roby's academy, Manchester, 1803–08', *Transactions of the Congregational Historical Society*, 13 (1937–9), 41–53.

'Leaf Square Academy, Pendleton, 1811–1813', *Transactions of the Congregational Historical Society*, 13 (1937–9), 77, 107–17.

'Students at the Yorkshire Independent academies during the eighteenth and nineteenth centuries', unpublished handlist.

Swaine, S. A., *Faithful Men; or, Memorials of Bristol Baptist College, and some of its most distinguished alumni*, London, 1884.

Swaish, J., *One Hundred Years of Village Preaching by the Bristol Baptist Itinerant Society founded in 1824*, Bristol, n.d. [1924].

Sykes, N., *Church and State in England in the XVIIIth Century*, Cambridge, 1934.

Terpstra, C., 'David Bogue, D.D., 1750–1825: pioneer and missionary educator', Edinburgh, Ph.D. thesis, 1959.

Thomas, R., *Report on a Survey of the Mining District of Cornwall from Chasewater to Camborne*, London, 1819.

Thomis, M. I. and Holt, P., *Threats of Revolution in Britain, 1789–1848*, London, 1977.

Thompson, D. M., *Nonconformity in the nineteenth century*, London, 1972.

'Denominationalism and Dissent, 1795–1835: a question of identity', *Friends of Dr Williams's Library Lecture*, 39 (1985).

Thompson, E. P., *The Making of the English Working Class*, London, 1963.

Thompson, J., *Lancashire Independent College, 1843–1893*, Manchester, 1893.

Thomson, D. P., *Lady Glenorchy and her Churches – the story of two hundred years*, Crieff, 1967.

Turner, J. H., *Nonconformity in Idle, with the History of Airedale College*, Bradford, 1876.

Underwood, A. C., *A History of the English Baptists*, London, 1947.

Urwick, W., *Nonconformity in Herts; Being Lectures upon the Nonconforming Worthies of St. Albans, and the Memorials of Puritanism and Nonconformity in all the Parishes of the County of Hertford*, London, 1884.

Voltaire, *Lettres écrites de Londres sur les Anglois et autres sujets*, Basle, 1734.

Waddington, J., *Congregational History, 1200–1850*, 4 vols., London, 1869–78.

Wake, W., *The Authority of Christian princes over their ecclesiastical synods asserted; with particular respect to the Convocations of the clergy of the Realm and Church of England; occasioned by a late pamphlet intituled, A letter to a Convocation man*, London, 1697.

Walker, R. B., 'Religious changes in Cheshire, 1750–1850', *Journal of Ecclesiastical History*, 17 (1966), 77–94.

Warburton, W., *The Alliance between Church and State: or, The Necessity and Equity of an Established Religion and a Test Law, demonstrated from the essence and end of Civil Society, upon the fundamental principles of the Law of Nature and Nations*, London, 1736.

Ward, W. R., 'The tithe question in England in the early nineteenth century', *Journal of Ecclesiastical History*, 16 (1965), 67–81.

'The French Revolution and the English churches. A case study in the impact of revolution upon the Church' in R. Peters (ed.), *Miscellanea Historiae Ecclesiasticae*, 4 (1970), 55–84.

'The religion of the people and the problem of control, 1790–1830' in G. J. Cuming and D. Baker (eds.), *Studies in Church History*, 8 (1972), 237–57.

Religion and Society in England 1790–1850, London, 1972.

'The Baptists and the transformation of the Church, 1780–1830', *Baptist Quarterly*, n.s. 25 (1973–4), 167–84.

Warren, M., *The Missionary Movement from Britain in Modern History*, London, 1965.

Watson, C. E., *The Story of Rodborough Tabernacle*, Stroud, n.d. [ca.1927].

Watts, M. R., *The Dissenters From the Reformation to the French Revolution*, Oxford, 1978.

Webb, R. K., *Modern England From the Eighteenth Century to the Present*, London, 1969.

Welch, C. E., 'Andrew Kinsman's churches at Plymouth', *Transactions of the Devonshire Association*, 97 (1965), 212–36.

'The registration of meeting houses', *Journal of the Society of Archivists*, 3 (1966), 116–20.

Welch, C. E. (ed.), *Two Calvinistic Methodist Chapels, 1743–1811: the London Tabernacle and Spa Fields Chapel*, London, 1975.

White, B. R., *The English Separatist Tradition from the Marian Martyrs to the Pilgrim Fathers*, London, 1971.

Whitehead, T., *History of the Dales Congregational Churches*, Bradford, 1930.

Whitley, W. T., *A History of British Baptists*, London, 1923.

Whittaker, M. B., 'The revival of Dissent (1800–1835)', Cambridge, M.Litt. thesis, 1959.

Whittingham, R., *The Works of the Rev. John Berridge. With an enlarged memoir of his life, numerous letters ... and his original Sion's Songs*, London, 1838.

Wickham, E. R., *Church and People in an Industrial City*, London, 1957.

Wicks, G. H., *Bristol's Heathen Neighbours: The Story of the Bristol Itinerant Society, 1811–1911*, Bristol, 1911.

Whitefield's Legacy to Bristol and the Cotswolds, Bristol, 1914.

Wilberforce, R. I. and S., *The Life of William Wilberforce*, 5 vols., London, 1838.

Willmer, H., 'Dechristianisation in England in the 19th and 20th centuries' in D. Baker (ed.), *Miscellanea Historiae Ecclesiasticae*, 3 (1968), 315–27.

Wilson, J., *A Memoir of the Life and Character of Thomas Wilson, Esq., Treasurer of Highbury College*, London, 1846.

Ziegler, P., *Addington. A Life of Henry Addington, First Viscount Sidmouth*, London, 1965.

Index

Abbotts Ann, Hampshire, 60, 119, 120
Aberdeen, 85
Aberdovey, Merioneth, 89
Aberystwyth, Cardiganshire, 46, 89
academies, Dissenting
 prosecution, 7
 new institutions, 14, 15, 68
 links with Methodism, 16, 23
 contribution to itinerancy, 48, 53, 84, 96
 financial stability, 71
 selection procedures, 72–3
 academic training, 73–7
 practical training, 77–84
 rising standards, 85–6
 respectability, 160
Act of Uniformity (1559), *see* legislation
Act of Uniformity (1662), *see* legislation
Acton, Middlesex, 217 n20
Adams, John, 26, 215 n44
Adey, John, 55, 94
Alcaston, Shropshire, 89
Aldbourne, Wiltshire, 148
Aldeburgh, Suffolk, 11
Alexander, William, 55
Allard, William, 108
Allerford, Somerset, 92
Allerton, Yorkshire, 205 n57
Alresford, Hampshire, 115, 151
Alston, Cumberland, 51, 152, 217 n27
America, religious revival in, 39, 51, 147, 163
Anabaptism, theological influence of, 4
Andover, Hampshire, 60, 119
Anne, Queen, 7, 8
Ansty, Wiltshire, 114, 120
Anti-Corn Law League, 17
Anti-Jacobin Review, 128
antinomianism, 108, 191 n17
antipaedobaptists, relationships with paedobaptists, 36–7, 69, 70
apologetics, arguments for itinerancy, 48, 126–31

Apology for Sunday Schools, 34, 127–9
Apology for Village Preachers, 22, 107
Apostolic Society, 76, 204 n23
Arianism, 188 n22
Arminianism, Arminians, 17, 18, 20, 36, 37
Ashton-in-Makerfield, Lancashire, 122, 189 n54
Aspland, Robert, 108, 209 n11
associations
 new county unions, 25, 31–3
 effect on polity, 29–31
 older associations, 30, 31, 32–4
 change of emphasis, 30, 43, 194 n67
 earlier introspection, 31, 32
 undenominational spirit, 33
 objectives, 33–4
 support for evangelism, 42–6
 ordination, 57
 and growth, 87
 finance, 99–100
 political attitudes, 131, 214 n42
 statistics and accounts, 143–7, 194 n77
Aston Sandford, Buckinghamshire, 37
Atterbury, Francis, Bishop of Rochester, 8
Avon valley, Wiltshire, 25, 26, 43, 101

Badingham, Suffolk, 47, 189 n43
Ball, Philip, 158
Bampton, Devon, 38, 91, 92
Banbury, Oxfordshire, 12, 54
Bangor diocese, 9
baptism, 36–7, 38, 144–6, 147, 185–6
Baptist Annual Register, 147
Baptist Eastern Association, 193 n56
Baptist Home Missionary Society, 35, 54, 153, 183, 200 n56, 219 n59
 see also Baptist Society in London, for the Encouragement and Support of Itinerant and Village Preaching
Baptist Magazine, 103
Baptist Midland Association

236